W9-CTB-481

# convergence

Brett Johnson

Convergence

Copyright © Brett Johnson

All rights reserved. No part of this book may be reproduced or transmitted in any form or by any means, electronic or mechanical, including photocopying, recording, or by any information storage and retrieval system, without permission in writing from the Publisher.

All quoted scriptures are from the NIV version of the Holy Bible unless stated in the text.

Published by Indaba Publishing

A division of

The Institute for Innovation, Integration & Impact, Inc.

www.inst.net

+1.866.9INDABA

Printed in Indonesia

0-9678541-5-6

To my life partner, Lyn

And my three children Fay, James and David.

# Table of Contents

# Acknowledgements

My first acknowledgement goes with gratitude to the one who has been a better friend, a constant comfort, and a genius life planner, Jesus. I think I am enjoying the journey with him more as each year passes. He has taken me on a path with inherent uncertainty, except for himself, endless surprises, and deep joy.

The second reality is that my life path would be very different without my wife of 27+ years, Lyn. It is no overstatement that she is "the secret sauce" that makes everything more spicy and interesting. The road of Convergence has not always been straightforward. She has been a wonderful partner in seeking a better way. She has grasped the nettle of integrating our lives and ministry, and she has been committed to living a life of intentional obedience. The story shared in this book is our joint story. Had she written it, the story would have been more peppered with people, sprinkled with passion.

Our three children, Fay, James and David, have their own perspectives on this whole Convergence idea. Sometimes the colorful blending of relationships and work and missions and growing up has been tough for them. I am thankful to them for the way in which each of them has enriched my life, kept me real, and sharpened my focus.

A final "Thank you!" to the many people who have had hundreds of hours of conversations about the promise and practice of Convergence. Truth lived out always speaks louder than truth told. I am encouraged by those who have routinely climbed out of the boat and walked an illogical path towards an irresistible person.

# Preamble

Imprinted in the core of our being is a desire for life to make sense. Somewhere in the back of our minds is the unwhispered prayer, "God, I hope that the unconnected islands in my life hold together in your view." When we press pause and are no longer propelled by the momentum of the mundane, we secretly say to, "I hope I am going in the right direction." Or in a quiet moment when we sink into a seat on a plane, on a train, or in an emergency room we say to yourself, "I hope my life isn't happening this way just because I willed it, just because I made it happen, just because I drove it forward myself."

Then, every once in a while, we cross paths with someone who operates in "the zone" and yet lives in faith. Whether on a page in a book or at a corner cafe we instinctively know that, for this person, life's pictures are in the same frame; they are telling one story.

Several thoughts immediately compete for the clear space in our minds. "I long for the threads of my life to form a discernable tapestry—perhaps even a noble picture." "I wonder if this is a random coincidence, or is there a lesser known path that might lead me to..." "But doesn't it say somewhere that many diligent seekers did not receive what they had hoped for?"

Our deep yearning cannot be quelled by busyness, self-help books or group therapy. One-minute-this, three-step-that, and seven-part-the-other will not satisfy. We have to go beyond the logical to find the glorious. We must push past the mechanics to know the mystery.

> "It is the glory of God
>
> to conceal a matter;
>
> To search out a matter
>
> is the glory of kings."
>
> —Solomon

## Things have changed since 2000

The need for Convergence is greater than ever. In 2000 few were talking about integrating work and faith; today talk of "marketplace ministry" is common. Business-as-missions is now a well-worn term. Books on the intersection of faith and work abound. Every day a growing cadre of business men and women heads to work with a new understanding that they are ministers, every bit as much as their pulpit counterparts. This is good.

Why do we still need the message of Convergence? Over the last five years my colleagues and I have worked with hundreds of business professionals and hundreds more business owners who are tackling the thorny challenges of integrating work and faith. In Africa, Asia and the Americas, the message of Convergence is one that lights their passions. They hear it, they embrace it, and they move forward with intention. Careers have been transformed, people have been empowered, life-as-usual has been changed forever. At the corporate level, we have seen business owners and working people find new meaning in their work. Many have wrestled through the alignment of their careers with their calling. The typical tensions between work and home have been eased. People have begun to work with God, seven days a week, rather than doing odd jobs for him on Sundays.

There have been many successes; people have seen the hope of their work taking on eternal significance, but somehow the reality of it has eluded them. With all the resources available to businesspeople, teachers, doctors and entertainers, with all the affirmation that business is a calling, and with all the momentum in the marketplace, one might think that a high impact life is inevitable. But it is not. Make no mistake, most of us want to have an impact on today and for eternity. There is plenty of talk about leaving a legacy. The truth is, we are still falling short of the impact we could be having.

## There is still a gap

Why are we falling short? First and foremost, *dichotomy* is still deeply rooted in businesspeople and in the world at large. This has various affects:

» If we do not come to fully believe that work is ministry, then we are open to perpetuating the lie that non-clergy are second class citizens in the kingdom of God.

» If we do not really believe that work is good and acceptable worship, then we do not integrate our Career and our Calling.

» The tension between work and worship continues, as opportunities to minister at work get neutered by demands that we fill a role in a local church or other non-profit organizations. Often these roles do not use our full potential.

» Even attempts at corporate social responsibility are deemed not good enough if there is any gain for the business involved. Some Non Governmental Organizations (NGOs) want to see pain and no gain. This too is a fruit of dichotomized thinking.[1]

*Integration* is another challenge. The second reason why we need the truths contained in this book is that a disintegrated life cannot lead to Convergence. This looks similar to the matter of dichotomous thinking and living, but the issue here is less one of worldview and more one of practical choices. You may be able to write a paper about why all that we do is good, why work is worship, and why business and ministry are essentially the same. But if you do not make the practical choices to integrate the different spheres of your life you will not reach Convergence. We can know the truth about Convergence, but we still have to make practical choices to integrate the different spheres of our life.

---

1  *The Economist,* January 19th, 2008, "A Special Report on Corporate Social Responsibility"

*Inoculation* is yet another obstacle to finding and fulfilling our life purpose. The downside of the groundswell of "marketplace ministry" is that there is enough going on to get working people excited but not enough to get them transformed. Revelation without application does not amount to transformation.

*Purpose* should propel us towards Convergence, but when our purpose is man-sized, the job we allow ourselves to have is much smaller than it should be. It is not about self-improvement, self-actualization or self-fulfilment. On the business side, it goes far, far beyond Corporate Social Responsibility. We are invited to align our agenda with God's agenda. We are called to fully align our purpose with his purposes for now and eternity. Responding to this call is far above the "What's in it for me?" of consumer oriented Western spirituality.

Finally, in order to progress towards Convergence at the personal level, we must have *practical tools* that help us identify and navigate the narrow road of obedience that could take us there. This book will give you practical tools that will help you understand the road to Convergence, mark off the signs along the way, and become soaked in the principles essential to integrated living.

Convergence was born out of our own story. It comes from a personal struggle to deal with the tensions resulting from:

» The compelling cord of Career

» The stretched bands of Community

» The delicate threads of Creativity and

» The silver strands of Call.

Convergence has been woven out of our attempts to do what God seemed to be telling us at a given point in time. Looking back, we can see some threads running through our lives. Our hope is to share them with you so that you, too, can see an integrated tapestry woven in your life.

# Defining Convergence

Before we dig into the book, let's take a moment to preview the definition of Convergence from three vantage points. This is covered in Chapter 2 in more detail, but contemplate these definitions for a moment. I will begin at the end.

## The End of Convergence

This is the apprehension of a tapestry which, when turned over at a particular juncture in your life, causes you to say:

> "Yes! This is me, this is what my life is for."

## The Sovereign Part of Convergence

This consists of the deliberate drawing together of those threads that have been woven into your life over the past 40-or-so years in a way that reveals your life Call.

## Your Part in Convergence

This includes your cooperation in simple steps of obedience that increase your understanding of, preparing for, and walking into your Creator's life purposes for you. It is your availability to be used by God as he pulls, pushes and polishes the strands of your being.

You may well ask, "How do you I this?" This book is aimed at helping you answer this question in a straightforward yet non-formulaic manner.

# What Others Have Said About Convergence

"Brett Johnson is "deep waters." He thinks and writes on broad scale relative to the issues confronting serious Christians who want to make a difference. *Convergence*, is a virtual training manual for such believers. Proceed with caution, because reading; this book will change you."
– **Dennis Peacocke, President, Strategic Christian Services**

"Up to this point in my life Convergence has to be the most relevant book I've read. I could personally identify with the seven seasons in my life – those I've been through, those I am going through and those that are still to come. It's a personal book that speaks to the individual in a real way giving greater understanding as to why things happen in our lives. Never before have I read a book where I could see myself and the journey I am on start to come into perspective as much as I could while reading Convergence."
–**Greg Cockrell, President of Bondsolve, South Africa**

"Brett has written an awesome book that pulls together vocation, global, and transformative issues in the world today.. I've always benefited when I've been around Brett and learned from him. There are few people who are writing and get what he does. Devour this book - then apply it."
– **Bob Roberts, Senior Pastor of Northwood Church, Texas**

"Convergence is the finest book on discovering and implementing a life that truly fits all the pieces together. Brett and Lyn are writing from years of personal experience and hundreds of successful projects, relationships and services. I have been and continue to be transformed by the insights of Convergence and urge all thoughtful people to engage this work with family, friends and colleagues. The results will be revolutionary - no more fragmentation of practical and spiritual; no more divisions between business and ministry - all facets of life are centered and growing!"
– **Dr. Charlie Self, Author, Lecturer, Historian**

"In this new edition of "Convergence" Brett Johnson has again given us terrific insight into how leaders develop and mature in their given roles. People serving in any sphere of society will gain major benefit from this cutting edge volume.

We live in an era when men and women are striving to excel and breakthrough to see how their breadth of gifting will fulfill their dreams. Johnson's depth and breadth of understanding our process of growth in real life scenarios will bring you into a much illuminated perspective on where you've come from, where you are now, and where you can get to. I recommend this book to any leader keen to succeed and to see fruitful convergence in life and work."
–**Iain Muir, International Director of YWAM**

"For the Christian who wrestles to find that spot where their gifts, calling, relationships, and career all come together...and who are frustrated by the inadequacies of the contrived steps and formulas touted in best sellers, Convergence represents sanity, wisdom, and perspective. It combines Brett's wide ranging expertise and his humble and transparent life to provide you with whole life and lifelong insights into how God brings you to that place of convergence. Convergence is practical as well as wise. You learn what you must do while grasping what God is doing through the various seasons and tests of life to shape you for His purposes. Be warned. In the end, you will not achieve a balanced life – which is impossible. But you will discover who you are and learn to live with alignment in your whole life around God and His purpose for you. Read it. Study it. Share it. And do it now!"
–**Dan Wooldridge, President of Insidework.net**

"Obedience to God results in a journey to 'convergence!' Brett's enormous insight and analytical talent helps to show us the way."
–**Gary Daichendt, former Exec VP Cisco Systems**

"Convergence is another great book from Brett Johnson. Lemon Leadership was my first real introduction to his style of management thinking. This is a great continuation of his approach. He shows us why every part of our lives must be integrated from work to our spiritual commitment. The best part: He gives us a way to go about it. As usual, refreshing...."
–**Ken Eldred, CEO, Living Stones Foundation and Author: *God is at Work: Transforming People and Nations Through Business.***

## Why We Need Convergence

I had just returned to San Francisco from a trip to South Africa, then turned around and headed for Houston, where I had a brief speaking slot at a breakout session at a conference. The topic was Convergence. An eclectic group had gathered in the classroom at First Baptist Church. I had no idea of their personal journeys, so I simply shared some high level concepts, took a few questions, and ended the session. Afterwards a man who looked to be in his mid-thirties pulled alongside me as I walked down the hallway.

"I have just called my business partners and told them that meeting you was one of the top five most significant events in my life."

His name was Mike, and he went on to explain:

"I have figured out how to integrate my Calling, my Creativity and my Career. But until today I could not figure out the Community bit. Convergence has given me the key."

Mike was like many other people. He had a heart for people; his idea of fun was going to the local pub with his wife, Kristie, befriending the down and outs, loving them, and eventually introducing them to Jesus. He also had a job. He ran an Information Technology consulting company in Dallas, Texas, and had a team of people who were serving clients around the country. They ministered through their work and tracked their progress with practical measures such as how often God brought people across their paths who needed their help. Mike also had a heart for missions and had built relationships in various overseas countries. He was on committees at this local church, and he and Kristie had three growing kids. After applying *Convergence* to his life, Mike had this to share:

> After being misled in believing that Balance in life was a Biblical concept, I was so relieved to be introduced to Convergence. I was spending so much time trying to manage conflicts between career and community that I had very little time to focus on my calling and my creativity. This left me in a constant state of frustration and robbed me of joy. God clearly put Brett Johnson across my path at a very significant point in my life. Not only was I able to incorporate my ministry activities with my business, but God providentially made it possible to incorporate my family into my business as well. My business is better, my marriage is better, my ministry is stronger and my kids are happier than they have ever been. Recently I spent eight months on a client assignment in Europe. At the same time, I mentored a leader and helped him plant an urban church in Kansas City, I was a husband to my wife, and a father to a sixteen year old, a twelve year old and a nine year old. Without Convergence, Skype, and God's grace, this would

have been impossible. I cannot imagine going back to a life of compartmentalization. I now prioritize all aspects of life into one bucket, leaving only one priority at any given time. [1]

## We are Pressed by Time

Have you felt the tension that Mike felt between his work, his home, and his dreams? Have you wondered what you would do if you had more time, less pressure? To say that life is pressured is to say that Everest is a hill. To say that key areas of our lives are increasingly in tension is a similar understatement. We have been bludgeoned by a barrage of time-squeezers that leave even the most astute time managers beaten down. Complicating things is the fact that many of us gain our primary sense of identity from what we do, or our Career. Any sense of a greater purpose for our lives—our Call—is often suffocated by our Career, which has wrapped its tentacles around who we are.

A 1965 U.S. Senate Subcommittee predicted that by 1985 the average American would work a 22-hour workweek and would be able to retire by age 38. Instead, since 1973 leisure time for the average American has decreased 37% and the...average workweek increased from 41 to 47 hours!

## We are Stressed at Work

The situation today is reflected in a study by the National Institute for Occupational Safety and Health where they examine stress at work. Northwestern National Life reports that 40% of people rate their job as very or extremely stressful. Consider what the research reveals.

» One-fourth of employees view their jobs as the number one stressor in their lives. — Northwestern National Life

1    Mike Cheves is President of Kairos Global; www.inkairos.com.

» Three-fourths of employees believe the worker has more on-the-job stress than a generation ago. — Princeton Survey Research Associates

» Problems at work are more strongly associated with health complaints than any other life stressor—more so than even financial problems or family problems. — St. Paul Fire and Marine Insurance Co.

In California, the number of workers' compensation claims for mental stress increased by almost 700 percent over eight years, and ninety percent were successful with an average award of $15,000 compared to a national average of $3,420. Many studies tend to focus on environment and organization as primary causes of stress. In some studies people reported that 37% of the work they did was meaningless, a waste of time. The fact is, when our work is devoid of purpose, we get stressed. Is it less a matter of how long we work, and more a matter of how we feel when we are working? A study of 3,020 aircraft employees showed that employees who "hardly ever" enjoyed their job were 2.5 times more likely to report a back injury than those who reported "almost always" enjoying their job.[2]

Will Hutton, Chief Executive of the Work Foundation in the U.K. says, "Many organizations have found it difficult to reconcile flexible working with the embedded culture of nine to five presenteeism. Indeed, Britain works the longest hours in Europe—and yet it lags behind in the productivity tables; the way of working we cling to isn't delivering the goods and yet we won't let it go."

## Creativity is a Casualty

True Creativity should not take away from our Call. But Call can be obscured by entertainment and endless imaginings. There's the fantasy

2    Bigos, S.J.; Battie, M.C.; Spengler, D.M.; Fisher, L.D.; Fordyce, W.E.; Hansonn, T.H.; Nachemson, A.L.; and Wortley, M.D.. *A prospective study of work perceptions and psychosocial factors affecting the report of back injury, Spine,* 1991.

that says, "One day I'm going to quit my job and become a _____"
(fill in the blank). Dreams and the pursuit of pleasure can sidetrack
us from Convergence. We undoubtedly have subscribed to the Work
Hard/Play Hard philosophy. Americans spend 11-12% of their income
on leisure as opposed to 1.5% on charitable giving. So the tension
between Career and Call is probably overshadowed by the work/
pleasure cycle of: work, play, work, play. While we have seen trends
of "Cashing Out"[3] and "Cashing In"[4], for many on the treadmill there
just doesn't seem to be enough time or encouragement to stop and ask
whether the work hard/play hard game is the only one in town.

If you have a family, you will most likely feel tension between Career
and Community. I define Community as including family, friends and
affinity groups such as church and clubs. For most people, once the
battle to fight this tension has begun there is hardly enough time to
clean the weapons before next week's recurrence of the fight, let alone
energy to open another battle front.

If you are part of the burgeoning single-and-thirty-something set, the
pulls and pushes will be centered around your identity. Who am I?
How do I define myself sans children, et al? How do I create legitimate
goals so that I am not consumed by the avoidance of aloneness? Can I
achieve Convergence without a life mate? Without the disciplines of
dependents shaping my calendar, how do I focus on the right things?

Every now and then I run into someone who has a notion to do
some great feat of faith, but their family doesn't want to fall in line
behind the vision. When one cuts to the chase, the family members
do not oppose the Call, but they legitimately fear the cost to their
Community. The absence of an integrated framework leaves them
insecure, and suspicious that they will be neglected while the Call is
being pursued. This Call/Community tension is common.

---

3       Lys Marigold and *Faith Popcorn, Clicking, Harperbusiness*, 1998.

4       This is the term *Newsweek* uses to describe the trend of yuppies who cannot afford to
        retire altogether, but are willing to take lesser paying jobs in organizations where they can
        do more meaningful work.

## We are Easily Polarized

The net result in our battle to keep all our "buckets" full is that we have become a polarized people. The points of disconnect between the major areas of our life seem to outweigh the strands of integration. One good choice—such as the decision to follow Jesus—does not guarantee that the rest of our decisions will be as sound. As long as we have breath in us, we will have the ability to do our own thing. Some of our choices will be of little consequence; others will nudge us onto a path that meanders towards mediocrity. Few people seem to possess enough grace and grit to respond to God's apparently absurd initiatives over a long enough period of time to enjoy Convergence. The alternatives are just too appealing: successful career, nice cars, kids in "right" schools, looking good, big corporate/church title, fitness fanaticism, job security. Many travel these highways yet miss the off-ramps that could lead to Convergence. In our attempt to keep it all together, we lose it. Big time.

We often hear "God loves you and has a plan for your life" but there are two extremes in figuring out just what that plan is. On the one hand, Short-term Teri faces every grocery purchasing decision as though her spiritual life depended on it; on the other hand, Nebulous Nick doesn't believe he can ever know God's plan. Convergence counters both nearsightedness and fatalism. Convergence helps us wear spectacles that have two different lenses. With one we see the big picture, the horizons, and delight in God's big design. Through the second we see the minutia of today - drudgery and all - and worship God in it. And yet there is an encouraging new wave of people asking how we can connect life's strands in a way that meets our deep longing for context while simultaneously living in the now of everyday life.

## The Rate of Change, the Increase of Alternatives and the Avalanche of Distractions

Breakthroughs in information sciences are creating tremendous opportunities, not just in the digital revolution, on the worldwide web, or for full-blown nerds. The implications are coming to a grocery store near you.

» Consumerism: The number of different items (SKU's or Stock Keeping Units) in food stored in America increased from 10,000 in 1986 to 35,000 in 1996. Every day, catalogues flood into homes around the world offering stuff, stuff, and more stuff.

» Biology: Thanks to the field of genomics—the blend of biology and information—130,000 new strands of corn were created in 1997.

» Technology: The explosion of information technology and information is re-raising the 1980's issue of the difference between data and information. Until filtering and smart technologies advance, individuals are left to sift through the rubble on their own.

» Confluence of information, communications and entertainment: This leaves individuals—particularly younger people—needing discernment to figure out what's real and what is hype in the game of life.

» Economics: The 1997/98 Asia economic crisis quickly became a global crisis. The economic rules for the 21st Century have yet to be written. The medium of exchange is even uncertain—will it be information, intellectual property, food...?

» Career opportunity/uncertainty: depending on whether "every silver lining has a cloud," or vice versa, there will be a surge of new opportunities for the "information haves" and a less bright future for the "information have-nots." Deciding how to chart your future when the job you will do may not have yet been invented, causes career anxiety.

Information, alternatives, distractions. Life's highway has evolved from a straight road with periodic, predictable markers to one lined with flashing neon signs, exits, on-ramps, and cheap motels. If that were not enough, the inside of the vehicle has surround sound, a 6-stack CD changer, telephones, intelligent guidance systems and talking control panels. We should be better guided. Yet we are desperately in need of a True North. How do we sift through the mire of muchness? We need to know our Call. We need life-skills that give us a shot at Convergence.

## Global Business Culture

Globalization used to be a buzzword, but because of the boundaryless Internet, we are now starting to see quick inter-continental ripples; when a pebble drops in Asia, Silicon Valley or Washington DC, its ripples are felt by the rest of the world. Organizations are learning to create global impact but lack the skills to manage it, if indeed it is manageable. The opportunities that are open to us nowadays are similarly global. We travel more, have instant information about what is going on in the world, and we can share our ideas and experiences with people across the planet. A popular website announced in July 2006 that 100 million videos a day were being downloaded from its site. This statistic may be radically out of date by the time this book is printed.

With this comes an emergence of a global business culture. As I travel to Indonesia, India, China, South Africa or Silicon Valley, there are some differences, but the shared language, experiences and processes are increasing rapidly. "Businesspeople" has become, in my view, an *ethnos*, a people group with common characteristics worldwide. Beyond this, you no longer have to travel to India or Mexico to find out how they do things. In San Mateo County, where I live, there are over 80 different groups learning English as a second language.

Will this increase in opportunity propel us forward, or will we be overwhelmed by the options? Once again, unless we practically know that God is for the whole of life, we will have to limit ourselves to that which we can manage.

## Hope is Fleeting

No sooner have pundits declared world peace than the headlines read Global Recession. Technology breakthroughs promise quality of life while the millennial bug or virus du jour eats away at our security. Unimaginable wealth from stock appreciation is followed by rumors of crashes. If we look to things around us, we will be hopeless. If we look within us, we will be no better off. "Hope deferred makes the heart sick," says the Proverb. But if we listen to God's voice through the babble of the world, we will have hope. Not only must we listen to God's voice, but we must also seek to understand his patterns of doing things in the world so that we are strongly rooted in "the God of all hope."

## Marketplace Ministries

Businesspeople around the world are waking up to the fact that they are ministers, that their business is their ministry, and that they can get into God's business. The big picture is The Kingdom of God. Societal Transformation is a subset of this, and is really just current language for what Jesus called "making disciples of all nations." I have come to view what God is doing in the marketplace as a flower with many petals that include:

» Tentmaking – using one's trade to support oneself financially in doing missions work. Many English as a Second Language (ESL) programs fall in this category.

» Great Commission Companies – establishing businesses among unreached people groups; an emphasis on being an ethical business.

» Marketplace Ministry – focusing on evangelism and discipleship.

» Kingdom Investing – making investments in businesses for redemptive purposes. The anticipation is a more modest return on investment, and a deliberate opportunity to fund businesses so that they can grow in influence, and ensuring that this influence is deliberate and positive.

» Trade – using trade as a means to access and influence communities or countries.

» Business as Missions – deliberately using the business as a vehicle for extending the kingdom of God.

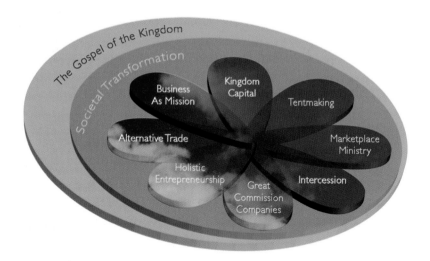

Taken at face value you would think that this makes the lives of businesspeople easier. In our work with hundreds of businesspeople through **rēp** we have seen something different. Those leaders who do not grasp the nettle of integration are left with a thorn in their side. When it becomes known that Mr. Businessman is passionate about

God's work, then the demands on his time increase. He ends up on new committees, churches ask for his time, and charities request his money. He gets asked to be chairman of various initiatives. In no time he is worse off than he was before because he has agreed to do lots of ministry outside his business rather than determine how to minister in and through his business. Integration and Convergence are cousins. Unless one integrates Career and the other spheres of life, the marketplace ministry phenomenon could make your life worse.

I am sad to say that many businesspeople simply opt for dichotomy: they would rather have everything in neat little boxes than go through the challenge of integrating the different facets of their lives. Others fly the marketplace ministry flag but are somehow still doing things out of an old mindset. I have seen many people come to the brink of integration and opt for something safer. The rich young ruler who came to the brink, considered the cost and walked away sadly, but Jesus did not lower the price of entry. No matter how much marketplace ministry we do, if we do not choose to relentlessly pursue an integrated life we will be flotsam and jetsam bobbing along the surface of marketplace ministry without knowing the joy that comes from living in the deep. We will not know Convergence.

## Spheres, domains, mountains...and Convergence

In recent years there has been a resurgence of interest in spheres, domains or sectors of society. Some have called them the gates of the city, others the doors of society, others refer to them as mountains. The lists vary, and some have narrowed it down to seven spheres, starting with lists put together by Bill Bright and Loren Cunningham, but now popularized by Lance Wallnau and others. The earlier starting point for this segmentation of society was actually a Dutch man named Abraham Kuyper. He formulated ideas on "sphere sovereignty" which we must be careful to not misinterpret, lest we start a new branch of dichotomous thinking: domainationalism. A proponent of "I am from this mountain, and you are from that mountain" recently asked me, "What mountain are you from, Brett?" I replied, "I work across many mountains." Each of us has authority, under God, to operate across multiple spheres. Kuyper himself worked across many spheres of society including religion, government, media and education. Abraham Kuyper was quick to note, "Oh, no single piece of our mental world is to be hermetically sealed off from the rest, and there is not a square inch in the whole domain of our human existence over which Christ, who is Sovereign over all, does not cry: 'Mine!'"[5]

Why do we need Convergence in order to influence spheres and disciple nations? I believe that Convergence is essential to growing in conviction and authority to master our spheres of influence as we experience that we are 100% ministers and 100% businesspeople, politicians, artists, doctors, educators, etc. This then opens the way for us to have growing authority in other spheres. God is over every sphere. Do not let yourself get held captive in one slice of society. I am not primarily a businessperson. I am a subject of the Kingdom of God, and I work in many sectors to bring what I know and experience of the truth of the kingdom of heaven to earth.

I have classified society as having 10 Spheres, each with a distinct way of doing things. The wineskin, or Operating Model, is quite distinct for each sector. My list includes three that are not common: The first is Non-Governmental Organizations (NGOs), which have huge budgets and massive influence, especially in developing nations. They were not as big a factor in the 1970's, but if we do not transform them, we do not transform society today. The second is Capital. Most businesspeople should know that capital markets operate vastly differently from regular business. The liquidity issues of the global financial markets in 2008 should underline this. We cannot have a transformational influence in society without bringing a Biblical view of Capital into practical play. Third, I have broken out Law as separate from Government. A judiciary that functions independent from politicians is very helpful in building a foundation for an effective society. Did you notice that

5       Kuyper, Abraham (1998), "Sphere Sovereignty", in Bratt, James D., Abraham Kuyper, A Centennial Reader, Grand Rapids, MI: Eerdmans, pp. 488

I do not have Church or Missions as a separate sphere? The reality is that the Kingdom of God should pervade every domain. It is true, Religion is a sector of society, but not Church or Missions. Finally, I have lumped arts and entertainment under the umbrella of Media & Communications.

An element of Convergence is when who you are catches up with God's vision of the role you will play in serving society. To transform society we need to influence each domain. The Ten Spheres are government, education, law, capital markets, family, the social sector, media, religion, healthcare and business.

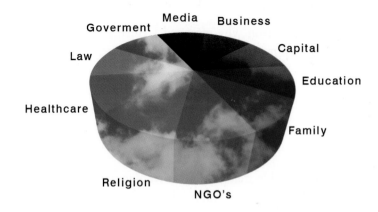

Let me end this section with a story. A good friend of mine is a money manager. She placed an investment in another nation hoping to deliver a good return to her investors over time. But the deal got bogged down and nearly a year later she was again asking me for prayer. Suddenly it dawned on me. I grabbed a napkin and sketched out the 10 Spheres of Society as I told her, "You thought you were going in to do a deal. You went into the nation through the door of Capital, but God has a greater plan. So he sent you a difficulty." The way things had transpired, she had discovered corruption and had eventually challenged even the President of the nation on the matter. She enlisted the help of church leaders (Religion sector) and prayed extensively in the nation. She became more aware of societal challenges in Business, Family,

Healthcare, and Education. She involved the Media in exposing the corruption, and of course was also engaged in the Law sector. I went on to say, "Your plan was to do a transaction; God's plan was to do transformation." The spiritual tools she had honed while working in Capital were applicable to many more spheres. A wrong notion of "sphere sovereignty" will limit our vision of the pervasive influence we can have in society. We find Convergence in the narrow path of obedience, and then God expands our horizon and sets a broader platform beneath our feet.

## We are Running Low on Margin

There is another reason why we need Convergence. Our segregation of Career, Community, Creativity and Call often manifests itself in the erosion of what Dr. Richard Swensen calls margin.[6] Margin is the shoulder of the road, the white space around the page, the slack in the rope of life. Rather than having a safe shoulder between danger and our vehicles, we often find ourselves scraping the median or driving into a ditch. We look worse for the wear.

It is difficult to tackle matters of Convergence when we have left no room for God to maneuver. You might say, "God is sovereign, so he can do whatever he likes." This is true. But it is also true that you have a free will, and he sees your heart, and he may not persistently badger you if you have decided to leave little space for his working deeper things in you. Before we can meaningfully develop strategies for Convergence, we need to assess the degree of margin in our lives.

Much work has been done to divide the human person into different categories. Mind, body, soul, spirit—these are typical components dating back to ancient times. My points here is not to debate the merits of this division, but simply to point out that people have tried to use this perspective to get a better handle on life. Scripture, of course, talks about many facets of life.

6    Richard A. Swensen, *Margin*, NavPress, 1995.

In Luke 2:52 we find a one-verse synopsis of 18 years of Jesus' life:

> And Jesus grew in wisdom and stature, and in favor with God and men.

Many of us would like to have that etched on our teenage years. In fact, whole teachings have been founded on this verse to promote the "Balanced Christian Life" that incorporates Wisdom (mental), stature (physical), favor with God (spiritual) and favor with man (social). For years I tried to plan my days on this basis. But this notion of "balance" was not enough.

## The 10-F Model® [7]

I personally needed a greater granularity for my planning to be more meaningful. So in the last ten years Lyn and I developed The 10-F Model to help analyze margin, assess contentment, and make planning more pragmatic.

I have a friend who has more talent than the average basketball team, twice as many kids as the average American, a mortgage to die for, a passionate desire to be something significant for God, and the day-to-day realities of keeping a larger-than-average family glued together. One morning as I drove along the San Andreas Fault, the phone rang in my car. It was my friend, let's call him, Kent, who wanted to meet at a nearby restaurant for a talk.

As usual, Kent had more pots in his kitchen than burners on his stove. Sensing a leading to give up a secure management position and create a new role for himself in his company, he would be walking out on a thin limb which seemed supported only by mist. While exciting for

---

[7]    *The 10-F Model®* is a registered trademark of The Institute for Innovation, Integration & Impact, Inc. – see www.inst.net.

Kent, there were a few complications. This mist-walk might require more time at work. He felt he didn't spend enough time there; his wife felt he spent too much. Second, he sensed that the job transition was part of a longer-term solution that would give him an opportunity to pursue his life dreams, but his dreams were his wife's nightmares that threatened family time and food on the table. As we had breakfast, I asked Kent a series of questions that were designed to give him the tools he needed to find his own future. He carefully outlined his rating of his life in the 10 areas. I then asked how his wife felt about these same areas. In some instances the results were markedly different. Looking at the gaps I could see that until Kent could create some margin, until he and his wife arrived at a place of grace together, he could not make many changes.

## What has Margin to do with Convergence?

Expecting to wake up one day and discover that we have arrived at Convergence is hugely unrealistic. We need to give ourselves—and God—the margin needed to make things happen. Some years ago I met a Jewish believer who had worked a steady job as a schoolteacher in New York. As a new follower of Jesus he realized that if he stayed in his job and failed to risk, there would be little opportunity for God to bless him. So he took a job for less pay, worked for a tough boss, and became a millionaire. I am not a "name it and claim it" proponent, but his advice to me has stuck: put yourself in a position where God can bless you. Make yourself available to God in a practical way. Absence of margin works against this principle. What is true for Finances is valid for the other 9-F's.

A rabbi told a story that went like this: A religious man stood in the synagogue and asked God to help him win the lottery. That week he won nothing. The next week he was back in the synagogue asking a bit more fervently. Silence from God, and no big win. By the third week he was prostrate before the Ark, begging God to help him win the lottery. Just then a voice came from the Ark. "Would you mind meeting me half-way—buy a ticket!" We've all been like that man. We all want the miracle, but we don't want to be in a place where we need a miracle. We want the joy when God does great things in and through us, but we are so busy in the locker room that we never get in the game. To win, you have to be in the game. To get in the game, you have to make the time and space to play. That's why Margin is important to Convergence.

## The Root and the Fruit

How did we become so short on margin? How did we become a people with our Career, Call, Community and Creativity at war with each other? The root of our fragmentation is in our thinking. Unless we address the root of dichotomized thinking, we will reap the bad fruit of fragmentation (and the associated loss of margin) in our lives. You may hear the words "dichotomized thinking," and think they are just another phrase. To me it is an enemy. We are commanded to "be transformed by the renewal of our minds." We have eaten so long of the fruit of the Greek tree that has its roots in dichotomy that we are left with the habit of dividing things into unconnected pieces. While we may intellectually assent to work and family being integrated, or God and business being intertwined, in practice we keep separate fruit baskets in our head. It is time we asked God to press the blender button and give us a smoothie.

# Defining Convergence

Sculptor Korczak Ziolkowski was invited by Sioux Chief Standing Bear to carve a memorial to the Indian people. A television documentary covered the progress of the carving of Crazy Horse into a huge granite face of the Yellow Stone Mountains. Clearly this work was going to exceed the life span of the sculptor. He has since died and the sculpture is far from complete. Yet his children continue the work. Current estimates are that it will be completed without Federal funding by the year 2050. The sculpture of the warrior astride a stallion will be 563 feet tall. That's eight feet higher than the Washington Monument and nine times as high as the faces of the four American presidents carved in Mount Rushmore, just a few miles north of Crazy Horse.

Why go to this effort? In an interview the late Korczak Ziolkowski said that:

"When your life is over, the world will ask you only one question: 'Did you do what you were supposed to do?'"

When Michelangelo was painting the Sistine Chapel he was told, "This may cost you your life!" His reply? "What else is life for?"

These two artists from different eras had a similar view of their work. The question to you is, "What is your life work?" It's a tough one to answer.

## Thesis

The basic thesis of Convergence is this: following God's leading reduces the tension between the major areas of life, and following God's leading is easier if you recognize and understand the road signs along the way. The road signs take the form of seven major seasons. These are covered in subsequent chapters. Convergence is about completeness, about being in the zone, about contentment.

Some people do great things, but have no contentment. Others know that they have done what they came to do. Paul, the great pioneer of the Early Church, said, "I have fought the good fight, I have finished the race." Yet Michelangelo had no assurance of his spiritual prospects in the after life. John Wesley founded a movement that far outlasted his years. His counterpart, Whitfield, built in his own words "a rope of sand." He did amazing things (much of it in conjunction with Wesley) but was not too content with the life results. Jesus prayed "I have brought you glory on earth by completing the work you gave me to do." By contrast, Pancho Villa's last words when the U.S. Military finally tracked him down and he was dying were, "Don't let it end like this. Tell them I said something." How about you: will you be searching for something meaningful to say on your death bed, or will you be able to conclude, "I have done what I was called to do"?

# Convergence: Definition

*Roget's Thesaurus* offers an explanation of Convergence that is short and sweet: "to direct towards a common center."

I have expanded that definition to include three aspects of Convergence: your part in Convergence, the Sovereign part of Convergence, and the end of Convergence.

## Your Part in Convergence

This includes your cooperation in simple steps of obedience that increase your understanding, preparing for, and walking into your Creator's life purposes for you; your availability in God's hands as he pulls, knots, pushes and polishes the strands of your being.

## The Sovereign Part of Convergence

This consists of the deliberate drawing together of those threads that have been woven into your life over the past 40-or-so years in a way that reveals your life Call.

## The End of Convergence

This is the apprehension of a tapestry which, when turned over at a particular juncture in your life, causes you to say, "Yes! This is me, this is what my life is for."

Convergence is not necessarily about setting out to do great things. Convergence comes through setting one's face towards a walk of obedience that is carried to completion. In this book I hope to direct four separated areas of life towards a common center: our Career, Community, Creativity, and Call.

## The Components of Convergence

An absence of Convergence is often the result of the fragmentation of four key spheres within our individual world. I call them The 4-C's of Career, Creativity, Community, and Call.

The tapestry of Convergence comes about as a result of the weaving of the inter-relationships of these areas. It is essential that we do not snip the threads when they cross preconceived boundaries in our minds. Our God is One. So when he makes connections between the disparate segments of our lives, let him do this work of reconciliation. The fact is, to discover Convergence one must understand Integration.

My own background includes the field of "systems integration" and a company I worked for was known as a "systems integrator." This embodies the notion of getting different "things" to work together efficiently to achieve some business purpose. Organizations need systems integrators because of the complexity of aligning people, processes, software, hardware, communications networks and other technologies to work together. The idea is to not just be functional but to deliver a specified result.

The concept of Integration reaches well beyond the realm of systems integration. It's a centuries old life framework that has been a key organizing principal of philosophers and green grocers alike. In the March 29, 1999 issue of *Newsweek,* an article by Kenneth L. Woodward entitled "2000 Years of Jesus" pointed out that Jesus Christ changed many things. He caused an "inversion of values" with his focus on the poor, the "discovering of the individual" and the "redefining of male and female." Jesus was not about "business as usual." He made a radical difference in the world. The first thing that Woodward notes is that Jesus introduced a "new conception of God." Quoting theologian David Tracy of the Chicago Divinity School, he says:

> Now, as in modern physics, we are coming to see that all of reality is interrelated. The doctrine of the Trinity says that even the divine reality in all its incomprehensible mystery is intrinsically relational.

Integration is inherent in the nature of God. He is perfect, and that perfection includes the perfect inter-relationship of the Father, Son and Holy Spirit.

Despite this foundational truth, during this past century we have emphasized specialization and the never-ending quest to sharpen our focus, be more precise. The explosion in knowledge has forced professionals in many fields to filter out everything that detracts from a narrow specialty.

Add to this the increased competition in the macro and micro work environment and the demands this places on one's career, and we have the ingredients for a fracturing of the once interrelated areas of life. Work, family, church and relaxation strain and tear. When these areas become disconnected, we have "disintegration."

In the business world, Michael Hammer and Jim Champy pointed out that disintegration was inefficient and, therefore, costing companies lots of money. Their writings caused a wave of "business re-engineering" across Corporate America. At the center of re-engineering was the integration of processes across business functions. The results were often spectacular, but not always spectacularly good. The human toll was enormous. Unfortunately, the executors of re-engineering projects often lacked a comprehensive philosophical framework that considered integrating other areas into this changing mass.

On a broader scale, the tight fiscal policies of the International Monetary Fund (IMF) in Asia are said by some to have caused the Asian Economic Flu in part because they ignored the cultural, political and people issues in those nations. Optimization is not the same as Integration. Optimizing one area can yield good short-term results for individuals and organizations. Sustained Impact comes, however, from continuous Innovation, focused Investment, and Integration.

Integration emanates from the understanding that God is for the whole of life. In a letter written to a group in Corinth, the writer makes an amazing statement:

> So from now on we regard no one from a worldly point of view. Though we once regarded Christ in this way, we do so no longer. Therefore, if anyone is in Christ, he is a new creation; the old has gone, the new has come! All this is from God, who reconciled us to himself through Christ and gave us the ministry of reconciliation: that God was reconciling the world to himself in Christ, not counting men's sins against them. And he has committed to us the message of reconciliation. We are therefore Christ's ambassadors, as though God were making his appeal through us. We implore you on Christ's behalf: Be reconciled to God.[7]

In the past my focus on this text had been on the individual. "Be reconciled to God." My problem was that I had equated this exclusively with my personal "day of salvation" (although I cannot tell you exactly when that was) and assumed that reconciliation had to do with a mostly one-time mending of an estranged relationship. But I now see

---

7    2 Corinthians 5:16-20

more: "God was...reconciling the world to himself." Several things have changed in my thinking:

» "All things are from God" and reconciliation—or integration—includes the alignment of all elements of life to him who is eternal.

» Reconciliation is an ongoing process of bringing into alignment anything in my life that is out of alignment with Truth. It is a process of integrating the many aspects of my life by overcoming, through Christ, the sin that has caused separation.

» The world is broader than individual relationships. Here the word is *kosmos*. This means "an apt and harmonious arrangement or constitution, order, government; the world, the universe; the circle of the earth, the earth; the inhabitants of the earth, men, the human family; the ungodly multitude; the whole mass of men alienated from God, and therefore hostile to the cause of Christ; world affairs, the aggregate of things earthly."[8]

People are desperately hungry for integration. They cannot always put a name to it, but they want the whole of their lives to have meaning, seven days a week. The Bible verse most displayed at football games, John 3:16, says "For God so loved the world..." Once again, the word used is *kosmos*, and when we begin to align our lives with this broad focus that God himself has, it draws us onto a bigger playing field.

## The Future is Almost Present

When the rate of change is very, very fast, as it is today, the future is almost now. When society is reinventing itself every three to five years the person with the six-year forecast is a futurist. Today someone predicts a technological or societal breakthrough at some future date; tomorrow you read about it in the newspaper. There are now blogs that opine on every topic, and websites that contain "prophetic words"

8    *Strong's Concordance*, # 2889.

about everything from presidential elections to future oil supplies. With all this chatter and clatter, is it worth trying to understand the times? Given that God is all-knowing, can we not just trust him and not worry too much about our lives?

> Therefore do not worry about tomorrow, for tomorrow will worry about itself. Each day has enough trouble of its own.[9]

The context of this "do not worry" verse is that we ought to seek first the kingdom of God. In other words, the verse is a caution not to get hung up on material possessions or, one could imply, the labor that will produce the cash to buy those possessions. The verse is not saying, "Don't try to understand what God is doing in the world." On the contrary, the earlier part of the passage states clearly, "So do not worry, saying, 'What shall we eat?' 'What shall we drink?' 'What shall we wear?' For the pagans run after all these things, and your heavenly Father knows that you need them. But seek first his kingdom and his righteousness, and all these things will be given to you as well."

The fact that we have a partial picture of something should not stop us from trying to understand it to the best of our ability. That is why we read and re-read passages from the Bible. Every time we read them, we are not the same reader, and the Holy Spirit is able to show us a different angle on the same passages. When Paul said, "For we know in part and we prophesy in part"[10] he wasn't encouraging us to not even try to understand. Consider these verses:

> My people are destroyed for lack of knowledge.[11]

> ...the sons of this age are shrewder and more prudent and wiser in relation to their own generation than are the sons of light.[12]

---

9    Matthew 6:34

10   1 Corinthians 13:9

11   Hosea 4:6

12   Luke 16:8

Following the trend is not necessarily a path to Convergence. Sometimes God asks us to walk in the opposite direction of a series of major trends. Nonetheless, it is generally helpful to understand the major trends so that we can better understand what God is up to (or sometimes up against), and how he might be leading us. By the time you read this, some of what follows may be out of date. But if you pick up the habit of trend spotting, you will have learned a skill that will serve you well as you seek to make wise decisions.

## Career Trends

Almost everything is changing on the career front. The job market has undergone radical shifts since the 1990's. The old career rules no longer apply. What used to be respectable stability is now lack of marketability. It's not yet clear whether the new trends are better, but it is clear that they are very different. Re-engineering has both helped and ravaged companies. The number of people employed by FORTUNE 500 companies has dropped from around 16 million in 1990 to 11 million in 1995. The fundamental shift to an information-based economy is in full swing. The Internet in particular has exceeded all growth projections and will continue to be a yeast that alters the shape of many industries. It is an enabling technology that is allowing huge changes to take place in the way that we see and do work. Many of the jobs that will provide our income in the 21st century do not even exist yet. The location of these jobs is also up for grabs. Jobs that can be done electronically can be done anywhere.

In the Appendices I dig into the trends and their implications in more detail. A key point to note is that things are shifting: by "shift" I don't mean a slight tweak, but a potentially major change in the way things are defined and done. The definitions of family and community are changing, the boundaries between work and leisure are moving, and the hard edges between work and home are blurring.

One should not be too quick to predict that a blurring of Career and Community is a good thing. Some corporations will jump on this trend for their own benefit. "Corporate America harbors a dirty secret," says *FORTUNE* magazine. "People in Human Resources know it. So do a lot of CEO's, although they don't dare discuss it. Families are no longer a big plus in a corporation; they are a problem."[13]

Regardless of whether corporations have holistic approaches to family and work, the fact is that our Career still gets the bulk of our energy. This is not necessarily a bad thing. Scripture has much to say about working hard and honestly. The question should not be whether we love our work, but whether it has become our primary point of significance. For many, the worship of work indicates that we are still finding our identity in our work, and not in our God.

Work—*occupacio*—is good. Call—vocation—is better. Convergence is about making the choices that maximize the harmony between these concepts.

I sat opposite a successful businessman at lunch one day. As a fairly young millionaire he had reached a critical stage in his career. He wasn't taking a rest between periods, as some would suggest, he was in meltdown mode. After 20+ years of career success he was struggling to face the prospect of coming out of the locker room for the second half. Others saw him as successful, but he knew that the money trail did not lead to a settled identity. When work saps the energy out of our soul, then we have probably been doing the wrong thing, or the right thing the wrong way for too long. When we hurtle down the hollow hallways of our jobs desperately seeking for identity, our pace becomes more and more frantic for fear that we will be overrun by the deafening echo of our own empty steps.

The Career trends could lead to two distinct possibilities: one is meaningful work without sacrificing the other areas of life. The other possibility is a redefinition of work as being the place 'where it all happens' and family as a source of utility-type services such as food, laundry and sleep. "For many people today, home has primarily

---

13    Betsy Morris, *"Is your family wrecking your career?"* FORTUNE, March 17, 1997.

become the place where a lot of routine work has to get done—duties that won't wait: doing the laundry, cooking dinner, and taking care of the kids. Home has become a treadmill. At work, there is a higher level of service; people have time to talk and have fun."[14]

There are Career trends that point to a more family friendly world, but we must be warned that the benefits are not automatic. If we carry any seeds of fragmentation out of the locker room, then instead of a more fruitful second half, they will spill on our field of dreams and we will spend the rest of our lives pulling weeds. In short, we will reap the same crop we had going into half time. The question is not, "How much money do you have in your pocket coming out of the locker room?" But "What is the quality of the seed you have in your pocket?" The fact is that you get good seed from a renewed mind, a refined character, and a life of obedience, and not from success in business.

A final word of caution: you may be thinking, "But I am very important to the corporation where I work!" An August 1997 article in *Fast Company* spoke of a Paul LaFontaine who left Bertelsmann Music Group in March 1997 to advise other businesspeople about radical honesty. His candidate for the top lie in business: "People are our most important asset." The truth, as he sees it, is this: "People are our most worrisome and unpredictable asset. Our most important assets are really our financial assets." He even has a lie detector: "When management starts talking about how important people are," LaFontaine says, "you can bet there is going to be an unpopular human resources decision coming soon." I am pro-business. Every day I enjoy the products and services produced by businesses. I love the fact that they can create jobs and further human dignity. But when we let our Career destroy the other facets of our lives then we have either deceived ourselves, or swallowed the lie.

Which leads us to a discussion of Community.

---

14    Rolf Jensen, *The Dream Society* (1999) McGraw-Hill.

# Community

Community looks a little different for each of us. Traditional definitions of peer, support and accountability groups are up for grabs. The jury is out on electronic communities, the impact of technology on relationships—good and bad—and the role of traditional nuclei of community. Regardless of how one defines Community, it is often at odds with Career. Somehow Community takes second place to our love affair with doing. The net result is that we are increasingly isolated. The larger the city, the quicker the pace, the greater the isolation. Without Community we suffer.

*Newsweek* magazine reported radically different health effects of simply being in relationship with supportive people.[15] Women who answered the question "Do you feel isolated?" with a "Yes" were three-and-a-half times as likely to die of breast, ovarian or uterine cancer over a 17-year period. "Does your wife show you her love?" According to *Newsweek*, men who answered "No" suffered 50% more angina over a five-year period than men who said "Yes." And heart patients who felt the least loved had 50% more arterial damage than those who felt the most loved. Unmarried heart patients who did not have a confidant were three times as likely to die within five years. "Do you live alone?" Those heart attack survivors who said "Yes" were more than twice as likely to die within a year.

Independence is a two-edged sword. In the U.S. it is prized right along with "life, liberty and the pursuit of happiness." In fact, many probably confuse the pursuit of happiness with independence, and independence with leaving one's social and family structures as quickly as possible. Said another way, American parents may be far too quick to push their children out of the nest. Friends once told us that others would view them as suspect if they said that their 17-year-old daughter was going to attend a community college and stay at home during that period. "What about the Big 10, the Ivy League...all will be lost!" We

---

15      *Newsweek*, March 16 1998, "Is love the best drug?"

prematurely dismantle the social infrastructure of our children, and then wonder why they struggle to create community of their own.

Have you noticed that many of the successful TV sitcoms are simply about people in community? Seinfeld, Mad About You, Friends, Fresh Prince of Bel Air, Growing Pains...A newer series, The Office, involves community at work. Inwardly we seem to long for community. Outwardly it is often quicker and easier to turn on the TV and meet our pseudo-friends who care for and get mad at each other, rather than take the time to build our own community. Yet week after week millions of people turn on the tube because of a deep longing for community. And much of the Community depicted on TV nowadays is based around work: Career and Community are converging.

So what are some of the major trends impacting Community? Let me pick just one point from the trends contained in the Appendices. The "Roll-your-own Community" trend which I noted in the First Edition of Convergence has accelerated. "We used to accept the menu of primary community-providing groups, such as a local church. More and more people are defining their own small groups and not paying much attention to the formal prescriptions of organizations."[16] People have a deep hunger for authentic Community. But lifestyles and demographic changes are challenging the traditional assumptions about where we find Community. For believers, the traditional place of community has been the local church. I don't believe that the definition of Church has really changed since the First Century. The institutional church has, however, often meandered away from the essence of Church. Today we see that people are exercising a greater degree of self-management in forming or joining groups that meet their needs. This extends to areas of fellowship traditionally organized by a single local church. This Chinese Menu approach goes something like this: I will attend Sunday services at Church A, I like the evening worship at church B, and I do not like the fellowship groups (home churches, Bible studies, care groups) of either. So a group of us

16    ibid.

from various churches will get together when it suits us. This lack of local church community cohesion has potential downsides and upsides. Nonetheless it reflects the tolerance, independence and self-management of our times. A possible expression of this trend is what some call "the emerging church." This isn't limited to any stereotypical group: people of all ages including late-career businesspeople are "rolling their own" in an attempt to experience authentic community. There are many other factors that feed into this phenomenon such as the empowerment to create your own online community, and the huge up-swell of single working people, which I will cover in a later chapter. This Roll-your-own Community trend has therefore become more of a survival mechanism than an altruistic choice. It is also something that will not go away.

A final trend I would like to highlight here is the "Integration of Family" trend. The "going to work" / "having spare time" separation that came about in the Industrial Age is beginning to reverse itself. There is a window of opportunity for the Church to become a community of relevance as society is once again in the throes of redefining itself. To do this we need a better theology of work, and we need to rethink the simplistic "God first, family second, church third, and work fourth" view that is preached all too glibly. As my friend Al Lunsford points out, "God worked before there was family. And, by definition, there was family before there was church." Unless we understand and practice an integrated expression of work-ministry-worship-family, then the church (by which I mean the local, institutional church) will be a community of irrelevance.

The bottom line is this: it will be hard to get to Convergence without Community. We discover ourselves in the context of community. Others shine a light on our gifts and grim realities. People inspire us, refine us, and multiply our efforts innumerably. The deliberate integration of one's family into one's business life, in whatever form that may take, paves the way for Convergence. No Community, no Convergence.

# Creativity

Some years ago Lyn asked a young intern what he had learned in his three-month stay with us. "I don't like maintenance!" came the quick reply, a fact born out by the fact that he had not changed his bedding for the same period. A group of adults had to take turns jumping down his throat with me concluding that "God spends a lot of time maintaining you." He had a point, however, because we were born to create. It is wired into our nature to do things that go beyond the maintenance mode of everyday life. Creativity is part of our DNA. Before we go on, a clarification on what I mean by Creativity might be helpful.

"In the beginning..." God heads the Creativity Department. Far from being the stodgy figure of history that once had a go at making things, he is still actively at work. What's more, he longs to engage us, mere humans, in his ongoing creative process. This God-man collaboration can be one of our highest joys. "Keep company with me and you'll learn to live freely and lightly."[17] In our dichotomized thinking we erroneously exclude God from our creative processes at work. One of our **rēp** clients in Cape Town woke up one night and God, step by step, revealed the design of a new water regulator to him. He was up the rest of the night sketching it out. He then built a prototype from "garden variety" components, and when he took it to a local water department they said, "This solves a problem we have been wrestling with for five years. We would like to place an order for 36,000 units."

So how does God create? At first glance his general modus operandi was to create something out of nothing. He simply stated it, and things came into being. Now if you don't subscribe to creation as articulated in the early chapters of Genesis, this book will probably do nothing to change your views. I have to point out, however, that Creativity is key to Convergence. And the creative process that we employ today is not

17    Matthew 11:30 *The Message*

so different from God's creative process. In fact, it derives from him and therefore looks like his process.

Before we explore this further, notice that the creativity of which we speak has little to do with leisure. It is essential to relax. The leisure industry has grown in leaps and bounds. We spend a huge percentage of our disposable income on travel and entertainment. In short, we work hard, and we play hard. At least that's the way we justify our wild fluctuations and adrenaline dependencies. But is it good for us, and if not, is there another way?

Creativity is not the twice a year pleasure rampage. The starve/binge approach to "creativity" is not healthy. Second, if we are talking about leisure and being built up, there is another way: entering a rest, Sabbath. With our grocery stores open 24 hours a day, malls and gas stations open on Sundays, and the ripple effects of "separation of church and state" spilling into commercial life, it is hard to maintain the sanctity of a holy day. (This is not a grand religious statement; it is an observation of reality.) Strict observance of the Sabbath as a day when no work can take place was maybe once a bondage. Today it appears much less of a bondage than the enslavement that people have to work—followers of Jesus included. We are also enslaved to communications. How many of you have forgotten to turn your cell phone or pager off when you are in church? Who takes their cell phone on a bike ride? Likewise many other things keep us enslaved and our engines running on high. It's hard to be creative when you are worn out.

When looking at Creativity I am including what we do with a paintbrush and palette, a pottery wheel or software code. These and many other areas are essential to our well being, but I am probably not the person most qualified to talk about them. There is great pleasure in reflecting God's creativity in the everyday, particularly in doing what the scripture calls "practicing hospitality."

Beyond this, I want to unpack the joys of getting alongside God and finding out what he is up to, then climbing on his bandwagon. This is where we go back full circle to the process of creation: seeing something where others see nothing, articulating it, and causing it to come into being.

> God is the God who gives life to the dead and calls things that are not as though they are.[18]

But I am not a visionary! You say? So what? God called you out of one thing to something else. You at least need to get a picture of yourself being wrapped around the form of Jesus. That involves some change. Then the wonderful privilege of being called to be co-workers of Jesus Christ means that we all have the responsibility of figuring out what he is up to and how we can serve what he is building. You may not be wired to be a trailblazer or a pioneer. You may be a settler who comes behind to establish the infrastructure and law and order that creates a place where others can live. But this too requires vision. It involves creativity. It involves faith.

So the Creativity of which I speak is a creative faith. And we need to integrate this creativity into our homes, our work and the pursuit of our Calling.

> Now faith comes by hearing, and hearing by the word of God.[19]

He speaks and things come into being—in creation and in you and me. This Creativity is definitely not limited to what we do outside of work. In fact, God's creation was his work! Today there is this same quest for creativity in work and meaning in play. "In the Dream Society, free time will occasionally be difficult to distinguish from work and—above all—it will be imbued with emotional content..."[20]

Before leaving the subject of Creativity, some will read into Creativity an advocacy for "the contemplative life." Contemplation is good, but

---

18   Romans 4:17

19   Romans 10:17. The word here is *rhema*, not *logos*. It is the spoken word of God, not the written word of God. Reading the Bible raises our hope level; God speaking something to us gives us faith, the faith to create. This once again reinforces the importance of the season where we learn to hear God.

20   Rolf Jensen, *The Dream Society*, McGraw-Hill, 1999.

when it leads to isolation and the relegating of everyday life to a so-called secluded life, we open ourselves to distortion. In the writings of the early Church there was "the perfect life" and the "permitted life."[21] An over-emphasis on a "secluded being" as distinct from an "everyday being" is as dangerous as the elevation of doing above being, or being above doing.

## Call

"Everyone has a call upon his or her life."

This is easy to say, but when someone asks how to discover the call of God on their life, it is not so easy to answer. Like personality, gifts and character, the call on our lives has two different, but equal facets: it is the same for everyone, and it is different for everyone.

What is the same for everyone? The Westminster Confession states that the chief purpose of man is to glorify God and to enjoy him forever. This is universal. We are made in the image of God, and we understand ourselves and our context as we get to know him better. This is the fabric of every believer's tapestry.

But "call" seems to go beyond this broad purpose. It takes on a flavor of something specific to you and to me. So the flip side to our common purpose is that this God is infinitely creative, and he has made each of us unique. He has decided that each of us is best off when we reflect the unique facet of his character that shines only through us.

The ways in which people have "received a call" are many and varied. In the old days we seemed to hear more about "receiving a call" than we do today. And when we heard about it the context was generally someone explaining how they were "called" to "full-time Christian ministry" or to a particular "tongue, tribe or nation." If it was "spiritual" it was a call, or if the location was remote and preferably African-sounding, so much the better. The rest of us didn't talk about our Calling that much.

---

21    Os Guinness, *The Call*, Word Publishing, 1998 - page 32.

How often have you heard someone say, "I was called to IBM." Or "I was called to General Electric."

Well, I was called to Price Waterhouse and San Francisco. Seriously. When I was completing my undergraduate work at the University of Cape Town, the Big 8 accounting firms did their spiel on campus. I don't recall seeing any of them. I simply prayed and felt that God would have me go to Price Waterhouse. My friends lined up interviews with many companies. I went to one. During the interview the Staff Partner, Anthony Coombe, asked where else I was interviewing. I replied, "Nowhere else. I believe I am to work here." He graciously extended me a job offer.

I then spent 14 years with Price Waterhouse before being called on to my next skills building situation at KPMG Peat Marwick. My calling to these particular jobs enabled me to rest in the fact that "promotion comes from the Lord." It freed me from the pressures of needing to carve my own career, politically speaking. In the creative sense, I did carve my own career as both firms provided wonderful opportunities to trail-blaze in new areas, and also left me the freedom to leave when I felt God wanted me to move on.

The move from KPMG to Computer Sciences Corporation was another such move. Logically speaking, it was a little crazy: Less money, more work, less prestige...a potential CLM (career limiting move.) But through prayer and much confirmation from my Bible readings, I felt I had learned what I was to learn at KPMG, and it was time to move on for other reasons too. I wanted to travel less. Fay was entering her pre-teen years, and I would not have the opportunity to repeat them. In addition it turned out that there were wonderful aspects to the culture, skills and quality of people at CSC that complemented what I had learned at Price Waterhouse and KPMG. The main point is that I felt called to move. How is a call to First Baptist Church or XYZ Missionary Movement any more real or valid than a call to business? Not in my book.

# Business is a Calling

"What is my calling?" This big question with a vague answer has been simplified in my mind. Not long ago I sat with the head of a major denomination and asked him, "What percentage of people in San Francisco and nearby counties attend church?" "We don't know," he said, "but we estimate 3% to 4%." I went on to ask, "What percentage of these people attend work?" "Nearly 100%...", and the penny dropped. Unless we teach people how to live a called life in their workplace, we fail them. Second, unless we reach those who are engaged in work, we miss the market. Third, unless we ourselves are convinced that business is a calling, and a high one at that, then we will not have the faith to embark on mighty exploits with God through business. God is in business. Jesus said, "I must be about my Father's business." He further told us through the parable to "do business until I return." One of my favorite verses is John 15:15 where, near the end of Jesus' life, he explains the nature of his operation and the call on the disciples:

> I no longer call you servants, because a servant does not know his master's business. Instead, I have called you friends, for everything that I learned from my Father I have made known to you.

Take the negative out of the verse and it paraphrases something like this: "I call you friends because everything I have learned from my Father about his business I have made known to you." If you are a friend of Jesus the proof will be that you know his business. And you do it. As Dennis Peacocke reminds us, God doesn't want you to invite Him into your business, he wants to get you into His business!

As much as I felt led to work in each of those organizations for different seasons, they were not in and of themselves my Calling. My call includes being a living example of the integration of business and missions in a way that creates a bridge for others to find a way to walk out their vocation without necessarily abandoning their occupation. It is a people business, and God is in the people business.

When I planned to leave CSC and start The Institute, I met with the President of the Consulting division. After a few sentences of explanation, he interrupted my dialogue to state that he would: "go to his grave believing that I made a mistake leaving CSC." Less than an hour later he remarked, "We want you to stay, but if you have this higher Calling on your life..." I hadn't used the word "call." I did not lay out the alternatives: God's way or your way. But he saw it clearly. How did he recognize the call on my life? Like some other things, call can be hard to explain, but you know it when you see it. In later years a colleague at The Institute asked me, "Are we a business or a ministry?" I replied, "Yes!" God wants those of us in the workplace to be 100% ministers and 100% businesspeople, educators, government officials, or whatever our work may be.

## We Need a Call, and We Need a Context

Without a frame of reference outside ourselves, we will implode on ourselves. Without an external voice calling us beyond ourselves, we will lack the realistic vision to be other than who we are at the moment. God calls us to be and do, not because we are able, but because the Calling itself will require us to stretch and go. Call is not just a validation of who we are, it is an appeal to grow to the next level. I used to think God gave me a Calling because of who he had made me to be. I was wrong. He rather seems to set a stretch goal that will inevitably require that I be melted down and flexibly reformed in the image of his Son... or I will simply come apart at the seams trying to get there in my own strength.

The second thing to note is that our Calling comes in a context. Each of us is placed in a context, or frame of reference, or sphere of influence. For some it is the Arts, for some the Sciences, for some Education, and for others Government. For many it is Business, yet they hanker for the other side of the fence where "real ministers" have "real calls." Come to terms with your context, then minister 100% to God and others in it.

I have come to see another facet of Calling which is overly obvious in Scripture, but in our age of individualism has somehow been lost: the Family Calling. God is the God of "Abraham, Isaac and Jacob." Abraham is the father of our faith, and his story comes to life in Genesis chapter 12. He is living with his dad, Terah, in a spot up river from modern day Iraq. All of a sudden God calls him and tells him to take off for the Promised Land. In my own thinking I had the notion that Abe probably had no clue where he was going:

> The Lord had said to Abram, "Leave your country, your people and your father's household and go to the land I will show you. I will make you into a great nation and I will bless you; I will make your name great, and you will be a blessing. I will bless those who bless you, and whoever curses you I will curse; and all peoples on earth will be blessed through you." So Abram left, as the Lord had told him; and Lot went with him. Abram was seventy-five years old when he set out from Haran. He took his wife Sarai, his nephew Lot, all the possessions they had accumulated and the people they had acquired in Haran, and they set out for the land of Canaan, and they arrived there.[22]

If you read back in Genesis 11 you will find, however, that God had actually called Abraham's dad, but he got halfway and stopped:

> Terah took his son Abram, his grandson Lot son of Haran, and his daughter-in-law Sarai, the wife of his son Abram, and together they set out from Ur of the Chaldeans to go to Canaan. But when they came to Haran, they settled there. Terah lived 205 years, and he died in Haran.[23]

The fact is, Abraham did not start something totally new. He had more of a re-call than a call![24] Another way to say it is that his calling was

---

22      Genesis 12:1-5

23      Genesis 11: 31-32

24      For more on this topic see my booklet titled *Beyond Halfway* which lays out a challenge to business people to go the distance in their following of God, and equips church leaders to understand the businesspeople in their congregations. See *www.repurposing.biz*.

a Family Calling. God had already told his father where to go, but he got held up either by a good real estate deal, or perhaps he was still hindered by the hurt carried from losing a son. After all, he named the place Haran after his deceased child. When I realized that my children will probably have callings that have the DNA of my own call intertwined in them, it changed my thinking. No longer would I expect that they would be searching for their own Calling in a context-free environment. No longer would I try to bury the threads of my history and future under the ruse that they should start from scratch. I now pray regularly that my children will pick up and take to a new level and scope the Calling that God entrusted to me for a season. I don't want them to be mini-me. I am jealous, however, that the kingdom DNA that God has deposited in me will be stewarded across multiple generations.

## Our Call Must Come From God

The word "call" can be used loosely by those inside and outside the Church. Despite the many sources of inspiration, there are numerous reasons why our call must come from God:

» Only he can create a vision beyond us and provide the grace and power to ratchet us beyond superficiality and slothfulness.

» He provides a goal—it is him, his likeness.

» He provides a source—it is his being.

» He provides a reason—it is his love.

» He provides a path—it is his Son, Jesus.

» He provides a means—it is his Spirit.

» No one, nothing—not ourselves or this world—can ever begin to make us this offer.

"From him and through him and to him are all things."[25]

Convergence is not the result of a decision you make once. It is not the outcome of a single planning session. It is more often the fruit of an integrated mind, the harvest of lots of little decisions. Some of your decisions have pushed you in the direction of Convergence; others have sidetracked you. The older you get, the lengthier those side-roads seem to be, and the less you can afford to take them.

Convergence is an all-too-rare phenomenon. Sadly, I have met many chronologically gifted people who have done many things, traveled to a plethora of places, seen lots of "ministry," but have yet to experience the fullness of God's purposes for themselves. There is no formula that predicts or explains when individuals will experience Convergence. God works differently with each of us.

Discovering the wisdom spoken of in the book of Proverbs has some parallels to the journeying into Convergence. If we learn to listen, we will hear it cry out to us. If we learn to read its road signs, we will begin to see the path it is taking us on. If we are aware of its principles, it has a way of drawing us towards it. This, I suppose, is part of the mystery. It happens in God's time and in his way, but we can understand it, accept it and even hasten it by God's grace.

> If you accept my words and store up my commands within you,
> turning your ear to wisdom
> and applying your heart to understanding,
> and if you call out for insight
> and cry aloud for understanding,
> and if you look for it as for silver
> and search for it as for hidden treasure,
> then you will understand the fear of the Lord
> and find the knowledge of God.

---

25    Romans 11:33-36

Words, commands, wisdom, understanding, insight, hidden treasure, fear of the Lord...knowledge of God. This is our goal:

> I will give them singleness of heart and action, so that they will always fear me for their own good and the good of their children after them.[26]

26    Jeremiah 32:39

# What Convergence is Not

## Convergence is Not Balance.

I'm not sure that balance is a Biblical concept. While it was helpful to me as a new believer to compartmentalize my life and make plans for each area, I'm not sure that the goal of balance was altogether trustworthy. Obedience sometimes demands that we be unbalanced. When I meet people I often ask, "What's your passion?" I seldom ask "Are you balanced?" For well-rounded people the question is a non-issue; for unbalanced people…what's the point in asking?

"Convergence is not Balance" is a statement that some people love. It releases them from an impossible juggling act. Mike Cheves is an example of such a person.

Others dislike it because they know that, left to their own devices, they will tend towards misalignment, so they need safeguards to "keep in balance." They solve the problem of time debt by allocating scarce resources in even payments to the creditor compartments in their lives. What I like about this is that they hopefully allocate time for God and family early in their time budget. I would call this "priority setting," which is a good thing, and not "balance" as Christian-speak generally describes it. What I don't like about our implementation of "the balanced life" is that it reinforces dichotomy, puts us in the driver's seat, and skews us towards Christian Humanism rather than simple daily obedience. This striving for balance is unlike the prototype that Jesus exemplified:

> I tell you the truth, the Son can do nothing by himself; he can do only what he sees his Father doing, because whatever the Father does the Son also does.[27]

## Convergence is Not a Formula

Second, Convergence is not designed to be formulaic or prescriptive. This is no "Three-Easy-Steps-to-Life" program. Simple answers to life are often just that.

During Jesus' three brief years of public function, many adept religious people scurried left and right trying to box him in. And yet the Jesus of the gospels carefully escaped the predictive packaging of the establishment. Jesus was clear, yet mystical. He was fresh, yet established in eternity. He was single-minded, yet vigilantly avoided the narrow-minded arguments with which his followers and opponents sought to tether him.

27    John 5:19

I recognize the dangers of The 4-C's and The 10-F's[28] and other tools in this book. So I ask that you not look to these ideas as a "way out," but as a "way to." Should you find yourself becoming formulaic in your thinking as you read these pages, stop to rediscover where Jesus is taking you.

Convergence is about the mystical. It's about fine-tuning your senses to the mysteries of an unboxable Creator. It's about discovery—discovering yourself, learning to know and tell your story, gaining a perspective of how that story fits into the grand sweep of your Father's story.

To gain this perspective it helps to have pens and a palette. To better participate in what God is initiating, it's useful to recognize markers and milestones that illuminate what has happened in our lives. So don't think of Convergence as the day planner for the next century, but as the toolbox of the mystical. We all need to sharpen our tools to understand, not just God's plan for eternity, but what the Bible calls his ways, his paths, his dealings. We need a forensic kit so we can rediscover the fingerprints of our Creator on the seemingly random pieces of our short lives.

One of my favorite verses comes from Proverbs 25:

> It is the glory of God to conceal a matter;
> To search out a matter is the glory of kings.

Come be a king for a day.

In a letter to Chuck Colson, Father Tom Weinandy wrote:

> The true theologian or church body wishes to know ever more clearly the mysteries of the faith so that... we know better what the mystery is, not that we comprehend the mystery and so

---

28    The 10-F Model® is a registered trademark of The Institute for Innovation, Integration & Impact, Inc. See www.inst.net for more information.

deprive it of its mystery...with the clarity [of doctrinal purity] comes more mystery—more awe, more reverence.[29]

Our goal is to bring clarity to the mystery—not to reduce the mystical to a formula—and cause us to be more in awe, more reverent, more fearful of the living God.

## Convergence May Not Lead to Significance

My wife, Lyn, says that people have an invisible sign hanging around their neck that says, "Notice me!" Each of us likes to feel special; most of us would rather be a "somebody" than a "nobody." We often express this as a need to feel significant or to have significance. In and of itself, this is not bad. But the quest for significance can be dangerous. In his book, *Perilous Pursuits*, Joseph M. Stowell opens by saying:

> We are built for significance. Our problem is not that we search for it, but that we search for it in all the wrong places.

Believers in business are facing an unprecedented opportunity to find significance in all the right places. The Founding Partners of the *Life@ Work* magazine, Tom Addington and Stephen Graves, state their belief that "for the past 20 years, family has been a front door through which the Gospel has been introduced to Americans." But they see the early decades of the next century belonging to the world of work. This would not be the first time God has birthed mission waves out of the business incubator. The stage has been set for businesspeople to have worldwide influence. Writings and organizations that spur others on to find meaning in life beyond the sometimes lucrative daily grind have emerged in recent years. I am generally heartened by the desire to do business God's way. My caution is that it may not lead to significance if one is defining significance the old way.

---

29    Charles Colson, *The Body*, Word Publishing, page 98.

# Convergence is Not Success

Convergence is not "success" as it is generally defined. There have been many attempts to define success in a way that separates it from wealth, but in the back of our minds the definition of success seems to be a two part equation, and the second part is "...and made money doing it." If you are in the business world and doing exactly what you want to be doing, you generally do not get bonus points unless there is the creation of wealth included in the mix. We know that it makes no real sense, but the moneymaking element hovers like a mist over our definition of success. A friend, Kim Daus-Edwards puts it this way:

> One thing I have learned is that there is an enormous tension between worldly success and Godly success. Psalm 49 says, "But man, despite his riches, does not endure; he is like the beasts that perish. This is the fate of those who trust in themselves, and of their followers who approve their sayings" (v 12-13). And "Do not be overawed when a man grows rich" (v 16). Worldly success for sure, but even success from a Christian mindset, is often equated with money, titles, fame, power, and possessions. Sometimes we add in legacy as a barometer of success, though often that is even connected to ego or self. As Christians, we don't like to admit that the world has influenced our definition of success. Looking back at several times in my life, I have seen the deception and denial in my own heart on this issue, though I would never have admitted it at the time.[30]

In order to remain at a place of contentment we have to continually ask for a renewing of our minds. We also have to look alternate definitions of success squarely in the eye and be willing to contrast God's view and the temporary view. The apostle Paul had to face the fact that not everyone thought he was a howling success. Where were the accolades, where was the string of great accomplishments? Why did they see this

30    Kim Daus-Edwards, *What is Success?* A booklet published by Indaba Publishing

www.repurposing.biz.

battered-about man instead of something, well, more successful? Here is his view which he expresses in detail in 2 Corinthians chapter 4. It is a long quote, but meditate on it and ponder how you would feel if your name, resume or reputation was encapsulated by this passage:

> Since God has so generously let us in on what he is doing, we're not about to throw up our hands and walk off the job just because we run into occasional hard times. We refuse to wear masks and play games. We don't maneuver and manipulate behind the scenes. And we don't twist God's Word to suit ourselves. Rather, we keep everything we do and say out in the open, the whole truth on display, so that those who want to can see and judge for themselves in the presence of God. If our Message is obscure to anyone, it's not because we're holding back in any way. No, it's because these other people are looking or going the wrong way and refuse to give it serious attention. All they have eyes for is the fashionable god of darkness. They think he can give them what they want, and that they won't have to bother believing a Truth they can't see. They're stone-blind to the dayspring brightness of the Message that shines with Christ, who gives us the best picture of God we'll ever get. Remember, our Message is not about ourselves; we're proclaiming Jesus Christ, the Master. All we are is messengers, errand runners from Jesus for you. It started when God said, "Light up the darkness!" And our lives filled up with light as we saw and understood God in the face of Christ, all bright and beautiful. If you only look at us, you might well miss the brightness. We carry this precious Message around in the unadorned clay pots of our ordinary lives. That's to prevent anyone from confusing God's incomparable power with us.

> As it is, there's not much chance of that. You know for yourselves that we're not much to look at. We've been surrounded and battered by troubles, but we're not demoralized; we're not sure what to do, but we know that God knows what to do; we've been spiritually terrorized, but God

66

hasn't left our side; we've been thrown down, but we haven't broken. What they did to Jesus, they do to us - trial and torture, mockery and murder; what Jesus did among them, he does in us - he lives! Our lives are at constant risk for Jesus' sake, which makes Jesus' life all the more evident in us. While we're going through the worst, you're getting in on the best! We're not keeping this quiet, not on your life. Just like the psalmist who wrote, "I believed it, so I said it," we say what we believe. And what we believe is that the One who raised up the Master Jesus will just as certainly raise us up with you, alive. Every detail works to your advantage and to God's glory: more and more grace, more and more people, more and more praise! So we're not giving up. How could we! Even though on the outside it often looks like things are falling apart on us, on the inside, where God is making new life, not a day goes by without his unfolding grace. These hard times are small potatoes compared to the coming good times, the lavish celebration prepared for us. There's far more here than meets the eye. The things we see now are here today, gone tomorrow. But the things we can't see now will last forever.[31]

Note the fact that Paul does not see the negatives only in light of today; we have to have one eye on eternity when we define success. If you own or run a business, then the matter of success must also be addressed for the corporation. The work of **rēp** is to help repurpose businesses and develop scorecards that we hope are "good for today, and good for eternity." I see a heartening new trend emerging. Generation-X and the Millennial Generation, perhaps predictably, want the direct route to significance, even if it means trading in old definitions of success. Many people with whom I speak want both, but the point here is that they want meaningful work right out of college. Others are exiting Corporate America to find something more lasting.

---

31      2 Corinthians chapter 4, *The Message.*

## Convergence is Not Business-as-Usual

*Convergence*, like other writings around this subject, can be prone to a formulaic interpretation. We don't want the "Seven Habits" or the "Ten Laws" or the "Five Whatevers." One of the best ways to miss what God is doing in a situation is to take your tried and true template and overlay it on the raw material of the next phase of your life. Please recognize that there are no fixed time lines for Convergence, there is no particular sequence to the Seven Seasons. You get from one season to the next based on some blend of listening to God and obeying, on the one hand, and his sovereign choices on the other. In Isaiah 55:8 we are reminded:

> "For my thoughts are not your thoughts, neither are your ways my ways," declares the Lord.

Regardless of what stage of life we have reached, if business has a mandate for missions in this century, we will have to be a people who are finding out what it means to do things God's way. The rest of the Isaiah 55 passage gives us insights into the key to Convergence:

> As the heavens are higher than the earth, so are my ways higher than your ways and my thoughts than your thoughts. As the rain and the snow come down from heaven, and do not return to it without watering the earth and making it bud and flourish, so that it yields seed for the sower and bread for the eater, so is my word that goes out from my mouth: It will not return to me empty, but will accomplish what I desire and achieve the purpose for which I sent it.[32]

When sharing the word of God with people we can claim as a promise that the Word won't "return void." But sometimes things are spoken and they do not come to pass. This can be a good thing if the credibility of the source is dubious. We need to note, however, that this statement that "it will not return to me empty" follows a clear understanding that

32    Isaiah 55:9-11

God does things his way. And his way is not our way. And his thoughts are not our thoughts.

It is also important to note the phrase, "so is my word." The chapter entitled "Fearing and Hearing God" elaborates on this truth. Convergence comes as we respond to God's initiative. God's initiative is revealed in what he speaks, and these "words from God" produce the faith to follow God:

> Faith comes by hearing the word of God.[33]

Convergence therefore has much more to do with obedience to God's word—written and spoken—than a specific pursuit of significance or any business formula for missions. In fact, in many instances obedience leads to insignificance. If God's leading in your life parallels the life of John the Baptist, Jesus will increase, and you will decrease. You may end up with a downwardly mobile career. If obedience to God's call means significance in the eyes of the world, well and good. But this is the wrong measure. For our significance results from our secure identity in Jesus and not in the dubious views of success or the accolades of people. Our secure identity leaves us free to serve. And service, among other things, leads to a sense of satisfaction. "Lose your life and you find it."[34] Allusions of significance can rob us of contentment. Likewise, caring too much about what others think of us leads to consternation, not Convergence.

> Do nothing out of selfish ambition or vain conceit, but in humility consider others better than yourselves.[35]

Jesus is the best example of a secure person laying aside an easy route to significance in selfless obedience:

> Jesus, knowing that the Father had given all things into his hands...

33        Romans 10:17

34        Matthew 16:25

35        Philippians 2:3

[He was secure in his positional authority.]

...and that he had come from God

[He knew his roots and identity.]

...and was going to God...

[He was very clear on his destination.]

rose from supper and laid aside his garments... and began to wash the disciple's feet.[36]

[He was able to follow a path of service, precisely because he was so secure.]

Our question should not be, "How do I find an outlet for my great gifts and talents?" Our question should be, "How has God created me to best serve others with my unique collection of talents?"

Now that we have considered what Convergence is not, let's begin to explore what it is.

## Leaders Throughout History

While still resisting the urge to reduce Convergence to a formula, let's take a closer look at some historical leaders whom we admire. It's often easier to figure out what happened in their lives than in our own, and almost always easier to do so in retrospect. I want you to consider the patterns of key figures in history and reflect on what this may mean for your own life. Noah, for example, received a highly unusual mandate from God, and persisted with his project for 120 years. Finally the vindication came as his calling became a reality. Sadly, it appears he did not end well. Others fared better.

| Leader | Early life | Skills/Call | Character | Convergence |
|--------|-----------|-------------|-----------|-------------|
| Joseph | Dreams | Duties | Dungeons | Dynasty |
| Moses | Abandoned at early age | 40 years in training | 40 years in desert | 40 years of national leadership |
| Esther | Exile, training by uncle | Selection as queen | Rejection (for a season) | Rule |
| David | Duties | Anointing | Desert | Kingship |
| Daniel | Exile | Training | Lion's den | Governing |
| Jesus | Suffering, exile | Launch, Divine commissioning | Desert | Ministry |
| Mary | Promise | Relocation | Mother of Messiah | Place in history |
| Paul | Training | Call | Desert | Effectiveness |

Joseph had dreams that got him into and out of trouble. Early on he dreamed of his brothers bowing down to him. This landed him a job as a slave. He then got promoted to lead servant in a prominent household, but his principles sent him to jail. Finally, his proven skills as a dream interpreter got him the top job in the nation. He got to know God at an early age, learned to hear and fear God, built skills repeatedly, had an internal integrity test in the form of Potiphar's wife, honed his gifts, had numerous years in the University of the Desert while in jail, and finally chose a wife. In the language of Convergence, he went through all Seven Seasons.

David wasn't the favored son. When the prophet came scouting for a future king, he was the only one left off the list. Samuel had to ask for him. He had been in the back, off beyond, looking after sheep and fending off predators. He was getting to know his God, finding out who he was, and learning how to lead sheep...a skill that would stand him in good stead when leading people.

Several things are worth noting about these and many other leaders in the pages of the Bible:

» They all began nowhere and yet somewhere: Moses floating in the basket on the river Nile, Joseph one of twelve sons, Mary a teenager in the village. Not many of them have noble beginnings, yet somehow we know that God began his work when they were "knit together" in their mothers' wombs.

» For many there was a definite commissioning of some sort—a dream, a choice of a leader, a prophecy, a word of a parent or relative. Sometimes others are more tuned in to our destiny than we are, especially when we are young: Convergence.

» For most there is a delay between the call or commission and the fulfillment of that call. This is perhaps the toughest thing for us to handle. We are so accustomed to immediacy. We get so wrapped up in "my career, my plans, my time line, my ideas of my life." Yet God is not bound in his thinking about time.

## The Inevitable Delay

One of the challenges we face is the delay between what we sense God has said to us about our lives, and the time it takes for that to come to pass. An extreme example of this is a man in the church I was leading who was traveling overseas when he received a "prophetic word" that God would make him a leader in the church. He definitely had leadership qualities, but he was very young in his faith, and there was lots of opportunity for character development. When he shared this leadership possibility with me I was happy for him. I knew it would take years before this came to pass, but he had something quicker in mind. He did not hear "you will be a leader someday." What he heard was that "God would make him a leader of my church...soon." A short while later I was out of town at a conference and received the phone call saying there had been a coup in the church. This man and a band of ready recruits had decided they were taking over and announced it at a Sunday morning service. I smile now, but we do crazy things when we feel God isn't doing things fast enough for us. You can ask Abraham, King Saul and Judas...they all experienced The Inevitable Delay.

In order to shape your expectations of The Seven Seasons, you may want to try to estimate the amount of time between God's call/word to these leaders, and their walking it out:

| Leader | From | To | Number of Years |
|---|---|---|---|
| Moses | Call to lead | Red Sea | |
| David | Anointing by Samuel | Public coronation | |
| Jesus | First acknowledgement as Messiah | Public Ministry | |
| Paul | Damascus road | Recorded ministry | |

For some of these leaders the delay is measured in decades, not years. If they are a pattern for our lives, what can we expect in our own walk with God? Many of us get mad at God because we don't like his timing. Others of us get wrinkled because we like God, we just don't like the way he does things. In fairness to God, he has tried to manage our expectations. Not only are there ample warnings that this is a "long and winding road," but there are also solid indications that the road has tollbooths.

## Unavoidable Tollbooths on the Road to Transformation

Convergence is not a country club where old boys are sitting around in smoking jackets smugly pondering the fact that they have arrived:

> Blessed are those whose strength is in you, who have set their hearts on pilgrimage.[34]

Convergence involves a commitment to stay on the road, even when there are distractions, hurts and apparent detours. A good example of this can be seen in Paul's references to his own journey in his second letter to the church in Corinth. A pinnacle of the letter is found all the way in the 10th chapter:

34    Psalm 84:5

For though we live in the world, we do not wage war as the world does. The weapons we fight with are not the weapons of the world. On the contrary, they have divine power to demolish strongholds. We demolish arguments and every pretension that sets itself up against the knowledge of God, and we take captive every thought to make it obedient to Christ.[35]

Wow! This is an impressive arsenal. Wouldn't you like to have him on your side in a spiritual battle? How did he get to be so equipped? Where did he get the big spiritual guns? If you are like me, you are more familiar with this verse than with the nine chapters that precede it. But as we study the letter we see that the road to 2 Corinthians 10 passes through many tollbooths. Likewise, the journey to Convergence has some inevitable seasons. Let's look at the tollbooths:

» Chapter 1: Suffering. "For just as the sufferings of Christ flow over into our lives, so also through Christ our comfort overflows." (v. 5)

» Chapter 2: Financial integrity. "Unlike so many, we do not peddle the word of God for profit. On the contrary, in Christ we speak before God with sincerity, like men sent from God." (v. 17)

» Chapter 3: Competence from God, not our own intellect. "Not that we are competent in ourselves to claim anything for ourselves, but our competence comes from God." (v. 5)

» Chapter 4: Transparency. "Rather, we have renounced secret and shameful ways; we do not use deception, nor do we distort the word of God. On the contrary, by setting forth the truth plainly we commend ourselves to every man's conscience in the sight of God." (v. 2)

» Chapter 5: New thinking, new ministry. "So from now on we regard no one from a worldly point of view...and gave us the ministry of reconciliation." (v. 16)

35    2 Corinthians 10:3-5

» Chapter 6: Hard work. "Rather, as servants of God we commend ourselves in every way: in great endurance; in troubles, hardships and distresses; in beatings, imprisonments and riots; in hard work, sleepless nights and hunger; in purity, understanding, patience and kindness; in the Holy Spirit and in sincere love; in truthful speech and in the power of God; with weapons of righteousness in the right hand and in the left; through glory and dishonor, bad report and good report; genuine, yet regarded as impostors; known, yet regarded as unknown; dying, and yet we live on; beaten, and yet not killed; sorrowful, yet always rejoicing; poor, yet making many rich; having nothing, and yet possessing everything." (v. 4-10)

» Chapter 7: Purity. "Since we have these promises, dear friends, let us purify ourselves from everything that contaminates body and spirit, perfecting holiness out of reverence for God." (v. 1)

» Chapter 8: Selflessness. "...they gave themselves first to the Lord and then to us in keeping with God's will." (v. 5)

» Chapter 9: Generosity. "Remember this: Whoever sows sparingly will also reap sparingly, and whoever sows generously will also reap generously. Each man should give what he has decided in his heart to give, not reluctantly or under compulsion, for God loves a cheerful giver." (v. 6-7)

You may find different tollbooths on the road to the victorious place of 2 Corinthians 10. I have extracted just one per chapter to simply illustrate that Paul's life was not a walk in the park. He had serious challenges, genuine suffering, real scars, and stark setbacks, even though he was doing the will of God. Of particular note are the frequent references to giving and generosity. We must make strides in overcoming our attachment to money before we can have the spiritual power we so long for.

There was a time in our lives when a series of bad things happened in such a way that only God could have orchestrated it. Clients reneged on debts, a book went awry, staff left and set up shop in opposition to us, and it felt like a vacuum cleaner had attached itself to our bank account. We had peace when we realized only God could have created this perfect storm, then we had peace in that storm. It did not go away; we just had calm. Once God breaks our attachment to money, he restores our ability to safely create wealth, and Joel 2:25 kicks in:

> I will repay you for the years the locusts have eaten—the great locust and the young locust, the other locusts and the locust swarm—my great army that I sent among you.

## Timing is Everything

We hear it so often that we forget its importance. The world's technology dump is filled with products that hit the market too soon or too late. "I was five years ahead of the times." "We were just three months too late to market."

"Timing is everything!" This is not a core Biblical truth, but an understanding of timing sure helps and, as followers of Jesus, we often run into trouble because we don't understand it. In my own life, after getting initial direction I am learning to ask the secondary questions. "When? How long are we talking about here? Long term, or short term? Way off, or pretty close? Any other clues as to timing?" I don't think God objects to these questions.

Don't get me wrong; I am often surprised by God's timing and how his plans and mine are out of sync. But I've found that it doesn't hurt to ask. One of my most valuable lessons in this area came in 1987 when Lyn and I were praying about whether to start **rēp**. In summary, we felt it was right. We were to stay in the U.S. as business-based missionaries to start an organization that would bridge the worlds of business, missions, and local church. In prayer with other leaders, I felt God say that he would give me the blueprints of the new ministry, which he did. As I meditated a while longer, I sensed God say that there would be a five year ramp-up period. So I stashed the ministry blueprints, and quietly enrolled in the University of the Desert. If I hadn't sensed the timing, I would have been frustrated and wasted a lot of people's time. The fact is, for the next four to five years I did not have the energy to do anything except wait.

While we may seldom know the exact timing, God takes most people through a series of major seasons. With the exception of the season dealing with choosing a spouse, I believe the remaining seasons apply to all people.

## Seven Seasons

**K**airos and Chronos.

Technically, I am an African. My father was born on a farm in Sea Point, a suburb of Cape Town, South Africa. While my mother only arrived in the city of Port Elizabeth when she was eight years old, she is an African. She has a South African passport, her formative years were spent in South Africa, and she lives in a small town in South Africa. My four older siblings and I were all born in South Africa, making us Africans too.

Practically, however, no one in my family is African, especially when it comes to a concept of time.

As a child I was amazed to watch real Africans interact. Many things can mesmerize you while in Africa: the gentle rhythm of women-folk walking with a load balanced perfectly on their heads and a child tightly wrapped in a blanket on their backs; the leisurely lilt of their voices; and the fact that a conversation with a pedestrian passing the other way began long before they were shoulder to shoulder, and continued until they were virtually out of earshot. The rhythm of Africa is different. It is not driven by time as we know it, but by events or seasons.

In the translation of Scripture to English we have lost the nuances of time. In the Bible *Chronos* and *Kairos* are two distinct words referring to time. *Chronos* is the root of chronology and chronometer, the official name of a watch or timepiece. We are driven by time. We have 101 ways to master it, make it go slower, get more out of it, put more into it, get more because of it. We have whole industries devoted to helping us slice and dice the 168 hours we have each week. We measure our worth in time. If we have money, we easily say, "Time is more precious than money," and almost mean it. *Chronos* we know; chronos knows us, and controls us.

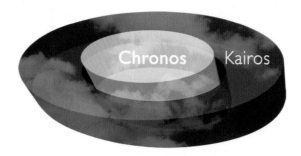

But cousin kairos is a stranger. *Chronos* ticks; *kairos* sings, it whispers. *Kairos* speaks of time as a season. It is the notion of the rightness of the timing of something that is greater than the calendar or the chronometer. In Biblical revelation, *kairos* controls *chronos*.

"In the fullness of time..."[36] Or, at just the right time, the right season. Africans know *kairos*; Westerners know *chronos*. The *James Strong Exhaustive Concordance of the Bible* defines *kairos* this way:

> an occasion, i.e., set or proper time; convenient, due season; (due, short, while) time, a while.

My daughter, Fay, is a Westerner. When writing the First Edition of this book she was morbid about the phenomenon of her 15th birthday because it reminded her of how young she was. She wanted to be older, anticipating the future, but not content with the season of being 15. I should not have been surprised, as this was nothing new. On her fourth birthday she announced with some concern, "I am four years old and I don't even know who I am going to marry yet!"

How about you? Are you driven by *chronos*, or sensitive to *kairos*? Where *chronos* is important, do you have it working for you or against you? To answer these questions we must first develop a grid that will heighten our ability to distinguish between *kairos* and *chronos*. A separate *Convergence Applied Learning* booklet contains most of the exercises for practical application of these concepts. I do want you to take a moment to dig into the Scriptures to assess your gut reaction to time: do you usually see *kairos* or *chronos*?

## Chronos or Kairos?

Take a look at the following scriptures and indicate which seem like *chronos* and *kairos* to you. (A Greek concordance, which you can find online, would help.)

36    Galatians 4:4 and Mark 1:14,15

| Reference | Scripture | Chronos | Kairos |
|---|---|---|---|
| Matthew 2:7 | Then Herod called the Magi secretly and found out from them the exact *time* the star had appeared. | | |
| Matthew 8:29 | Have you come to torture us before the appointed *time?* | | |
| Mark 1:15 | The *time* has come. The kingdom of God is near. | | |
| Mark 10: 30 | [no one] will fail to receive a hundred times more in this present age... | | |
| Luke 1:57 | When it was *time* for Elizabeth to have her baby... | | |
| Acts 7:20 | At that *time* Moses was born... | | |
| Romans 5:6 | You see, at just the right *time*, when we were still powerless, Christ died for the ungodly. | | |
| Colossians 4:5 | Walk in wisdom toward them that are without, redeeming the *time*. (KJV) | | |
| Rev. 12:12(b) | He is filled with fury, because he knows that his *time* is short. | | |
| Rev. 22:10 | ... because the *time* is near. | | |

# Life before Convergence

What do people usually go through before they get to Convergence?

This is the question I wrestled with as I lay in the sun on a deck chair in Cancun. (Someone has to do the hard work.) As I spent a good while chatting with God and reflecting on my own life I began to realize that I had passed through seven life-shaping eras before reaching the front gates of Convergence. With the background understanding of *kairos*, I was able to discern the major seasons in my life, some of which had run in parallel:

» Faith (and knowing God)

» Fearing and Hearing God

» Discovering Gifts

» Internal Integrity

» Skills Building

» Re-choosing my Spouse

» University of the Desert

I was about to launch my own company. This was something I had considered before, but sensing the season was not ripe, had set it aside. I had often started things in the past; I like to blaze a trail. But with The Institute a looming reality, I had to ask myself some tough questions: Was this just the Forty Year Itch? Hadn't my father left a secure job at about the same age and struggled financially after starting his own businesses? (Or was he really successful despite the economic down-scaling he had undergone?) Was I ready? Had I been through adequate preparation?

Some of the answers lay in The Seven Seasons. While I had been through some of the seasons more than once, not one of them was avoided. As I reflected on God's handprints on my life and what had transpired, I accepted that I was on the verge of Convergence, not implosion. The edge still looked a little scary, but Lyn and I had committed years before to live on the edge.[37] Convergence was "not the end, nor the beginning of the end" but just, in Churchill's words, "the end of the beginning." It was both the culmination and the start of our personal story.

Each of us has our own special story of how God is interacting with us and shaping our path. I believe The Seven Seasons are generally applicable to all people, with one season being an exception: Choosing your Spouse. Not everyone will get married, of course, and a subset of

---

37      Recommended reading: *Daring to live on the Edge*, Loren Cunningham. YWAM Publishing, September 1996.

these people are called to celibacy. I will expand on this in the chapter that covers this season.

If each of our stories is unique, it stands to reason that the order in which we experience The Seven Seasons differs from person to person. There is no particular merit to a specific order of things. Unlike the more linear demarcations of career progressions,[38] my observation is that *kairos* is no slave to *chronos*. Having said this, there are often two seasons that are bookends to the others: Faith (knowing God) and The University of the Desert.

It is easy to rationalize why Faith may not be the first season. In fact, the very instruction from Jesus to "go and make disciples" carries in it the implication that one can begin to disciple a person or a people group before they have come to have a faith encounter with the Living God. Some seek to hear God before they know him, and he meets them in their pursuit. Others seek to discover their wiring, and find that they are amazingly made by an amazing Maker. Others seek a wife and find her God instead. Clearly the season of coming to know God may come at any time. But, more often than not, it is the season that gets us going down the road to Convergence, or at least gives us confirmation that the God-road was the one we were seeking.

At the opposite end of life's bookshelf stands a volume labeled "The University of the Desert." This is God's Finishing School. Why is it often last? Because, as we will see later, when we have run out of words, God is ready to start talking. When we have exhausted our resources, he kicks into gear. By the time we get to surrender, we are surrounded by desert sand. Regardless of when this season is experienced, however, we don't get to Convergence without it.

So, get a handle on your own story as you read about The Seven Seasons. You will benefit as you scramble over the hurdles, past and present, that try to prevent you from grasping your own story. And,

---

38    Dr. J. Robert Clinton's book, *The Making of a Leader*, covers the sequential stages of development of leaders with a predominant focus on those in "full-time Christian work."

true enough, while your story is unique, it is the same. No matter; it bears telling. A later chapter provides some tools for telling your story.

As you learn to understand your life story in the context of Seven Seasons, don't make the mistake of viewing God's involvement in your life as beginning from the day you wrote your name on a card and "made a decision." God made a decision to love and pursue you before this earth was established.[39] While you came to know him at some point in your story—or perhaps you're not sure you know him yet—he has known you longer than that. As you explore your seasons, remember that his fingerprints were on your life long before you decided to follow him.

Having a good grasp of the seasons prevents us from taking shortcuts to the top of a mountain only to find we do not have the character and life experience to live on the rarefied air at those heights. Faithfulness through the seasons will prepare you to not only see mountain tops, or vacation there while at Christian conference, but to live there.

## Which Season Are You In?

"Been there, done that."

This is a common phrase that bothers me. It smacks of an unwillingness to be open to what God may have in store. You hear it from people eager to indicate that their resume is complete. The question is not, "Have you been there and done that?" But, "What happened to you when you were there and doing whatever 'that' happened to be?" After their first tour around the desert, how would God have responded if the people of Israel had said, "Been there, done that," when God told them to take another lap?

The seasons in our life are not measured in terms of some heavenly checklist. If you are half like me you'll be trying to mark off all the

39    Ephesians 1:3-12

sights on the Holy Land Map as you skim through this book. If we opt for this cursory crash course, we might miss the essence of The Seven Seasons. They are threads woven into the tapestry of our life as we "lay hold of that for which Christ laid hold of me."[40] Christ is the audience of our tapestry, but he is more than that. He is also the designer and weaver, and he weaves himself—his life threads—into your tapestry and mine.

Remembering that Convergence is not formulaic—we are not trying to "connect the dots" between Seasons—we will now begin to explore The Seven Seasons and give you an opportunity to consider where you've been and where you are today. So let's pull back the dustcover from your tapestry and see what God has been doing thus far.

40    Philippians 3:12

## Faith

Regardless of the timing of this season, it is the foundation of Convergence, for in it we get to know the essence of God's character. In many ways this is the logical place to start. Nowadays there is an increased spiritual openness, but some of it is faith in faith itself. Faith in God is directed and grounded faith: directed towards the person of Jesus, and grounded in a knowledge of his person and "work." For some, "faith" is marked by "the introduction."

"Jesus Christ, Mr. Jones."

"Mr. Jones, Jesus Christ."

For others there is a gradual revelation of the fact that there is more to life than meets the eye. It leads to knowing God. This is an exciting season.

## The Character of God

To experience a life of faith, we need to know in whom we are placing our faith. One hindrance to moving toward Convergence is that our concept of God is too small. He is not the all-powerful, creation-calling, sea-splitting, smoke-billowing, fire-falling, nation-naming, water-walking, death-defying, Life-living God of the Bible. We have shrunk him into someone we can safely understand and, better yet, contain.

Faith, however, is based on facts. We will risk our lives for one who is all-knowing, unquestionably good, undeniably able, and infinitely informed. The shrink-wrapped Savior we have sometimes espoused has little appeal to a world hungry for the authentic God of the Universe.

When God woos us, we begin to go through an intense period of discovering God and having our presuppositions and actions challenged to the core. Given the fact that God is infinite and we are imperfect, this process never ends.

## My Personal Story

In the small community of Llandudno just 20 miles south of Cape Town on the Atlantic side of South Africa, the church was, to our family, the center of life. In fact, like the local school, the church started in our home.

My dad and mom were business people. But they were more than that. They were strongly bi-vocational. I never heard them use that language, but I watched them preach, teach, superintend Sunday Schools, run youth groups and manage the affairs of the local church. There was no full-time pastor until J.L. Green, a Baptist Minister, retired and came to live in Llandudno. He was my grandfather.

It wasn't a hotly evangelical or a swing-from-the-chandeliers charismatic church, but it was church. Perhaps not surprisingly I grew up with a dichotomy: I knew what was right, but I didn't find myself doing it. In Llandudno "those Johnson boys" were accused of many of the maladies common to any village: broken windows, fruit stealing, whatever. Some of it was even true. On Sundays we were angels; the rest of the week we were just boys.

But we were churchy boys. I taught Sunday School from age 13, led a Bible Study in my boarding school every Wednesday night from age 14 (half the hostel professed a personal relationship with Jesus Christ), and began co-leading a Youth for Christ club at age 18. I was christened, confirmed, inoculated and membered. I knew much about God, but I didn't know him personally.

One night our youth group was attending a rally at the same City Hall in Cape Town where years before my grandmother had sung with the Cape Town Symphony Orchestra. The preacher, Dr. Frank Retief, said that when the crowds followed Jesus but later turned away, it was for one of three reasons:

1. Their motives in following him were wrong. ("Give us bread.")

2. Their understanding of him was wrong. (He'd be a political conqueror.)

3. Their repentance wasn't real.

Now I was trying to follow Christ for the right reasons. I knew there was something more to life that I didn't have. I had seen plenty and had seen want, and I wasn't after the goodies. I knew the synoptic gospels, the Gospel Light Sunday School materials, and the major and minor prophets by the time I was 13. But I came up short when it got to the bit about repentance.

By the time I was 18 or 19 years old, I was frustrated. I was trying to be a Christian. I went to Christian meetings—I led many of them. I read my Bible diligently. Yet I had no peace. I was striving to find God. But I wasn't finding him anywhere.

Repentance is a strange thing. It's a word we avoid...like sin, conviction, and commitment. The strange part is that it's a simple choice, a 180-degree turning around. But it requires that God show us our need to turn. And I was probably more self-righteous than a 100-person church choir.

I'm not sure how it happened, but shortly after that evening at the Cape Town City Hall, I knelt at my desk and had a peek into my own heart. It was not a pretty sight. I felt that for the first time I saw myself as God saw me, and my need for a heart change became all too apparent. Through no work of my own, I moved from remorse to repentance. Things I had known intellectually to be wrong, I now loathed. The miraculous gift of forgiveness was given and received.

Like countless people before me, from then on my reading of Scripture took on new life; the Book was in color. I could begin to live from the inside out. I didn't just know about God, I knew him.

## Different Names, Different Situations

Putting a label on the "faith experience" is problematic. Too little definition and we leave people in a verbal fog. Too many clichés and A,B,C's and people genuinely seeking to follow Jesus are disqualified in our minds because they don't know all the right jargon. But do we? What did Jesus say about our response to him? The Gospel of John records many expressions that Jesus used about ways we can engage with him: "honor me," "hears my word," "believes him who sent me," "cross from death to life," "that you may be saved," "come to me to have life," "accept me," "believe," "believe in the one He has sent," "eat this bread," "feed on me." This is just a sample of phrases from a few chapters in the Bible where Jesus seems to bend over backwards to describe all sorts of ways in which people can relate to him. He is clear that he is the only way to the Father, but the sweep of his language is not narrowly confined to "you must be born again."

Another way to look at this is to consider the variety of ways Jesus called people to himself. And to what did he call people who responded appropriately? Here are some examples:

| Situation or person | What Jesus said | Reference: |
|---|---|---|
| Simon and Andrew | "Come, follow me." | Mark 1:17 |
| James and John | Without delay he called them, and they left their father Zebedee in the boat with the hired men and followed him. | Mark 1:20 |
| Levi, son of Alphaeus | "Follow me." | Mark 2:14 |
| Rich young man | "Go, sell everything you have and give to the poor, and you will have treasure in heaven. Then come, follow me." | Mark 10:21 |
| Blind Bartimaeus | "Go, your faith has healed you." | Mark 10:52 |
| Teacher of the law | "You are not far from the kingdom of God." | Mark 12:34 |

We often hear it said, "Become a Christian" or "Join the church" or "Follow these four steps and you will know Jesus/be saved." But is Scripture asking us to become a Christian (with all of the historical baggage that the term can carry)? No. We are being asked to follow Jesus. Did Jesus ever say, "You must become a Christian?" Not once. The label "Christian" was rarely used in a positive context. How did believers in the early Church describe themselves? Usually as "followers" or "followers of the Way."

In most translations the word "Christian" appears two or three times. It is unclear whether the word was one chosen by the followers of Jesus or one that was placed upon them by those who didn't care much for their beliefs. Either way, today "Christian" is a loaded term that can create unnecessary barriers for people who simply want a relationship with Jesus Christ. We must be careful that the labels we use don't become obstacles for knowing Jesus. We must also be careful not to prescribe formula that even Jesus did not impose on those who sought to know him.

I love the many ways that Jesus describes this divine relationship. Within a few chapters in John's account it is as if Jesus is giving us many descriptions, lots of options for how this allegiance to him can be described.

» "honor the Son" (John 5:23)

» "whoever hears my word and believes him who sent me has eternal life" (John 5:24)

» "All that the Father gives me will come to me, and whoever comes to me I will not drive away." (John 6:37)

» "...the one who feeds on me will live forever." (John 6:58)

And then there is the famous line about how we can see the kingdom of God:

> I tell you the truth, no one can see the kingdom of God unless he is born again... No one can enter the kingdom of God unless he is born of water and the Spirit.[41]

## The Crux of the Matter

A young man and his sister came to see me some years ago. She was unsure of her relationship with Jesus and wanted some counsel. I pulled out all my verses on Assurance of Salvation and gave her a long pep talk. But I made the grave mistake of never making sure that she had actually made a decision to follow Jesus. I never asked her whether she believed the historical truth that the God-man, Jesus, had paid a price for her separation from God. I did not make sure that she had accepted his free gift of forgiveness for her sins. I did not stop to make sure that the moment of spiritual regeneration had actually taken place.

41    John 3:5

I talked long and hard, as I recall, about the things she had to do to live like a believer. I never did probe the simple question: "Have you actually made an eternal transaction with Jesus?" It wasn't long before she drifted into doing her own thing.

A lot of spiritual sounding stuff is floating around the marketplace today. Most of it masks the historical fact that Jesus chose to die to take the punishment for our wrongdoing. He died so that our misdemeanors could be forgiven. Then he was buried. After three days he came alive again and lives today to share a brand new type of life with us. This is God's plan; it is the way he has made. Our part is to decide whether we want to buy into this plan. In our day of self-help, personal empowerment and "I-want-to-be-in-control", there is this stark truth:

> The message that points to Christ on the cross seems like sheer silliness to those hell-bent on destruction, but for those on the way of salvation it makes perfect sense. This is the way God works, and most powerfully, as it turns out.[42]

Try to find a smarter way if you like, but Christ crucified is God's best and only plan. Put another way, there is a legal case against us; we have violated the innate laws of our Creator. He gets to decide the terms of the settlement. He has only one way that justice will be served. Our punishment has been laid on a substitute. His name is Jesus. Either we accept this, or we die with the legal case against us being unsettled. These are the facts of the case. People make crazy statements about the narrow-mindedness of God, as if he makes arbitrary decisions. We have already seen Jesus cast the net wide with language that says, "Come to, look to, believe in, follow, get born by the Spirit, hear my words and believe…" Find the language that turns on your light, but make sure that at the end of the day you have made peace with God on his terms.

42    1 Corinthians 1:23-25, *The Message*

## Following Jesus

The key to the season of faith is not the orderly arrangement of religious verbiage, but the deep alignment of our whole being with objective truth. It is easier to straighten a bone just after it has been broken. It is often easier for the Great Surgeon to straighten out damaged lives on the heels of the transformational experience of first coming to know him. Just this week a man spoke to me on this topic.

"I have led people to Christ, but I am not sure about their spiritual maturity," he said.

I asked, "How would you define maturity?"

He explained, "They must have a good knowledge of Scripture, be established in the Word..."

(So far most of the emphasis was on someone who was knowledgeable, not mature.)

He added, "They must be accountable..."

So I inquired, "So if they spent 20 years in a Bible Study and knew the Bible backwards, you'd be happy?"

He replied, "No, they actually have to be obedient."

Bingo...sort of.

The line of reasoning we follow in the Western world is this: if we know what to do, especially if we know lots of theological nuances, then we will do it. The fact is, following Jesus is not so much about knowing what to do, but knowing him enough to trust him when he tells us what to do. Growth in knowledge comes from revelation which flows as we obey in conjunction with that learning. As the saying says, "You will know what is right by practicing doing right."

On the shores of Galilee fishermen where called to become followers. What about us? What about you? Who are you following? Or are you asking God to follow you, providing, cleaning up, fixing mistakes, and making your life more liveable? Do you have role models of Christ-followers who will take you to a new level of practical obedience? Notice that I am not asking whether you have people who can take you to new heights of knowledge. We are a generation without excuse when it comes to having enough information. Most of us, however, lack a relationship with those who can challenge us to a new level of obedience. Or, when the path of following gets hard, we retreat to the safety of learning. "I don't have time for missions ventures because I am in a discipleship group."

There are many disciplines that are useful to a disciple. Prayer, contemplation, journaling, fasting, worship, personal Bible reading, hearing teaching, teaching others, celebration of the Lord's Supper or breaking of bread... these, and others like them, are essential. At the end of the day, however, we have less of a problem of "knowing" and a huge problem of "going." We are paralyzed by inertia. We have relegated "Go into all the world" to the chosen few, and especially to women, whom God seems to prefer for the tough jobs, as there have been twice as many women missionaries in the last few centuries than men.

Search the Bible, and expect a few surprises as you enjoy your season of Faith. And remember that it is not a summer vacation season, but the laying of foundations upon which much will depend in future seasons. These foundations are laid through obedience, not just information. Learning + doing + going = Knowledge. On the other hand, Learning + talking + staying = Information. The season of Faith and Knowing God should be a practical season. You have faith when you do what faith-filled people do. Take a leaf from Ezra's book:

> Ezra had committed himself to studying the Revelation of God, to living it, and to teaching Israel to live its truths and ways.[43]

43    Ezra 7:10 *The Message*

My friend Kasia is an example of this pattern of discovering as she obeyed. Her dad was an atheist and her mom an agnostic, so they left Kasia to choose her own religion. As a young girl she decided to raise herself as a Quaker. Through a series of events which included the death of her parents, she felt drawn to reconsider the community of faith and their leader, Jesus. She loved the community, she grew in knowledge, but she still had a problem with this "whole sin thing." This did not stop her from enrolling in the **rēp** training. ("What? You took an 'unbeliever' into missions training?" Jesus told us to make disciples, not converts... we left that work to him.) One day when Kasia was returning from a self-help group she had attended for some time (not connected to her church) she received a revelation that the thing everyone was struggling to get rid of was, in fact, sin! So she immediately went to a few friends and said, "I am ready! I get the sin and Jesus connection. Pray with me."

Her experience echoes that of a couple in Scripture who had the privilege of Jesus pulling alongside them on their walk:

> That same day two of them were walking to the village Emmaus, about seven miles out of Jerusalem. They were deep in conversation, going over all these things that had happened. In the middle of their talk and questions, Jesus came up and walked along with them. But they were not able to recognize who he was. He asked, "What's this you're discussing so intently as you walk along?"[44]

Sometimes we figure things out as we follow. Build momentum; become an avid follower.

## Not Without Opposition

Another place where the word "Christian" is used is in 1 Peter 4:16 where Peter says, "Yet if anyone suffers as a Christian, let him not be ashamed, but let him glorify God in this matter."

44    Luke 24:13-17 *The Message*

I would be remiss to close this chapter without pointing out that new believers have entered a war zone. A continuous battle wages over the lives of individuals seriously pursuing God.

Using the tapestry analogy, there is a war for the needle: who will be in control—God, Satan or us? There are constant assaults on the threads: tear them, twist them, and sidetrack them. There is the inevitable introduction of threads that are not included in God's design, be they from us or Satan "just wanting to add a little color" or give God a hand. There is the delay tactic: weave it later, let the needle hang, relax for a while... when you have made more money/had more experience/seen a bit more of the world.

The road to Convergence is chosen at a price. It involves tough decisions, and the right decisions are sometimes the result of battles. (Other decisions seem easy, particularly if they are the result of God's more visible sovereignty when we are left with little choice—more about this in the next chapter.) We will do battle with ourselves and our circumstances—"the godly in Christ shall suffer"—particularly as God combs through the tangles of our lives and brings them into alignment with himself.

We can have two equal but opposite errors: being preoccupied with Satan and being unaware of his schemes. Know your God, know yourself, and know your enemy.

## Faith, Risk and Business

Business is a life of faith. I have often said that it takes more faith to run a business than it does to run a church. This is not entirely true, of course, because the reality is that it takes faith to "run" or be part of a kingdom venture, whether it is a local church or a business. True faith and right business are, and always have been, inseparable. If you do not have a business background you may think of it as a world of science and precision where rationality is king. The reality is that business is a world of constantly changing variables, continual resource reallocation, and a great dependence on many uncontrollable factors. If we are doing business God's way, then it is exacerbated because we are taking on and turning down work that doesn't make total sense. We are extending our borders into areas where the kingdom needs to grow but where we may not make money, and we are sometimes placing ourselves at a short-term competitive disadvantage by acting with integrity and transparency. We depend on rain, on orders, on divine connections, and on imperfect people as an expression of our trust in God. Business is, or should be, a life of faith.

In fact, living as a follower of the Way is a faith journey in every sphere of society. As we saw in an earlier chapter, I have classified society as having 10 Spheres, each with a distinct way of doing things. To transform society we need to influence each domain. Convergence helps us experience victory in our starting point, which for the majority of people is their work. This builds a platform of faith from which we can springboard into other sectors.

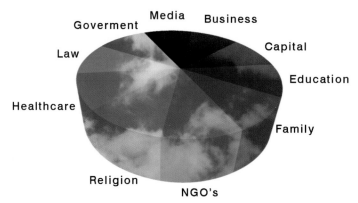

Know for sure that you don't have to leave what you are doing and "become a full-time minister" to live a life of faith.

> Belief is reassuring. People who live in the world of belief feel safe. On the contrary, faith is forever placing us on the razor's edge. — Jacques Ellul

Faith is not a place of feeling safe, however, but neither is it blind.

## Levels of Faith

A friend and marketplace colleague, Dr. Louis Rossouw, recently shared about different levels of faith. If we are to make headway on the Convergence journey we need to destroy the notion that only some people have faith. The Bible is very clear that we have each received some measure of faith and that it is a gift from God. It is a fact, not something we screw up by exercising our willpower:

> For I say, through the grace given to me, to everyone who is among you, not to think of himself more highly than he ought to think, but to think soberly, as God has dealt to each one a measure of faith.[45]

Every Christ-follower has some level of faith. Louis points out that the faith we have received is of equal quality. We have become those who please the Father through our trust in his Son. Father-pleasing requires faith:

> And without faith it is impossible to please God, because anyone who comes to him must believe that he exists and that he rewards those who earnestly seek him.[46]

Faith also seems to be held in different measures. Jesus refers to faith of different sizes, which is not to say that you can get faith in different sizes, like something off the shelves at Wal-Mart, but that faith can grow. Let me give some examples from the book written by Matthew:

» "O you of little faith" – Matthew 6:30

» "such great faith" – Matthew 8:10

» "You of little faith, why are you so afraid?" – Matthew 8:26

» She said to herself, "If I only touch his cloak, I will be healed." Jesus turned and saw her. "Take heart, daughter," he said, "your faith

---

45    Romans 12:3 *New King James*

46    Hebrews 11:6

has healed you." And the woman was healed from that moment. – Matthew 9:21-22

And he did not do many miracles there because of their lack of faith. – Matthew 13:58

Then Jesus answered, "Woman, you have great faith! Your request is granted." And her daughter was healed from that very hour. – Matthew 15:28

Now that you have the concept of faith of differing measures, let's look at Louis' table and allow it to raise our expectations about what God can instill in us in the Season of Faith:

| Type of Faith | Category | Measure of Faith |
|---|---|---|
| God-focused faith | Faith we live by | Miracle-working faith |
| | Faith as a gift | Great / Strong faith |
| | Faith as a fruit | Growing faith |
| Ineffective faith | Compromised faith | Little faith |
| | | Aimless faith |
| | | Denied faith |
| Absent faith | No faith | Faithless |
| | Dead faith | Faith without action |
| Man-focused faith | Humanistic faith | Faith in man |
| | | Faith in Nature |
| Dark faith | Infected faith | Unbelief |
| | Corrupted faith | Evil faiths |

The purpose of this table is to raise our expectations, knowing all the while it is not about getting some "faith diploma" but about readiness to obey and a willingness to have our faith grow. Hudson Taylor said, "God isn't looking for people of great faith, but for individuals ready to follow Him." Faith comes when God speaks; it grows when we obey.

# God's Marketing

It is important to mention that sometimes God chooses to woo people into a faith-based relationship with himself by performing miracles. This is especially true today among peoples where there is no openness towards Christianity. Stories abound of people having dreams, visions and other miraculous encounters with Jesus even when they have had no contact with his followers.

The other place where God uses miracles as part of his marketing is in the business world in particular, and marketplace in general. At **rēp** we are so expectant that God will do miracles in business that we have a Marketplace Miracle Form to document and authenticate the miracles we see when business leaders pray for miracles in their businesses. We have seen and documented:

» Business leaders, mostly CEOs, radically turned around

» People coming to Christ at work

» Millions of dollars of cash flow

» Products "healed" miraculously

» Equipment prayed over and starting to work again

» New products created after God downloaded product designs, overnight

» Miraculous sales, again and again

» New partnerships through divine connections

» New businesses created

» Government and other contracts and licenses granted

» Businesses "born again"

» Old debts repaid miraculously

» Land donated.

Families of employees have been healed—a young girl recently had a visitation from Jesus and was physically healed from epilepsy after we prayed with the mom in a business setting.

It has become a "best practice", which is actually better described as an essential survival practice, to have intercessors pray for and with the businesses throughout our consultations with clients. For some business leaders the intellectual frameworks are transformational enough; most, however, are deeply touched through the integration of the intellectual and the miraculous and the relational. We need truth, we need grace, and we need the miraculous. We need, as the song says, "wisdom, power and love."

This is nothing new, of course. We are simply following the pattern that we saw Jesus model for us:

> When he had finished speaking, he said to Simon, "Put out into deep water, and let down the nets for a catch." Simon answered, "Master, we've worked hard all night and haven't caught anything. But because you say so, I will let down the nets." When they had done so, they caught such a large number of fish that their nets began to break. So they signaled their partners in the other boat to come and help them, and they came and filled both boats so full that they began to sink. When Simon Peter saw this, he fell at Jesus' knees and said, "Go away from me, Lord; I am a sinful man!" For he and all his companions were astonished at the catch of fish they had taken, and so were James and John, the sons of Zebedee, Simon's partners. Then Jesus said to Simon, "Don't be afraid; from now on you will catch men."[47]

You may be thinking, "This is a nice story" and miss the facts about business and faith and how God woos practical people in the marketplace. First, he visited their business, he didn't ask their business to come to him. Next, he formed a relational connection, made use of

47    Luke 5:4-10

their business assets for a while, and taught truth from the platform, literally, of their business: he stood in the boat and taught. This may be like saying, "Do you mind if I use your conference room to do some teaching?" Third, he the told them to do something counter-intuitive in their business: he gave them an opportunity to exercise faith. Then he produced a miracle directly relevant to them in their business. In fact, it was such an extraordinary thing that others got drawn into the picture. The business guy came unglued, it seems. "Go away from me, Lord; I am a sinful man!" Not every businessman wants a holy God in his business. Then Jesus gave Peter's career a tweak; he repurposed Peter. If you are a preacher you are probably thinking, "Then he called Peter out of business and into ministry." If you thought that, you are wrong. It is true that the passage does go on to say, "So they pulled their boats up on shore, left everything and followed him." It is also true that we see them fishing again, and not just after they had deserted Jesus.

Being in business is not "backsliding" as it used to be called when someone fell away from following Jesus. Jesus didn't "backslide" between ages 12 and 30. He did business, growing "in wisdom, and stature, and in favor with God and men." When Peter encountered the miracle-working Jesus in his place of business, Jesus didn't chastise him for being a businessman, but said, "Don't be afraid..." and then there is this wonderful Repurposing statement, "from now on you will catch men." He transformed him from fisherman, to fisher of men.

This wasn't the first time God had done this, of course. God knows Return on Investment, or ROI, as we say in business. He invests in our skills and training, and he looks for a return on his investment. If you work, which most of us do, he has invested in your skills, your education, your work experience and training. He is entitled to a return. When you came to faith it was all of you that came, not just your "spiritual life." So it stands to reason that he wants a return on all of your life. He invested 40 years in training Moses to be a political leader. He added 40 years of character development, then he got 40 years of good service from Moses.

You can see the pattern again and again. David is a good example of the connection between occupation and vocation:

> He chose David his servant and took him from the sheep pens; from tending the sheep he brought him to be the shepherd of his people Jacob, of Israel his inheritance. And David shepherded them with integrity of heart; with skillful hands he led them.[48]

Your business is a great place to grow in faith. It is also an excellent place to find God's life work. If you are faithful with your sheep, he may give you a nation to shepherd. You can develop both competence ("skillful hands") and character ("integrity of heart") in your workplace. Stop thinking that you have to find faith outside your work:

> Isn't it obvious that God-talk without God-acts is outrageous nonsense? I can already hear one of you agreeing by saying, "Sounds good. You take care of the faith department, I'll handle the works department." Not so fast. You can no more show me your works apart from your faith than I can show you my faith apart from my works. Faith and works, works and faith, fit together hand in glove. Do I hear you professing to believe in the one and only God, but then observe you complacently sitting back as if you had done something wonderful? That's just great. Demons do that, but what good does it do them? Use your heads! Do you suppose for a minute that you can cut faith and works in two and not end up with a corpse on your hands?[49]

If you separate your work and spirituality, if you compartmentalize your Career and your Calling, you will "end up with a corpse on your hands." God doesn't do miracles in business to get us out of our business but to get us into his business. God is an "AND" God. You can be in his business, and you can be in business, and he can be in your

48      Psalm 78:70-72

49      James 2:17-20, *The Message*

business. For most people, and I mean most people, the marketplace is the exact place where he wants them to be living this faith life.

## George Müller

Born in Kroppenstaedt, Germany on September 27, 1805, Müller quickly got in trouble. After being bailed out of prison he went to divinity school, primarily as a means of earning a living. When invited to a Bible Study in 1825 he accepted Christ as Savior. He then moved to England and eventually pastored a church in Bristol for over sixty-six years. He is best known for his work among orphans which was one of five branches of The Scripture Knowledge Institute which he founded in 1834. Müller explained why he started the orphanage:

> The three chief reasons for establishing an Orphan-House are: 1. That God may be glorified, should He be pleased to furnish me with the means, in its being seen that it is not a vain thing to trust in Him; and that thus the faith of His children may be strengthened. 2. The spiritual welfare of fatherless and motherless children. 3. Their temporal welfare.[50]

John Piper writes that there was a deliberate order in these aims: "And make no mistake about it: the order of those three goals is intentional. He makes that explicit over and over in his Narrative. The orphan houses exist to display that God can be trusted and to encourage believers to take him at his word. This was a deep sense of calling with Müller."[51] Müller, in his own words, said:

> It seemed to me best done, by the establishing of an Orphan-House. It needed to be something which could be seen, even by the natural eye. Now, if I, a poor man, simply by prayer and faith, obtained, without asking any individual, the means

---

50  George Müller, *A Narrative of Some of the Lord's Dealing with George Müller*, Written by Himself, Jehovah Magnified. Addresses by George Müller Complete and Unabridged, 2 vols., Muskegon, Mich.: Dust and Ashes, 2003.

51  John Piper. *Desiring God*. www.desiringGod.org.

for establishing and carrying on an Orphan-House: there would be something which, with the Lord's blessing, might be instrumental in strengthening the faith of the children of God besides being a testimony to the consciences of the unconverted, of the reality of the things of God. This, then, was the primary reason, for establishing the Orphan-House. . . The first and primary object of the work was, (and still is) that God might be magnified by the fact, that the orphans under my care are provided, with all they need, only by prayer and faith, without any one being asked by me or my fellow-laborers, whereby it may be seen, that God is FAITHFUL STILL, and HEARS PRAYER STILL.[52]

You might say that George Müller's remarkable Season of Faith was more than a season. It is as if God used his life as a magnifying glass to highlight the truths about faith contained in Scripture. By the time he died, "He had read his Bible from end to end almost 200 times. He had prayed in millions of dollars (in today's currency) for the Orphans and never asked anyone directly for money. He never took a salary in the last 68 years of his ministry, but trusted God to put in people's hearts to send him what he needed. He never took out a loan or went into debt. And neither he nor the orphans were ever hungry."[53] Faith comes from Hearing. Let's explore the season where we learn to hear God.

52      Ibid

53      Ibid

## Fearing And Hearing God

Those who fear God, hear God. What is not so clear is the manner in which we hear the invisible God speak to his creation. A while ago I sat backstage at my son's school play. I had made myself comfortable reading a book that had to do with hearing God. One of the moms came by, and a discussion ensued about what I was reading. I eagerly shared with her stories about how God speaks today and some specific examples of how he spoke to some of the Scottish Presbyterians in the 15th and 16th centuries. Prophecies foretelling martyrdom, words of knowledge about how much people earned in their businesses, speaking out judgment, halting plagues…we covered some interesting examples.

As the dialogue progressed, she felt safe enough to offer that she was not really a Christ-follower. She had her kids at a Christian school, but she "wasn't there yet." We then went on to have a conversation as she wiped away the tears, not about becoming a Christian, but about becoming a follower of Jesus. Several things about the conversation stuck in my mind:

» You cannot follow one whom you do not hear. "My sheep hear my voice."

» The pattern of the discussion did not follow the typical "friendship evangelism" pattern. She felt safe talking to me because I was open enough to share what some might call the more wacko ways in which God speaks.

» Right at the outset of our conversation there was a hint as to where she was coming from. The title of the book I was reading was *Surprised by the voice of God.* When I told her the title, she asked, "Why surprised?"

Friends, the unchurched world is often less surprised about the fact that God speaks than we are. And they are certainly more open to the variety of ways in which he speaks than we who are "grounded in the Word." By way of contrast, I recently spoke with a seminary-graduation-Bible-reading pastor who didn't really expect God to speak to him, other than through the Word. Consequently, like young Samuel, he was somewhat oblivious to the voice of God.

## Looking Back

It was one of those special moments. Lyn and I were flying back from Washington D.C. having witnessed perhaps the largest gathering of men in history on the National Mall.[53] On the return to San Francisco

---

53    On October 4, 1997 perhaps as many as 1 million men gathered in a sacred assembly to repent, pray and commit themselves to the principles of godly character. This Promise Keepers event moved us as we witnessed people kneeling, standing and sitting before God in prayer.

at 30,000 feet Lyn and I began to list the major decisions we had made in our almost 25 years together: starting to date each other, Lyn's first job, getting married, buying our first home, taking a trip to Europe when we didn't have the money, taking another trip six months later to Chile and still no money. Having children, moving to America, staying in America, spending $375,000 on a fixer-upper, several job transitions.

We asked ourselves what the dominant factors were in each decision. It was a holy moment (lasting two or three hours). Slowly the patterns began to emerge. With me, the still, small voice. With Lyn, the impulse. For me, the restlessness and an unfolding of "the big picture." For Lyn, just the picture. For both of us, confirming Scripture. As we progressed through each decision we made a grid so that we could better understand God's ways with us.

| Decision | Dominant factor | Other factor | Result | Primary mover |
|---|---|---|---|---|
| Salvation | Bible preached (Brett) | Believers | Conversion | Holy Spirit |
| Career | Still small voice | Basic research | Job at Price Waterhouse | Brett |
| Dating | Desires of hearts (Ps. 37:4) | Match of gifts | Began dating, October 5th, 1975 | Lynelle! |
| First Home | Desires of our heart | Impulse | Bought first home (before we were married) | Lynelle |
| Starting a family | Lyn: ready for this stage of life. Brett: not ready - God had to do heart surgery first | Prodding from friend ("You better ask God why you aren't ready...") | Fay Maree born March 29, 1983 | Lyn, later Brett |
| Trips to Chile, Austria | Others: offer from Lyn's parents to accompany them | Circumstances (rented out house for summer to get money) | Great vacation in Europe | Elton and Cynthia Möller |

| Decision | Dominant factor | Other factor | Result | Primary mover |
|---|---|---|---|---|
| Coming to the States | The trip: Price Waterhouse. The location: "God, where should we go?" | Timing: readiness of church, pregnancy with son, James | Came to San Francisco in June 1986 (for one year) | Sovereignty. I had no way of knowing that choosing SF was God's plan; he worked out the details. |
| Buying the Belmont house | Impulse (Lyn and Fay) | Our children, our friends | Bought $375,000 house with -$1,000 in the bank | Lyn |
| Starting at Creative Memories | Impulse | Brett's prayer | Started successful business | Lyn |
| Brett leaving Price Waterhouse | Still, small voice | Circumstances (couldn't afford to stay) | New career at KPMG | Brett |
| Leaving KPMG Peat Marwick | God's whisper; sensing a new season | Family priorities | Different type of skills building season at CSC | Brett |
| Starting rēp | Vision, Call | Gifting, own story | An organization that bridges the world of career and call | Brett |
| Starting The Institute | Asking stupid questions: "God, got any good ideas?" | Prompting of wife; godly counsel of friends | A new type of vehicle for ministry | Brett and Lyn |
| Moving to San Carlos | Impulse, generosity | Our children | A house move | The whole family |
| Moving to Woodside | A friend, Frank, had a vision | Co-workers | Another great house to rent | God, Frank and praying friends! |

What was also clear to us was that sometimes neither of us was going to "get it." No matter how hard we prayed or dreamed or thought, we were not going to envisage the broader plan that God had in mind. So God just had to do something in his sovereignty, usually creating circumstances over which we had no control. For example, when buying our first house the mortgage broker made an error on early calculations leading us to believe we could actually afford the house. Another example was our "one year trip" to the U.S. which has, so far, become a twenty year "trip."

## Principles of Hearing God

Other writers have expounded the principles of hearing God. Because hearing God is so crucial to following his initiative, some reminders are worth mentioning:

» Understand past patterns of guidance in your life. Don't go with the standard experiences of others; examine your own walk to uncover the Infinite God's ways with you.

» Open your life to your spouse. God in his fairness will sometimes provide key points of guidance only through your husband or wife. Part of this is his way of ensuring that you remain inter-dependent. It is easy to slip into the habit of sharing your needs with people other than your life-mate. The excitement of talking to someone who doesn't know you but finds you interesting can be intoxicating. The downside of this habit is that when a big decision comes along and you need guidance, God may be hiding it in your wife or husband, yet you have blunted the cutting edge of hearing God together.

» Listen for God in children. This is true for children generally, but it is especially true that he speaks to us through our own children. We are not advocating that parents be held hostage to the whims of their children, but too often we fail to ask God to speak to us through our kids, particularly as they grow older. Natural pressures pull teenagers away from this role in the family (like thinking that their parents are IQ-deprived). Stick with it; children often hear God clearly. We once received a request from the twelve-year-old daughter of missionary friends. She was raising support for a summer of working in an orphanage in Eastern Europe. We asked the children to pray with us about how much we should give. I was thinking $50 would be plenty but Fay, who was nine at the time, announced that we should give $150. "Why $150.00?" the rest of us asked. "I saw a check with $150.00 written on it flying through the sky." The young girl was all packed and ready to go, but without her full fees she could not leave. Within an hour or two of her departure, our check arrived. She needed exactly $150!

» Be prepared to "go to the mat" alone with God to find out what he has to say about a situation or decision. At times our Father wants us to wait things out with him. This is his prerogative. I have experienced a number of times when he spoke to me, and I sensed that going to others would have been a travesty of God's confidence. "Be still in the presence of the Lord, and wait patiently for him to act."[54] When our precious daughter had the alarming signs of a seizure we went to God in desperate prayer. The doctors wanted to perform a series of sleep-deprivation tests to re-induce the condition so that they could observe her. In and of themselves the tests might have been harmful. As a deeply concerned father I went to my Father. After some time I felt God say, "In two years she will be completely healed." Many times we would hear her in the night, go to her, and observe that she was having another seizure. It was a long two years, but she was indeed healed and there has been not so much as a hint of another seizure.

» Open your life to others. This may appear to be the paradox of the previous point. The fact is that we need both our family and others, in that order. The confirmation, if not the impetus, often comes from the outside.

» Communicate constantly. "Pray without ceasing."[55] Ask God about the little things. Hearing him speak about small things builds faith for the larger challenges that will come.

» Separate the short-term (near-term) from the long-term. Understand timing.

If you used to hear God but have not known his guidance for a while:

» Go back to where you last clearly heard God's voice. Perhaps God has asked you to do something that you need to follow through on.

» Consider whether you are in the desert. If so, look for relationship, not lots of forward direction.

» Acknowledge and turn away from any known sin.[56]

» Make sure you are not responding negatively to the situations God is placing in your life. He sometimes uses the unpleasant to accomplish his plans. Suffering produces perseverance, perseverance character, character hope, and hope lets us "see" the love of God in our lives.[57]

## The Wild Ways Some Folks Hear God

Ask a group of people how God speaks to them. Really. We've been taught some pat answers, and they're good (through the Word, counselors, etc.) But isn't God infinite? And isn't he the essence of creativity? And isn't communication at the essence of his being? Consequently there is a diversity of ways in which he speaks to his children today. God could speak to you in ways he's never done before!

Lyn gave a talk at a church and asked the participants to list the ways in which God speaks to them. Some of this may be familiar to you. We

---

55      1 Thessalonians 5:17

56      Ps. 66:18

57      Romans 5

have categorized the lists and added a few things that we have known to be true in the lives of friends.

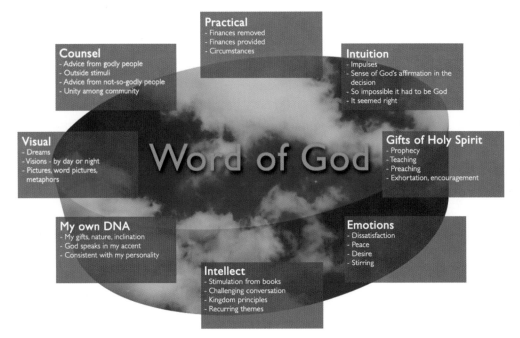

We are constantly bombarded with messages and words. How do we filter what we hear to discern whether it is from God?

I want to resist the temptation of telling too many stories that are on the dramatic end of the scale, but at the same time I must illustrate ways in which God speaks. Some years ago I was chatting with my friend, Brian, who had decided to rearrange his life to allow more time with his growing family. His career took him away from home at night, and also kept him from pursuing his Calling. He was contemplating a risky move that eventually included selling his house, starting some businesses, and following a path that wasn't quite there yet. One day we were chatting and I shared an experience I had that could well have involved a few angels. This was new to him, but he was at a critical juncture in his career. He had cut the umbilical cord on his prior job and was taking some drastic steps in moving towards his dream. This included a switch from a lucrative TV career to become a radio talk show host. He had sensed that he was to get a job on a local radio station, but was not totally convinced yet. He needed to hear from God. God spoke in two ways. First, some friends were praying for him and two people saw a picture in their minds of Brian's face in the clouds above San Francisco International Airport. When they compared notes they realized they had both seen the same thing. When they shared this with Brian he immediately knew what it meant. He asked them, "What do you call the airport?" To which they replied, "SFO." Brian then explained that what they had seen in their mind's eye meant "Brian in the air over SFO"—he was meant to be on KSFO, the radio station he had felt God speak to him about.

A short while after our angel chat Brian was buying a cup of coffee from a sidewalk vendor after an early morning TV appearance, still pondering the risky move to radio. Just then a rather plain looking middle-aged lady walked up to him and said, "Hi, you're Brian Sussman." He greeted her politely. She went on; "I recognize you from KGO/KSFO." He immediately thought to himself, "She must be mistaken—you cannot recognize what someone looks like from the radio. She must mean the TV station, KPIX." So he asked her, "And who would you be?" "I would be one of your listeners," she replied, and turned and walked away. When he looked again, she was gone. Brian immediately called me and when I answered my phone he said, "Brett, I have just seen an angel!" A short while later Brian was invited to a be a radio host on KSFO. When Brian received his first paycheck it read, "KGO/KSFO" just as the lady had said.

One of our **rep** teams recently had a hard time getting through to a businessman who, by his own admission, was not hearing what was being shared. Our team prayed that God would speak to him. A few days later his two children, aged eight and six, began to counsel him on what to do with his business. He was so struck that he asked them to pause so he could get a note pad to record their observations and recommendations. His life has been transformed.

Clearly God is not limited to our preconceived notions of how he speaks, but whatever we think we hear God saying, we need to run it through some form of filter so that we are not misled by our own enthusiasm, fears or fantasies.

## Run That One Through the Funnel

The picture of the funnel is a series of filters with three major sections through which we "run" our decisions:

» Compliance: does this comply with the broad strokes of the written Word of God, what God has already spoken to me, and who he has created me to be?

» Community: how does it affect others? What do they have to say about the matter?

» Commitment: are we/am I willing and able to commit the resources suggested by this decision?

A word about the "Community" piece of the filter: the evangelical tradition of the past 150 years or so has emphasized the notion of "personal salvation" and the importance of the individual's relationship with Jesus. While this is true, it is not the whole truth. Further, it is not the dominant truth of the New Testament or Old Testament for that matter. Walking out the life of Jesus in us—being a follower of the Way—was never intended to be a "just Jesus and you" experience as the old song suggests. The Community filters therefore need to be considered carefully.

Hearing God is often a matter of learning to ask the right questions, expecting that he hears, listens and answers. Let's take a closer look at some of the filters involved in hearing God.

| | Filter | Questions to Consider |
|---|---|---|
| **C O M P L I A N C E** | Word of God | Is it consistent with the written Word of God? Has God already spoken to us on this subject? <br><br> Have we obeyed what he said? |
| | Your Values | Is it consistent with my Values (and my philosophy of ministry)? <br><br> How does it reinforce these values? |
| | Your Purpose, Call or Vision | Does it move me in the same direction as my call, or is it a divergence? <br><br> How does it underscore or clarify the vision God has given me? |
| | Consistency with gifts or talents | We have listed this as a "major filter" even though at times it is less important. For example, during the Skills Building season when we are discovering our gifts and adding to our tool box, it can be less important to have an exact fit. "Whatever your hand finds to do, do it with all your might" (Ecclesiastes 9:10) can be more appropriate. <br><br> For sustainability, however, we do well to ask, "Is this consistent with my gifts and talents?" <br><br> If I do not have the skills, is this an opportunity to grow skills I need? |
| **C O M M U N I T Y** | Consideration for others | Who are the key stakeholders? How are they affected? What is the cost to them? A note of caution: there are critical junctures on our journey when God asks us to obey him and not hide behind the cost to others. This should be sensitively factored into our decision-making. |
| | Unity among all stake holders | Is there agreement? If there is not unanimity of thinking, is there at least a "unity of the Spirit"? <br><br> Have we tested for alignment among stake holders? How? <br><br> Do we need to consider our roles and responsibilities should the decision go through? |

| | Filter | Questions to Consider |
|---|---|---|
| **C O M M I T M E N T** | Action | Are we committed to the action this decision demands? |
| | | Do we have a short-term or long-term view? What does this decision require of us? |
| | Grace | Will I have the grace? |
| | | Does my "grace barometer" soar or leak on the floor? |
| | | God's smile... is there a settledness beyond what the circumstances might suggest? |
| | Margin | Does it sap or supply margin? |
| | | Do I have the resources, or what are the alternate resources? |
| | | Am I willing to make trade-offs to increase Margin? |
| | Timing | Is the timing right? Should we wait? |
| | | Is this the right decision for this season of my life? |
| | | Are there prerequisites that need to be set in place first? |

After all this filtering of the avalanche of rocks and rubble and mud, we are left with the diamonds.

# Fearing God

It's fun to talk about how God still speaks to us today. No doubt some people will take exception to this, but for me it is no problem that the One from whom all communication flows is still communicating. Interaction is wired into the Godhead; the three-in-one cannot help but communicate.

Some of us seem to have more "words from the Lord" in a week than some authentic saints have in a lifetime. ("God said this, then he said that...") This might disturb some, but what should concern us more is the absence of a true Fear of God in our lives. Many of us make plans and decisions as if life were simply ours to plan and live. We can also gradually tighten the circle of things about which we allow God to speak to us. The inevitable result is a lack of Convergence.

Am I saying that an absence of Convergence is an indication of a lack of fearing God? Absolutely not. I am saying that an absence of the Fear of God will stunt Convergence. If we do not fear God, we lessen the chances that we will know his leading.

In *The Joy of Fearing God* Jerry Bridges subscribes to the common definition of the Fear of God, namely, reverential awe. Why does it take a book to unpack this topic? In part because we have become so familiar with God that we lose sight of his awesome greatness. In our quest for Abba-intimacy, we forget he is the King of Kings.

## Alternatives to Fearing God

What are some of the alternatives to fearing God?

» Fearing man, but remember that, "the fear of man brings a snare." [58]

» Doing our own thing; leaning on our own understanding.

» Fearing our circumstances (Seeing evil coming when it is not really there).

» Fearing the future.

» Fearing change.

Paul gives Timothy some counsel that is much needed in a world where doctors' offices are overflowing with people who are filled with fear: God has not given us a spirit of fear, but of power, of love and a sound mind (self-discipline). [59]

---

[58]      Proverbs 29:25 (NKJV)

[59]      2 Timothy 1:7. Note that Scripture sometimes sees fear as a spirit. In extreme cases of fear, we do well to recognize the spiritual forces at work and deal with them appropriately.

Convergence is, in part, the outcome of many small decisions. Decisions are often directly related to our ability to hear God. Hearing God is linked to fearing God:

> Now what I am commanding you today is not too difficult for you or beyond your reach. It is not up in heaven, so that you have to ask, 'Who will ascend into heaven to get it and proclaim it to us so that we may obey it?' Nor is it beyond the sea, so that you have to ask, 'Who will cross the sea to get it and proclaim it to us so we may obey it?' No, the word is very near you: it is in your mouth and in your heart so that you may obey it.[60]

## Routine Responsiveness

Look at this through the window of responsibility or responsiveness to God. Scripture indicates that we will know God's will when we plan to obey God's will. For the most part, God will speak to us [consistently, in a growth mode] when he sees "routine responsiveness" in our lives. This is not to say that we are perfect, only that we are willing, despite our unbelief and inability to follow through. Because of the importance of routine responsiveness to God's voice, accountability can make an enormous difference in one's walk to Convergence. It is a rare person who stays the course without others holding him or her accountable for the best use of God's gifts. One question we should ask each other is, "Are we keeping a soft posture towards God's desires for our lives?"

## Church Leaders Hearing God

Lyn and I were asked to speak at a leaders' retreat for the staff of a local church. A group of about 25 gathered at a retreat center among the redwood trees in Northern California. The subject was "Hearing the Voice of God." The leaders came from a variety of backgrounds:

60      Deut 30:11-14

Catholic, Brethren, Baptist, Covenant, Athletes in Action, etc. I shared my discussions with the school mom whom I mentioned at the outset of this chapter. There was mixed receptiveness from the church leaders. I tried to set some context and said:

> "I will refer to the topic of the Word of God throughout our time together. Let me say a few things up front just to prod you out the bleachers and draw you right onto the playing field with me from the outset of the game.

» I believe that the Scripture is the inerrant Word of God, and that he speaks through his written word.

» I also believe that nothing he says to us today will contradict the written Word, and everything he says should be tested against the Scriptures.

» I believe that God still speaks today in a wide variety of the ways, just as he did in Old Testament times.

» I believe that since the coming of Jesus, we have certain advantages over the people of the time before Christ's coming:

- We have the Holy Spirit to lead us into all truth.

- We have the canon of Scripture collated and readily available to us in many sizes, shapes and colors (although this is not yet true of every tribe, tongue and nation).

- We know the Living Word. Look around you; the person to your left and right actually knows God. They talk to Him; he talks to them. That is quite amazing. And we know this without a shadow of doubt because of Christ's work.

- Another advantage we have is that the incidence of the 'word of the Lord' is far more than in Old Testament times. It is common in New Testament times for everyday people—not just priests and prophets—to:

- Hear a "still, small voice"
- See visions
- Dream dreams
- Prophecy
- Have words of knowledge
- Discern spirits
- Cast out demons

» Much less common, but also part of the normal Christian life, if we take Scripture to be a pattern for us, is:

- Seeing angels
- Hearing an audible voice from God
- Having a personal visitation from Jesus

Having recognized our advantages, we need to also recognize that we are not in too dissimilar a position than the religious leaders of Jesus' day:

» They had the scriptures ("You search the scriptures..."[61])

» They spent much time pondering its interpretation; whole groupings had emerged based on these differences in interpretation.

» Their interpretation of scripture kept them from knowing God, even when they saw him in the flesh. (We need to be careful not to assign the Pharisees an inevitable support role in the melodrama of heaven, and therefore lose sight of the lesson they teach us.)

Which brings me to remind you of a key point for our time together: Information without revelation does not lead to transformation.

Some of the participants liked what they were hearing. Others were curious. One or two were not so happy because they believed that God only speaks through the Bible. I went on to caution them about the religious leaders in the time when Jesus walked on the earth.

## So How did the Pharisees Hear God?

Whenever we have a disconnect between our theology and our experience, we begin to explain things away, and we then run the risk of losing the voice of God. Stated another way, when what we preach is not consistent with what we practice, we can slip down the slope to becoming hypocrites because we have to create an explanation for the disconnect. That explanation entraps us. We have the word, but we do not do it. We find a description of ourselves in James 1:22-25, which says:

> Do not merely listen to the word, and so deceive yourselves. Do what it says. Anyone who listens to the word but does not do what it says is like a man who looks at his face in a mirror and, after looking at himself, goes away and immediately forgets what he looks like. But the man who looks intently into the perfect law that gives freedom, and continues to do this, not forgetting what he has heard, but doing it—he will be blessed in what he does.

But what about the faculties that God has given us? You may say, "God has given me a brain, I should use it. God has given me his Word and a fine mind, I should join them together. I spent big bucks getting a theological degree—my particular views cost me a lot of money. Surely you don't want me to abandon them! I have a rational mind!" The rational mind... ah, the rational mind. Having spent so much on seminary—a better educational track record than even Jesus and the early apostles—we hold that we have the Word, so we don't need that inferior stuff that the uneducated people of Bible times needed. We place the Word in preeminence over Him who speaks today.

Those who hold this view—three chapters a day plus a large dose of personal discipline—are hardly different from secular humanists. In fact, they are what I call religious humanists: Christians who are enmeshed by a humanistic mind set.

Sometimes we can have our nose so deep in the *logos* that we cannot hear the *rhema*. And then we wonder why we end up with a theology of faith, without faith, "the assurance of things hoped for, the proof of things not yet seen." Do you have faith, or do you have just a theology of faith that frees you from living in daily dependence of manna (the word for today) from heaven? Are we Pharisees? Do we have the word of God without the power of God? We need to become far more passionate about expanding the Kingdom and let Jesus build His church. "The Kingdom of God is not a matter of talk, but of power."[62]

## What We Really Believe

An interesting thing happened at the end of the staff retreat where we spoke on "Hearing the Voice of God." God gave Lyn mental pictures in her mind for five of the staff. She shared them and prayed over each person. People were visibly moved. A short while later I heard that there was internal debate among the staff. One of the senior members had two complaints. First, he believed that God only spoke through the written Word. The staff member replied, "Either the picture Lyn shared with me was given to her by God, or she has been reading exact words from my journal." His second objection: "Why did Lyn only have pictures for the younger staff?" You see the disconnect, of course. These objections highlight the fact that even those who hold the intellectual view that God "only speaks through his Word" rely on a host of other evidences and means of God speaking to them.

All of us long to hear from our Creator. How does God speak? However he wants to speak. He is God, after all. He whispers to us through creation, he sings through the words of a song, he moves on the imaginations of our mind, he gives us dreams, he makes the invisible visible through visions, he sends angels that look like everyday people to assist us, he sends people that don't look like angels, he makes the words on the pages of our Bibles jump to life again and again, and he whispers quietly to us in our own accent. He speaks however he wants to speak, and he attunes our ear in the season of Fearing and Hearing God.

## Discovering Your Gifts

The self-help sections of bookstores are brimming with books that promise to propel you forward in every possible way. Unfortunately, their premise is that you can make yourself whatever you want to be. The self-help view puts us at the center; God's view has him at the center and encourages us to discover and exercise, within the context of a relationship with the Godhead, the gifts he has given us. Discovering our gifts involves lots of trial and error; doers do well in this season.

Jeremiah was a young man when God called him to be a prophet to the nations:

> The word of the Lord came to me, saying, "Before I formed you in the womb I knew you, before you were born I set you apart; I appointed you as a prophet to the nations." "Ah, Sovereign Lord," I said, "I do not know how to speak; I am only a child." But the Lord said to me, "Do not say, 'I am only a child.' You must go to everyone I send you to and say whatever I command you."[56]

Because Jeremiah was young, he was probably untainted by the religiosity and corruption in Israel and Judah at the time. He was God's kid for the job. There was only one problem; even prophets need some skills building. In the following paragraphs we see Jeremiah receiving a few revelations and interpretations, which was a confidence builder for things to come:

> The word of the Lord came to me: "What do you see, Jeremiah?" "I see the branch of an almond tree," I replied. The Lord said to me, "You have seen correctly, for I am watching to see that my word is fulfilled." The word of the Lord came to me again: "What do you see?" "I see a boiling pot, tilting away from the north," I answered. The Lord said to me, "From the north disaster will be poured out on all who live in the land."[57]

Notice how God put Jeremiah through the paces and gave him a taste of his new calling and gifting.

Personally, I didn't know myself until I knew God. I therefore had some inkling of my gifts, but a truer reflection of these began to emerge when this first penny of identity dropped. This is not atypical. Young people seem to try on different personae like clothes at a shopping mall. "Is this me? Does it fit?" This process is healthy and normal. It is also subject to

56    Jeremiah 1:4-7

57    Jeremiah 1:11-14

certain risks. If we are not content with who we are and are not secure in the love of Jesus, there is the danger that we'll fashion images of ourselves designed to mask the cracks. Further, we cultivate some notion that we are people of our own creation. If we are particularly pleased with who we are (which probably means that we haven't seen ourselves as God sees us) we become proud. If we don't like the end product, we reject ourselves. Worse still, we cut ourselves off from the wonderful process of discovering how our Creator fashioned us. Since the Garden of Eden, God has enjoyed sharing his creativity with man. Discovering your own gifts is a wonderful continuation of that process.

## Principles of Gift Discovery

Recently I discussed with a psychologist friend the wide variety of personality profiling tools on the market. He cautioned that most of these tests are designed to meet the needs of the researchers and not those filling out the forms. The Sophie's Choice questionnaires do not always yield a fair result. ("Would you rather keep your daughter or your son" type questions sometimes leave one without a fair answer. "Both" would render you indecisive, of course.) I have made no attempt to duplicate the many gift tests that are available; they are widely known and can be very helpful. Instead I offer some simple steps to get you on the road to gift discovery.

1. Find a need and fill it. Particularly in your early years, try to do a variety of things. Don't wait for the perfect job or the ideal assignment. Park some cars, copy cassette tapes, change a diaper or two.

2. Develop a willingness to serve. Don't let your ability outstrip your availability. Few of us pop out of the womb with finely honed gifts. Refinement takes practice and dedication. There is nothing quite so frustrating as highly gifted people who hold back on the deployment of their gifts.

3. "Don't think of yourself more highly than you ought."[58] *The Message* puts it this way: "The only accurate way to understand ourselves is by what God is and by what he does for us, not by what we are and what we do for him." In an age where young (and not so young) people seem to be taught more about packaging than content, don't believe your own press reports. Develop a healthy scepticism for your own opinions. As a modern sage has said, "The goldfish doesn't always have the best perspective of the fish bowl."

4. Take a good gift identification test. I recommend the "Modified Houts Questionnaire" as one way to understand how you are wired.[59] Then speak with people who know you well who can verify your self-assessment, providing encouragement and refining perspectives.

5. Don't get pigeon-holed by tests: Meyers Briggs did not write the Bible. There may well be things that God has planted in your heart that are not yet apparent. Pray, wait, and serve where you can.

6. Find older mentors. Older people are not threatened by your brilliance, you are less likely to try to impress them, and they would hope for nothing better than to see you blossom. Include older people in your life.

7. At the same time, avoid those who assume you lack gifts because you are young. There are plenty of examples of people who were called by God at an early age, such as Moses, Samuel and Jeremiah. Hang around those who will smile on your gifts and extend grace to you where your character is not quite as sharp as your insight or tongue may be.

8. Ensure character development stays in step with gift development. Gifting does not guarantee success. Unless it is tempered by humility and character, it can be lethal. Glory is "full of grace and truth."[60]

---

58   Romans 12:3

59   See http://www.mccgsl.org/PDFs/SpiritualGiftsInventory.pdf

60   John 1:14

9. Be part of a team. The Bible calls it a body. The Lone Ranger had some glorious moments on his own, but when the going got tough, it was "we." You won't discover your gifts without discovering your inter-dependence with others.

10. Be more concerned with obedience than Career. We often wonder, "What shall I do next?" Campbell McAlpine said, "There are more crises of obedience than guidance." Keep your heart supple and your will flexible.

My final recommendation on this is that you be willing to lose site of Calling if there is an overshadowing opportunity for gift discovery and skills building. This may sound counter-intuitive, but often God does not reveal Calling until he has seen the faithfulness in service.

## A Season, Not a Test

Just in case I am beginning to sound formulaic, remember that gift discovery is a season. I spent about ten years developing and discovering my gifts. I had a running joke with a friend with whom I had the privilege of co-working for about five years. When we taught ten and eleven-year-olds in Sunday School he said, "You should never stop doing this. You are gifted with this age group." Shortly thereafter, I stopped teaching that class and he took it over. A while later he again said words to the effect of, "You should never stop teaching a youth group. You are gifted at leading teenagers." It wasn't long before my ten or so years of leading youth were over. Some time later, after we had pastored a church together, he said "You should stay with the local church and I should go and do missions." I knew it was time to start packing. It wasn't long before we left Hout Bay, South Africa and came to the San Francisco Bay Area.

Was my friend misguided? Not at all. It's just that sometimes, particularly when we are young, we see a talent as our life-long Call when God sees it as an opportunity to grow our gifts. "Whatever your hand finds to do, do it with all your might, for in the grave, where you are going, there is neither working nor planning nor knowledge nor wisdom."[61] But remember, you could well just be doing it for a season.

While this is true, there is a corollary: God is not trying to get us through a pipeline of seasons; he is trying to get us. Period. No matter what season we are in, the issue is not the passage of time, but the preparation of our whole person.

## The LEMON Leadership Model®

As a new believer I attended leadership training courses, read the recommended reading, and proceeded to do what leaders do. It wasn't bad stuff, but it suggested a singular view of leadership that is not only unreal, but also robs unconventional leaders of their place in life. In the world of business, for example, much of the leadership literature focuses on two categories: Entrepreneurs and Managers. Within the latter category there is some dissection to deal with the differences between what are fondly called "executives" and "general managers." But are these the only two types of leaders?

Over the past 25 years I have worked closely with hundreds of senior executives in a variety of organizations. There is no way that these people fall into just two categories. I believe that there are five different yet complementary leadership types. These are not styles of leadership, but fundamentally different DNA that influences the way leaders see situations, communicate, hear information, respond to pressure, and shape organizations. Before we review these, note that each category is a category of Leadership; in other words, all are leaders. They simply lead from a different perspective.

61      Ecclesiastes 9:10

I have named this the LEMON Leadership Model®.[62] The topic is covered in depth in the book, *LEMON Leadership*. My recommendation is that you get to know these types of leaders as you will stand a better chance of knowing your gifts if you appreciate and nurture them in the context of how you are wired; or in this case you know your LEMON Leadership profile.

My final challenge on the topic is this: most leadership theories affirm your one type of leadership and give you a free pass on the others. I disagree. The last chapter of *LEMON Leadership* explains how Jesus is the perfect five-slice LEMON, and that it is sin that prevents us from developing the slices of the LEMON that do not feel natural to us. The "easy" antidote is to die to yourself, to lose your life, to regard others as better than yourself—or at least as good as yourself.

When you read about LEMONs, don't say, "This is me, and forget the rest!" Make sure you discover gifts across the LEMON.

| Type of Leader | Characteristics | Locus of Leadership |
|---|---|---|
| Luminary | • Believe that ideas precede activities<br>• Thought leaders: value concepts and fresh thinking<br>• Often long range thinkers<br>• Inspire organizations through the power of their ideas<br>• Care more about "Why" than "How" | Ideas |
| Entrepreneur | • Believe that opportunities precede activities<br>• Short-to-medium term thinkers<br>• Inspire organizations through energy and enthusiasm<br>• See "failure" as learning experiences<br>• Care more about results: "What" | Opportunities |

62    The *LEMON Leadership Model* and *LEMON Leadership* are registered trademarks of The Institute for Innovation, Integration & Impact, Inc. - www.lemonleadership.com

| Type of Leader | Characteristics | Locus of Leadership |
|---|---|---|
| Manager | • Believe that proper planning precedes activities<br>• Long-term thinkers<br>• Implementers of vision<br>• Will build a team to get tasks done rather than do the tasks themselves<br>• Understand process, planning, profits | Systems |
| Organizer | • Action oriented<br>• Have an "unconscious competence": they intuitively pick the right things to focus on<br>• Love to bring things to a close<br>• A quick result is usually always the best result<br>• Care about "When" | Loyalty to leader |
| Networker | • Love to bring people together<br>• Instinctively build networks, even if they are not always sure what to do with them<br>• "If we get enough smart people in the room, the right thing is sure to happen."<br>• Their communications is "event driven"<br>• Care about "Who" | Connecting people |

None of us are solely one type of leader or another. We tend to be a blend of a few categories, and we have to work at building our own capabilities and adding other LEMONs to our teams. The LEMON Leadership Model® is included here, not to box you into a category, but to cast new colors on your reflection about yourself and your leadership. We understand our gifts in the context of who we are.

## Hindrances to Gift Discovery

The top reasons why we don't discover our gifts:

1. We do not have a context that is calling out, coaching, and applauding our gifts. Who are your cheerleaders? I am blessed to have friends,

intercessors, and colleagues that spur me on. "The Lord is with you, you mighty man of valor!"[63] Along these lines, have you thanked your parents and past bosses lately for giving you work to do as a child?

2. We are waiting for the "perfect" job to come along before we do anything. Life involves grunt work. Get on with it.

3. We are willing to serve, but not yet. Procrastination. "Let me first go and bury my father."[64]

4. We are not willing to serve. False advertising tells us we can start at the top without having to pay our dues. "He who is faithful in little...trustworthy in a very small matter"[65]

5. Schedule pressure and fatigue rob us of courage and creativity. Vince Lombardi, the famous football coach, is credited with saying, "Fatigue makes cowards of us all." Time pressure is also true during the teenage years when children are asked to keep the daily schedules of adults—and still have time to discover who they are. It is true for adults who confuse activity with work. If Jesus said to Martha, "Mary has chosen what is better," what would he say to you?

6. Internal insecurity causes us to shrink from trying. Insecurity can cause us to (a) put down the gifts of others so that we feel better about ourselves, or (b) undermine our own gifts. Fear of failure paralyzes us. As the saying goes, "Better to try and fail, than to not try at all."

7. An inadequate understanding of the different types of gifts.

8. You are too gifted for your own good! But is it possible to be over-gifted? I have met many highly talented people who are 40 years old and do not know who they are. Many of them are highly gifted. I

63     Judges 6:12
64     Matthew 8:21
65     Luke 19:17

sense, however, that the real hindrance is #1: No one "called them out." They did not have earthly fathers or spiritual fathers who did the job, and this was masked by their abundance of gifts. So they look good on paper—are even successful by many measures—but they do not know who they are.

All the gifts in the world will not get you to Convergence, however, if you do not have integrity. That is why there is a short season called "Internal Integrity" that we must all go through at some stage or another.

## Internal Integrity

What do you do when no one is looking? Who are you when no one else is around? How would you respond under pressure to comply, give in, conform? Do you really know? Can we ever know for sure? C.S. Lewis says:

> Surely what a man does when he is caught off his guard is the best evidence as to what sort of man he is.

As in many things, there are two seemingly opposing perspectives on these questions. We are taught, "...if you think you are standing firm, be careful that you don't fall!" [62]

We should never be too cocky or self-assured, especially when it comes to sin. A healthy distrust of our sinful nature is useful. The corollary is that we should not be focused on our now-dead sinful nature. If we remain preoccupied with sin we will not be free of it.

A second reason why we go through testing is this: God needs to assure us that he has built character into us. He wants us to have a level of certainty, not so that we can be proud, but so that we can have the courage to cooperate with him in new ventures.

A third reason why the Internal Integrity season may be key to our journey to Convergence is that it helps amass spiritual capital when we choose obedience. When we overcome temptation, it adds to God's cause and plunders hell. This may sound dramatic, but the early pages of Genesis outline this conflict:

> "Why are you so angry?" the Lord asked him. "Why do you look so dejected? You will be accepted if you respond in the right way. But if you refuse to respond correctly, then watch out! Sin is waiting to attack and destroy you, and you must subdue it."[63]

Sin has the potential to destroy us; we have the capacity to subdue it. When we subdue it, we build spiritual capital. We take a success to the bank, if you like, and we can draw on it in future times of need.

## More Than a Jiffy Lube Checkup

We'd like to check this season off our list quite quickly. Judging by the experience of men and women who were close followers of God in history, it's usually not that simple. Somehow when it comes to the seasons of Skills Building and Internal Integrity, God's timetable is slow and relaxed. Later in this section we will review a few characters who knew this to be true.

63    Genesis 4:6,7

Back in the mid-1980's, I attempted to launch a consulting practice in a new area of thought. "Executive Information Systems" were hot—or at least the market predictions looked that way. Price Waterhouse had agreed that we should pursue the practice, and I had decided that it wouldn't hurt if I was a nationally-known speaker. A software company approached me to do a road show in 17 major North American cities to launch their new product. It was a great opportunity.

Naturally I had to clear it with the folks at "Corporate." I spoke to a colleague who assured me that he had cleared it with the partner-in-charge, and I could go ahead. I sensed a check in my spirit—"Was everything okay?"—but went ahead anyway. After all of the invitations were printed with my name on them and many distributed across the country, all hell broke loose. Price Waterhouse had signed a national alliance with another software company that they deemed to be a competitor of the company I was working with, and the partner-in-charge was livid. There were daily interrogations, unpleasant phone calls, and people questioning my integrity. After the first few days I implored God to ease up. I had learned my lesson. Enough was enough. But it continued for a month or more. I felt as if God had his foot on my neck, and I had the sense he was in no rush to remove it until the lessons of listening to God and not giving him a helping hand were baked into my being.

## A Season, Not a Sentence

Less than pleasant times are not always the result of punishment. If this were the case, we would spend our lives avoiding difficulties to stay "in God's will." Apart from an observation of Scripture, my experience is that God leads us into tough times. It's true that while he does not tempt us to sin, he does lead us into difficulties.

At about 24 years of age, I had the privilege of pastoring a wonderful group of people. The job wasn't one I chose—it was more like a wartime "field promotion" which is what happens when the guy in front of you gets shot. With a very committed team of volunteers, we rebuilt a local church over a five year period. By many accounts, it was a successful venture.

After we moved to the United States we were approached by a group of people who wanted to meet for fellowship. All of them had been in some position of church leadership; some had served effectively in foreign missions. It should have been easy. For months we spent social time, worshipped and prayed together. Then some people in the group felt that we should "start a church" rather than just be the church. They wanted posters, flyers, rented space, the whole deal. For a variety of reasons it never happened. On top of this, the fellowship group folded. In short, it was a failure. While it's a longer story than I have explained, the question remains, "Were we led into this experience? Did God want us to fail?" I think so. Bob Mumford says, "There is nothing quite so dangerous as a string of unbroken success." I am glad to have both the apparent success and failure on my resume.

Tests of our integrity are needed to make us strong. And they don't always come because we messed up. Often, it's to the contrary.

## Out-Jacobing Jacob

We have established that God is not vindictive. At times, however, there are things deep in our being that require uprooting. Often the infinitely creative God uses the University of the Desert to heal us of these maladies, but sometimes he lets us get outdone by someone who is like us. If we are not prepared to hate our own sin, we seem to be willing to hate it in others, and then, by grace, recognize that we are riddled with the same thing. Jacob knew all about this.

Jacob was a schemer.[64] He was the quintessential entrepreneur. By hook or by crook he would find an angle. And it's not that God wasn't in some of the schemes. But when Jacob hatched a plan to make Rachel his wife, Laban, his would-be father-in-law, outdid him. When Jacob

64    You find his story in Genesis 27.

planned an escape, Laban cut him off at the pass. This sparring went on for 14 years. Jacob lunged, Laban ducked. Eventually Jacob left with much material wealth—not everything always goes bad at once—but he still had to face a past nemesis. En route to see his brother, God met Jacob. The culmination of a 14-year Internal Integrity project resulted in a struggle with God. Jacob passed the test, but in the process he was forever marked. Thereafter the self-made achiever walked with a limp.

We are only really safe to do God's bidding when we walk with a limp. Furthermore, I am convinced that we cannot come to Convergence until we limp from having been broken by God. Before this point, we say we will never deny him. After this point, we are less cocky about ourselves and have a more tender heart for our Lord Jesus:

> Happy are those who know they are spiritually poor; the Kingdom of heaven belongs to them![65]

## A Strange Thing Happened Today

You never know when the Internal Integrity season will begin. It comes without fanfare and warning. Occasionally we get a glimpse ahead, but very often it simply comes. Then it does not help to pray, "God, what do you want me to do?" Because the heavens will be silent. The fact is, we already know what to do. The question is whether we will do it. When Satan tempted Jesus in the desert we do not see Jesus praying, "Father, is it your will to turn these stones into bread?" The Internal Integrity season is not a matter of inquiring but doing, or not doing.

## This Might Hurt

One of the dangers we face in this season is that the test intended to bless us gets twisted, and it then becomes a source of hurt. The Internal Integrity season, like some other seasons, can involve something that we

---

65    Matthew 5:3 Good News Translation

interpret as hurt. I experienced something in my life that left a wound. Others could probably see and feel the effects of it more clearly than I could. I knew that what I had experienced at the hands of brothers and sisters in the church was part of God's plan to move me on. What I did not know was that this hurt had festered and I was experiencing residual effects. As part of the healing process God caused me to think through the "model of hurt" that you see diagrammed and explained in the following paragraphs.

The essence of the model is this: hurt does happen. We cannot avoid it, but our responses to it can be different. God can use hurt for good, and because Satan has come "to steal, kill and destroy" he wants to take the same incidence and use it for harm. What influences whether we see the pain as being "for good" or "for harm"? In many cases it is our view of God. We have a filter that causes us to sift the pain and see it as being for our good, or to our detriment. That filter is our view of God. Some people believe he is good, all of the time. He does not have bad days, he is never in a bad mood, and he is not out to get us. He is simply good, and consequently, there is no shadow or change in him. His every thought, action and motive is pure. And he likes us.

Our enemy, on the other hand, does not have good things in his mind for us. This fact should not cause us to panic, but we should be aware that his basic tactic is to get us to question whether God is good, and whether he wants the best for us. This is not new thinking, but it is as old as the Garden of Eden. "Did God really say...?" We have to decide who we are going to believe if we are to get through the Internal Integrity season effectively...if we are to get through life joyfully. If our switch us set to "God is good" then fewer pains will wind up in the "For Harm" bucket. We must be aware of the enemy's schemes so that, along with Joseph, we can say, "What you meant for harm, God meant for good." We must ask God to clean our filter so that when hurt happens, which it will, we are not tempted to question God's intentions towards us.

Let's explore the path of pain more closely.

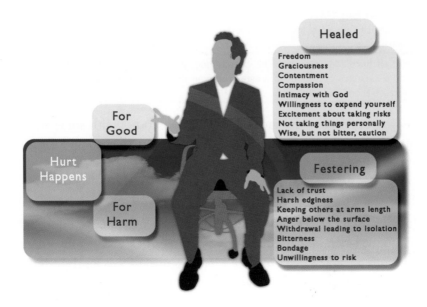

**Healed**

Freedom
Graciousness
Contentment
Compassion
Intimacy with God
Willingness to expend yourself
Excitement about taking risks
Not taking things personally
Wise, but not bitter, caution

**For Good**

**Hurt Happens**

**For Harm**

**Festering**

Lack of trust
Harsh edginess
Keeping others at arms length
Anger below the surface
Withdrawal leading to isolation
Bitterness
Bondage
Unwillingness to risk

Hurt Happens. It is a normal part of the human growth process. But it enters us with a tilting towards good or harm depending on a number of factors which, I believe, include (a) our past experience, (b) our self-image, self-perception, and level of security, and (c) our view of God: whether he is good or bad. Hurt is like an "egg"–our bias is like the "sperm" that predisposes that hurt towards "For Good" or "For Harm."

God intends that the hurt be used for his purposes in our lives.

Satan has come "to steal, kill and destroy." He plans to use hurt to "de-commission" us. God often intends that hurt, especially friendly fire, should "re-commission" us.

Hurt touches us in many places such as:

» A. Our Head – an attack on our ability to think and lead properly.

» B. Our Hands – the type and quality of our work is assaulted. "What they are building—if even a fox climbed up on it, he would break down their wall of stones!" (Nehemiah 4:3)

» C. Our Feet – the scope of our kingdom work is assailed. "You are going where?"

» D. Our Loin – Satan wants to hinder our ability to reproduce kingdom initiatives.

» E. Whatever the point of hurt, it finds its way to our Hearts.

» F. Our ego – saving us from believing our own Public Relations / advertising.

> Unhealed hurt festers and causes a slew of symptoms that ultimately taints many aspects of our lives. Instead of the hurt producing antibodies, it produces death. There is no denying the painfulness of hurt, but it must eventually be healed.

> Healed hurt adds strength. The overcoming of challenges creates spiritual capital, and this empowers us to do greater things in the future. We cannot wallow in hurt because there is a work to be done.

As you experience the inevitable pain that comes with some seasons, make sure you leave each season with your hurt healed and the truth about who God is intact:

> You will know the truth, and the truth shall set you free.[66]

Joseph had a perfect opportunity to harbor a hurt. He had done what was right when he passed his Internal Integrity season by resisting the constant advances of Potiphar's wife. His reward was a prison term of indeterminate length. He could have become bitter and useless to God, but he hung onto the dream. We have a choice whether we will forego our pity party and press forward to "lay hold of that for which Christ Jesus laid hold of me."[67] This is also true in the season of Skills Building when we are inevitably looked over for promotion and, like Joseph, spend time in prison learning skills that are invaluable to leading a nation.

## Who Do You Really Believe?

Do you think the Internal Integrity season is about you? Is it a season that highlights what you believe? Or could it be about *who* you believe? The obvious challenges of this season are about morality, ethics, core beliefs. The bigger issues come when the facts, the data and the opinions are contrary to what God has spoken to your heart.

---

66       John 8:32

67       Phillipians 3:12

Consider Abraham as an example:

He believed God, and it was credited to him as righteousness.[68]

Was Joseph only tested about what he believed, or as the years rolled by and he was still in prison and the smell of Mrs. Potiphar's perfume was long gone, was it now a question of who he believed in?

Was the fruit of Daniel a religious determination, or was it the aroma of one caught up in steadfastly believing his God? Nebuchadnezzar, his boss and ruler of an empire, saw it this way:

Praise be to the God of Shadrach, Meshach and Abednego, who has sent his angel and rescued his servants! They trusted in him and defied the king's command and were willing to give up their lives rather than serve or worship any god except their own God.[69]

It is my pleasure to tell you about the miraculous signs and wonders that the Most High God has performed for me.[70]

When Daniel and his friends navigated the Internal Integrity Season with their hearts intact, the king fell in love with their God. Let's remember this season with an eye to the boundless goodness of God, not the greatness of our temporary trials.

---

68      Galatians 3:6

69      Daniel 3:28

70      Daniel 4:2

## Skills Building

The skills we most need for public work are generally developed in obscurity. In God's economy, this seems to be more the norm than the exception. So people in the United States who reach this season are faced with a dilemma. Our educational systems seem bent on teaching people how to package themselves well, regardless of the contents of the package. A high school student in Lake Minitonka has a longer resume than the average 35-year-old in Britain. Candidates become shallow; interviewers become suspicious. Can you actually do all this stuff on your resume? Do you have that many trials, triumphs and passions by 19? If you don't you won't get into college. Posturing is key to progress, it seems.

And the problem is not isolated to the U.S. A young lady from South Africa commented that an acquaintance had landed an internship in a prestigious management-consulting firm. He had no clue as to what he was doing, but he very quickly learned that things were fine "as long as you gave the impression that you knew what was going on." This kind of problem is then compounded by inflated expectations of career fast-tracking, stars who are writing autobiographies in their early 20s, and less-than-30-year-old millionaires.

## Competence

I don't believe you can arrive at true Convergence without going through the Skills Building season. You might argue that you are unusually gifted, a person graced with extraordinary talent. Gifts and talents do not guarantee character. "Ah! But I have character too!" you may well say. The fact is that the Gifts + Talents + Character variables are not enough to complete the Convergence equation. We also need Competence, and Competence is developed in the Skills Building season. King David is an example of a highly talented person who had a heart that was tender towards God. He was a musician and a poet. He was also the somewhat forgotten "Employee # 8" that his father overlooked when Samuel came calling:

> Jesse had seven of his sons pass before Samuel, but Samuel said to him, "The Lord has not chosen these." So he asked Jesse, "Are these all the sons you have?" "There is still the youngest," Jesse answered, "but he is tending the sheep."[68]

David had been assigned the low level job. He was not in the inner circle, schmoozing with the boss and top management. But God had him right where he wanted him, building his skills, ironing out his leadership kinks by practicing leading sheep:

---

68      1 Samuel 16:10-11

He chose David his servant and took him from the sheep pens; from tending the sheep he brought him to be the shepherd of his people Jacob, of Israel his inheritance. And David shepherded them with integrity of heart; with skillful hands he led them.[69]

In the book, *I-Operations: How the Internet can Transform your Operating Model*, my coauthor and I explain the longing that nations have for leaders that have both character and competence.[70] David was such a leader. *I-Operations* goes on to explain an illustration of the "Bicycle of a Leader" that integrates the essential elements of character and competence:

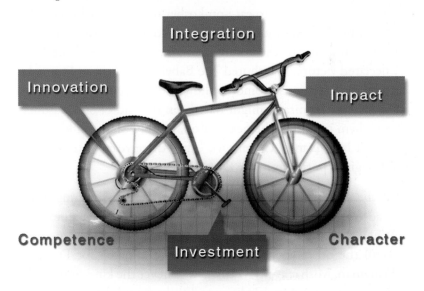

The basic premise of this $I^4$ Bicycle is that many factors need to work together for us to have sustainable Impact. Character is crucial, but we cannot ignore competence. I am tired of hearing, "I hire the best person for the job, and that usually isn't a Christian." It goes without

69      Psalm 78:70-72

70      Gary Daichendt and Brett Johnson, *I-Operations: How the Internet can Transform your Operating Model,* Indaba Publishing, 2002.

saying that we should hire people of excellent ability; it is time that these were people who claim to be followers of The Way.

Daniel is another example of someone well prepared for work. He was not just a "God said it, I heard it, that sealed it" prophet:

> In all matters requiring wisdom and balanced judgment, the king found the advice of these young men to be ten times better than that of all the magicians and enchanters in his entire kingdom.[71]

Wow! God did a miracle! Ten times better! How did he do it? In the early part of Daniel 1 we see Daniel and his three friends in the Internal Integrity season, refusing to eat non-kosher nosh. "Daniel resolved not to defile himself..." After just 10 days "they looked healthier and better nourished than any of the young men who ate the royal food."[72] So they declared victory, coauthored The Babylonian Diet, and toured the Christian radio stations promoting how you too could lose it all in 10 days! This 10-day miracle might have been the end of one season, but it threw them right into the next season, namely, Skills Building. How long did it last? Daniel 1:5 tells us, "After three years of training they would be given positions in the king's court."

> At the end of the time set by the king for their training, the head of the royal staff brought them in to Nebuchadnezzar. When the king interviewed them, he found them far superior to all the other young men. None were a match for Daniel, Hananiah, Mishael, and Azariah. Whenever the king consulted them on anything, on books or on life, he found them ten times better than all the magicians and enchanters in his kingdom put together. Daniel continued in the king's service until the first year in the reign of King Cyrus.[73]

---

71      Daniel 1:20 *New Living Translation*

72      Daniel 1:15

73      Daniel 1:18-21 *The Message*

Miracles will get you through some seasons, but Skills Building will add some sweat in the mix. Am I promoting the regular brand of Christian Humanism preached by many?

## Kingdom Truth versus Christian Humanism

Let's face it, Daniel must have learned some good things from his tutors, and they probably weren't good Jewish rabbis. We can learn from people all across the spectrum. I realize as I write this second edition, however, that it would be easy for the reader to slip back into what can be called "Christian Humanism," the dominant worldview of most people with a ticket to heaven. Christian Humanism is the mind set that says, "I will trust Jesus for the salvation of my soul, and, on a normal day, I will trust myself for my career and business." Most people who follow Jesus can adequately explain the basis for entering heaven; few can explain what the Bible says about marketing, product development or the purpose of business. They have given little thought to the business practices of Jesus, or why he described his work on earth as a business. Many are asking God to bless their business, few are genuinely asking how they can use their full range of skills and assets to get into God's business. A small fraction have searched the Scriptures to find their job in those Scriptures, or in the Godhead.

The Skills Building Season is not about reading the latest business or self-help books and becoming disciples of philosophies that come and go. I find more believers adept in chaos and chasms, in tipping points and tornadoes than in the best practices that come from God himself. Where do you get your best practices from anyway?

> Listen to me now. Give me your closest attention. Do farmers plow and plow and do nothing but plow? Or harrow and harrow and do nothing but harrow? After they've prepared the ground, don't they plant? Don't they scatter dill and spread cumin, plant wheat and barley in the fields and raspberries along the borders? They know exactly what to do and when to do it. Their God is their teacher. And at the harvest, the delicate

herbs and spices, the dill and cumin, are treated delicately. On the other hand, wheat is threshed and milled, but still not endlessly. The farmer knows how to treat each kind of grain. He's learned it all from God-of-the-Angel-Armies, who knows everything about when and how and where.[74]

I commend those authors who take eternal truths and package them in a manner that reaches the businesswoman walking through the airport. But the Christ-follower who doesn't do the legwork to find foundational principles and best practices for his or her work in the heart of God, in the pages of Scripture, is missing the essence of this season.

At a personal level, it took a few decisions to get me off the normal corporate road. They were big decisions at the time, but nothing like the hard work of getting the ingrained habits of the corporate way out of me. I am continually surprised at how much my presuppositions are counter to God's thoughts and ways. It's taking time, lots of time, to get my thinking renewed. Positionally I know I have "the mind of Christ." Practically I have the habits of decades of doing things my way.

## The Fast Track

The Skills Building season in God's plan seems to run counter to the Fast Track. My observation is that it often takes the form of 10 to 15 years of unglamorous work. The day in, day out drudgery that, bit by bit, hones our skills is part of God's plan. There are a number of implications of this season that will help us to rest in it, enjoy it, and be prepared for the long haul:

» Every job isn't a life-long career. When we feel led into a new career, we should consider why we are there. In one situation, I felt clearly that God had directed me to join a reputable firm. After about 18 months things did not look good. On the surface

---

74    Isaiah 28:23-29, *The Message*

everything was rosy. But at a lower level I saw an organization that had been built on money and not on values. After some time I asked God, "Why did you bring me here?" The reply was clear as a bell: "To learn what bad management is like." It's tough to learn the consequences of bad management when all you have experienced is positive leadership. Find out why God has asked you to do what you are doing.

» Marry yourself to God's long-term leading in your life, not to a career that looks good on paper. I have made numerous suicide career moves in order to grow into the person God wants me to be, rather than stay in a rut to achieve the status or position others thought I should strive for. Will money automatically follow such decisions? That's the wrong question, and it betrays our bias toward money as the only valid measure of worth.

» Let God be your promoter. When you wrap your white knuckles around your own career advancement, you set yourself on a collision course with God. As the psalmist says, "For promotion and power come from nowhere on earth, but only from God. He promotes one and deposes another."[75] God's pace of promotion varies greatly by individual. Learn to follow his pattern for you.

» Settle your identity. If you gain your sense of self-worth mainly from your job, you are at risk. If you are settled in being an obedient child of the King, changing fortunes in your career will less likely shake you.

» When others seem bent on ruining your progress, you can respond as Joseph did. "You meant it for harm, but God meant it for good."

» Ask yourself the tough question: Who has rights over my career? The right to a good (-looking) career and Convergence are sometimes diametrically opposed.

75   Psalm 75:6-7, *Living Bible*

» Recognize the risks of shortcuts. Don't try to bust the cycle of skills building just so you can say, "I am on a fast track." Fast tracks to nowhere just get you nowhere quicker.

Convergence is often many little things we have done in our lives coming together to be woven into a fine, rich tapestry. It is not uncommon for us to spend 20, 30, 40 years winding those threads onto their spools before the author and finisher of our tapestry is ready to work them all together. Don't abandon the spools before they are filled appropriately. Quicker isn't always better.

## Serial Career Tracker

Young people face a particularly difficult challenge in the Skills Building season. The "good old days" of predictable careers are over. If there is no such thing as job security, how do I commit myself to long-term skills building? If no one else is making long-term plans for me, how do I plan? The uncertainties in today's job market make it essential to get a grip on this season. Add to this the changing nature of work as we move from an asset-based to a knowledge-based global economy, and it is clear that we need fresh thinking about our careers.

Even when I left high school, the choices were pretty clear. One year compulsory military service, four or five years of university, join the best firm in your field, and hop on the partner track. Today is different. Recently Lyn and I observed that Generation Y high schoolers are embarking on careers as web designers and computer technicians while still at school. At the same time many of their counterparts in Generation X are leaving college with degrees but no clue about what they want to do. So how do you counter the uncertainties of career management in today's world? The answer lies in part in Hearing God, and in gaining a long-term perspective on your life. In a sense, Convergence is about developing what we call life-management skills as opposed to career-management skills. Insecurity in the marketplace need not mean insecurity within.

If you are stringing together a series of jobs that somehow build a picture of Career, it is all the more important that you develop a listening ear. Obedience to that quiet, inner whisper of the Holy Spirit is essential.

## Life is Work

Another point to consider here is one's definition of work. If we are to truly rest in a new definition of Career, we need to see Work as Scripture sees it. Back in the first chapter of Genesis, God worked. It is there in black and white: "And on the seventh day God ended his work."[76]

We live in an age when people are either obsessed with work or are Utopian in their dreams of avoiding work, or both. God worked. Creation is his work. It reflects his identity, ability and will. It was subjected to self-assessment and scrutiny. The quality of the output was the measure of his work—"He saw that it was good"—and not the size of the paycheck or how long he spent doing it. God didn't work because his boss told him to; he worked because he chose to. Work is not a punishment for the sin of Adam and Eve. "If only they hadn't sinned...I would not have to work." This is a myth.

> David, with Zadok of the sons of Eleazar and Ahimelech of the sons of Ithamar, divided them according to their offices for their ministry.[77]

> These were their offices for their ministry when they came in to the house of the LORD according to the ordinance given to them through Aaron their father, just as the LORD God of Israel had commanded him.[78]

---

76      Genesis 2:2

77      I Chronicles 24:3

78      I Chronicles 24:19

The Hebrew word for ministry, *abodah* or *avodah*, is the same as their word for work. *Strong's Concordance* describes it as labor, or service:

a. labor, work

b. labor (of servant or slave)

c. labor, service (of captives or subjects)

d. service (of God)

When Scripture speaks about God's work, starting in Genesis 2, the word *hkalm* means

a. occupation, work, business

b. occupation, business

c. property

d. work (something done or made)

e. workmanship

f. service, use

g. public business

h. political

i. religious

We will not come to Convergence if we hold to a view that some things are work and some things are ministry. This view is not supported by Scripture, and will either puff us up when we say, "I am in ministry because I am in full-time Christian service" with the implication that others are not ministers, or it will tear us down when we say, "I just work for a living...I wish I could be in ministry."

There are some truths concerning work that we need to have ingrained in our hearts:

» Work is a pre-fall reality. Descriptions of paradise are normally work-free, but real life embraces real work. When God and Adam and his business partner, Eve, walked in the garden and talked about the day, my guess is that they discussed work. "Adam, how are the strawberries coming along? And what did you decide to name those animals anyway? Aardvark...that's a pretty good start." I don't think they were discussing pre-or-post millennial reign or the role of women in ministry.

» We will work in heaven. What we do on earth is a preparation for the job we will have in eternity. When Jesus told the parable of the minas, he told the faithful servant that he would get the job of ruling over cities. The reward for a job well done is another job with greater scope.

» We should try to identify our work in Scripture. I spoke just recently with a private banking specialist who manages investments for wealthy individuals. He asked how he could learn more about integrating work and faith. I told him, "First, you need to find your job in the Bible. What does Scripture say about your work? How does it fit into God's plan?" He entered a whole new understanding of his work when he saw God as an asset manager, one who delivers and expects an incredible Return on Assets. He also saw the potential of challenging his clients to seek a return for today and a return for eternity. I encouraged him to speak with his clients along these lines: "We have discussed the immediate yield on your portfolio; have you thought about what it could yield in eternity? Could your investments "store up treasure for you in heaven?" Have you considered the Return on Assets that God might want to see? My job is just a reflection of God's job—how can this experience of investing your earthly assets prepare you for your work in eternity?"

» All of our work should reflect the character or nature of God in us. "So whether you eat or drink or whatever you do, do it all for the glory of God."[79] Whether you do spreadsheets, marketing or dish washing, do it all for the glory of God. Whether you study or surf the Internet, do it all for the glory of God. There are no second class jobs.

» The enjoyment of work is a gift from God to everyone, not just "full-time ministers." We are all workers, we are all ministers. We are all kings and priests. "The creature reveals the Creator in the quality of his work just as the Creator has revealed himself in the quality of his work. Community responsibility and creative solutions reveal the goodness of God to every level of our society. You have a call of God on your life. Like Joseph, you are part of God's revealing his ability to provide all that is needed in abundance. You are part of his plan to reveal the quality of the workman."[80]

» We should be content to judge the merit of our own work and not have our identity hinge on someone's decision about how much to pay us.

» We are entitled to a fair wage. God is not a cheap employer, but the returns may not come in this life.

Servants, do what you're told by your earthly masters. And don't just do the minimum that will get you by. Do your best. Work from the heart for your real Master, for God, confident that you'll get paid in full when you come into your inheritance. Keep in mind always that the ultimate Master you're serving is Christ. The sullen servant who does shoddy work will be held responsible. Being Christian doesn't cover up bad work.[81]

---

79    1 Corinthians 10:31

80    Landa Cope, *Old Testament Template*, www.ottemplate.org

81    Colossians 3:22-25, *The Message*

## Honor Those Who Help You Build Your Skills

There is a tendency among some in the Western World to take for granted the individuals or organizations that invest themselves in our skills development. Instead of being grateful we find ourselves feeling, "My employer owes me a job, life owes me a living, they should invest in training me, they should pay me more, I should work shorter hours, I should get more vacation time, I want more of the profits, they should have less, they should mentor me, they should give me more stock options..."

A friend of mine once told me that his grandmother used to say, "If I could sell you for what you think you are worth and pay you what you are worth, I would be a millionaire." At some stage of our lives most of us seem to have inflated expectations. It can easily become the big corporation against us. But to get the most from our Skills Building season we must do three things:

» Take ownership for our Skills Building.

» Keep a realistic assessment of what our present skills are.

» Remember that God is our real master and it is a privilege to work for him.

The ability to grow our skills is at once a necessity and a privilege. If we go back to the Bible and examine the relationship between the apostles and their work I believe we will see Paul choosing to work in support of his ministry so that he did not burden them, and so that he could be active among them in the marketplace, walking the talk:

> In the name of the Lord Jesus Christ, we command you, brother, to keep away from every brother who is idle and does not live according to the teaching you received from us. For you yourselves know how you ought to follow our example. We

were not idle when we were with you, nor did we eat anyone's food without paying for it. On the contrary we worked night and day, laboring and toiling so that we would not be a burden to any of you...we gave you this rule: "If a man will not work, he shall not eat."[82]

In the old days of trades and artisan apprenticeships, it was an honor to be trained by a skilled tradesman. In Silicon Valley some software developers will switch companies to work under a particularly gifted software engineer. In a Skills Building season we should honor those who are enhancing our skills. Their investment in us goes beyond what it costs them in time and money; they are imparting their values and vision. It is time they could have invested in others. Their investment helps ready us for the plans God has for us.

So go to your job to worship God with your work, appreciative of those who make your worship possible.

Finally, remember that God is in the people business. He is passionate about you developing to your full potential. He knows your particular combination of temperament and talent; he knows your past, your problems and your potential. Let him be the One who guides you in the Skills Building season.

# (Re-) Choosing Your Spouse

Who should I marry? How do I know if they are the right one? What if there is no chemistry? What if they don't love God as much as I do? What if we have different callings? What if someone better comes along...what if I choose someone and later meet my soul mate? These questions are pretty common in our household. Someone comes over to talk about a project, and pretty soon the conversation has shifted to the ever popular Choosing your Spouse season.

# Choosing Your Spouse

Not much serious writing is given to the choosing of your spouse. There's quite a bit on the do's and don'ts of dating—mostly the don'ts. But then, there's not much in the Bible either about choosing a wife or husband. I have concluded that this was one area where God got tired of taking the rap. After his provision of the perfect wife for Adam and Adam's admission that "she was good," God still ended up taking the heat. "The woman You gave me..." Now either Adam was little older than a teenager and was still in the mode of blaming his parents for even the best of things, or his newly found sinful nature was quick to blame others. Another factor is that in mankind's early history, marriages were generally arranged. So no need for great guidelines. "Son, this is your new wife." "Thanks, Dad." End of story.

Whatever the reason for Scripture's minimal coverage of dating, the choosing of a husband or wife is one of our most life-shaping seasons. With Isaac and Rebecca, God was involved. Jacob's choice of Rachel was equally important. The story of Ruth and Boaz is more a woman's pursuit of the husband-to-be. Samson made some bad choices. David, some good, some bad. Solomon, too many. Some were prophetic, some redemptive, and some just plain pathetic. Either way, our choice of a marriage partner makes a huge difference to our lives, positive or negative. Can God redeem bad marriage choices? Surely. Is it better to make a wise decision up-front? Of course.

One of the reasons that we make bad marriage choices is our own self-concept. Most of us grow up with some level of insecurity about ourselves. Too fat, too thin, too tall, too short. Too smart, too dumb, too pushy, too passive. In the stormy teenage years enough change is happening to our bodies, our brains and our beauty to leave the best of us feeling "not quite perfect." So we make a vow to ourselves that we will "show them" (whoever they are) that we really are quite cool and together and desirable by choosing the perfect marriage partner: blonde, blue eyes, unlikely to gain weight in latter years, a head turning, traffic stopping, to-die-for beauty. For Barbie, there's always Ken: tall, dark and handsome, sporting good pecs and (we even have a name for it) a Six Pack—with a nice personality, of course. A little money wouldn't hurt either.

Why do we have these fantasies? To look good. To feel better about ourselves. Twenty years later, if we haven't become a sad statistic at the nine-year average divorce mark, we are wondering why we are struggling to integrate our marriage and our Call. The big choice we made when we had more heat than light is coming back to haunt us.

## The Singles Phenomenon

In early 2003 Lyn and I became very involved with a group of young businesspeople that had something in common: they were single. We began to notice that singleness was rampant in the San Francisco area. We shared this with people from London, and they saw the same thing. Cape Town was no different. Shanghai, Johannesburg, Jakarta...the same was true there. We have since spent hundreds of hours speaking with these precious people about the situation. We have prayed with, married, comforted and kept hoping. Slowly we have begun to see marriages take place, not just any marriages, but what we have come to call "kingdom marriages" where the couples are committed to make a difference in the world. Before jumping ahead, let me unpack some of the observations a group of us have debated and discussed at length. Later I will list 15 reasons why people avoid marriage. But before we get to these I would like to explore a few more ideas.

First and foremost, one has to view the rampant singleness in major metropolitan areas around the world as a spiritual matter, not just some social quirk. We don't have to be that smart to realize that there will be a massive decline in the Church if Christians are not getting married and having children. We are, to put it crudely, being out-bred by Muslims, for example. "But isn't marriage all about me...what's this about children?" The book of Malachi is a challenge from God in four key areas: having a fair view of who he is, keeping faith with each other, how we treat our wives and marriages, and tithing. Let's dig into the marriage matter in Malachi 2:

> Another thing you do: You flood the Lord's altar with tears. You weep and wail because he no longer pays attention to your offerings or accepts them with pleasure from your hands. You ask, "Why?" It is because the Lord is acting as the witness between you and the wife of your youth, because you have broken faith with her, though she is your partner, the wife of your marriage covenant. Has not the Lord made them one? In flesh and spirit they are his. And why one? Because he was seeking godly offspring. So guard yourself in your spirit, and do not break faith with the wife of your youth. "I hate divorce," says the Lord God of Israel, "and I hate a man's covering himself with violence as well as with his garment," says the Lord Almighty. So guard yourself in your spirit, and do not break faith.[84]

Men, your wife matters to God. He sees her as your partner. When you treat her as anything less, then you are short-changing God on his dream for your marriage. The New Testament calls her a "co-heir of the grace of life," echoing the truth expressed by Malachi centuries before. More on this later.

Someone, and this was a smart person, said to me that the commandment to "be fruitful and multiply" only applied to Adam and Eve because they had to boost the population. This is a shallow view of children and shows a lack of understanding of the truth expressed by Malachi: "Because he was seeking godly offspring." God is not looking for perfect, sin-free kids—he took a risk with you, and he is prepared to take the same risk again with your children. But it is his prerogative to seek godly offspring. Not to put too fine a point on it, but a key difference between God and Satan is that God can create. He can make things out of nothing. Satan is impotent. He can deceive and woo and suck people into his schemes, but he cannot create. You, my friend, were made in God's image. A very basic way in which you reflect God's ability to create is reproduction. There are many other reasons why having a family is important, too many to contemplate here, but I want to point out that God has an interest in you Choosing a Spouse, and children are one of the returns on his investment.

"So guard yourself in your spirit, and do not break faith." Marriage is a spiritual matter. Avoiding marriage is spiritual matter. The inability of healthy, talented, nice looking, smart, godly single people to not see other similar people of a different gender who are right under their noses is a spiritual issue. These same people can spot, and be attracted to, a pre-believer in a millisecond. What's wrong with this picture?

Another point to ponder before we move on: we have to bust the "I can have it all" myth that pervades our thinking. "I can have my freedom and have lots of girlfriends." "I can stay single and good looking and independent and not be lonely one day." "I can have a stellar career and one day flip the baby producing switch, and have a few kids." "I can delay dating and, when I am 37-and-a-half, I can find a great person to marry." I have seen so many of these assumptions creep onto coffee tables during hundreds of hours of conversation. There are many, many more, and they follow the same mythical patter. "I can have it all." Friends, this is the oldest lie in the book. "Eat that fruit, and you will have it all." The net result was that they lost it. Jesus, on the other hand, said, "Lose your life, and you will find it." He basically said, "Unless you give it away, you have nothing."

Pornography is a false-promiser in the "you can have it all" category. I have met many Christian men who remain single because years ago they thought they could have it all from a magazine or an Internet site. Rather than giving them all the women they wanted, this deception took away their ability to relate normally to the everyday women they needed. Please note that not every fine man whom you know who is thirty or forty-something and single has had issues in this area. This is simply not the case. But some have told me that they suspect that as many as 50% of them have had past issues, and some have present issues in this area. If you are a young woman reading this book, may I appeal to you to dress in a manner that does not send young men in the direction of lust? I am not asking you to replace every tank top with a polo neck, but I am appealing to you to spur men on to godliness. A major downside of addictions is that they neuter our ability to make decisions. People who are addicted, whether to food or alcohol or gambling or sex, do not simultaneously make great, bold, godly decisions. So men stuck in pornography are less likely to marry. Do you see the Liar at work? "You can have it all..." and the fine print says "but you won't have the authority to make a big decision such as marriage requires."

There are a series of less heavy reasons, perhaps, why people avoid marriage. You may recognize some of them:

1. I'm too busy with my Career. Lyn was driving along a road in Cape Town with a young woman on a **rēp** venture when, out of the blue, she turned to Lyn and exclaimed, "I have been sold a bill of goods!" "What do you mean?" Lyn asked. "I have just realized the college professors who told me to get on with my career first and not get married are all single!"

2. I can't afford it. College debt encumbers too many people. Add to this the notion of wanting to afford and enjoy a very good lifestyle, and money becomes an obstacle. Not to mention the stupendous expectations in some parts of the world about the size of an engagement ring and the expense of a wedding; no wonder people cannot afford it!

3. Fear at losing freedom, or being burdended with responsibility or commitments. Fear by any other name is still fear. The "I will lose more than I gain" fear factor is too real for some people. Risk and faith are flipsides of the same coin. It blows me away to see entrepreneurs who are willing to start with nothing and make something of it, when it comes to business, apply a different standard when it comes to marriage. They want a sure thing, a

safe bet, a lifetime guarantee that there will be few wrinkles, good health, mental stability and a positive contribution to the gene pool.

4. Glittering images. Men more than women are afflicted by the image they have in their minds of some glamorous goddess whose sole purpose in life is to see to their every need. One woman put it this way: "Men want a cross between Mother Teresa and Christie Brinkley."

5. Keeping options open in case the perfect person comes along. This I have heard more than once. "What if I start dating her and next week someone better comes along?" Well, it may not be next week, but it will happen. Get over it. The point is not whether another bird will fly past your window next week, but what you are doing to serve your bird in the hand so that she or he becomes a bird of paradise and does not deteriorate into a pecking hen or a vulture.

6. Availability of single people – mentally, emotionally, physically. Young women are way too available to young men nowadays. You may think, "But he is a good brother in the Lord..." He will stay just a "good brother" if you don't stop providing him with the benefits of dating or marriage without having to step up to the responsibilities. "But we are not involved physically!" You don't have to be; we already covered that outlet. The fact that you are there for him emotionally, socially and spiritually—too available— simply delays the day when he has to grow up. If they want it all, they have to commit it all. Simple as that. Candice Z. Watters counsels women this way, "Are you the gal guys come to for advice about other women? Do you spend all of your time with a guy who's not your boyfriend? Are you an open book with a man who hasn't asked for a commitment? If you've answered 'Yes' to any of these, you may need better boundaries to protect your time and your heart. This will help you resist the temptation to spend your prime years and best self on counterfeits."[85]

85  Candice Z. Watters. "Finding a Husband" www.boundless.org/2005/articles/a0001220.cfm

7. Lack of vision – I don't have a good view of marriage. Lyn once asked a smart young man to think about his role models of Christian marriage. After a week he managed to come up with two fine couples: Billy and Ruth Graham, and George and Laura Bush. That's it! No more. Do yourself a favor, find some couples with marriages worth emulating and hang out with them. Get a fresh perspective on marriage.

8. Super-spirituality – spirit is good, flesh is bad. You won't believe how many believers fall for this expression of dichotomized thinking. We don't say it this way, but we compartmentalize to the point where the "spiritual" becomes more highly elevated than the "natural" and, pretty soon, it is quite easy to kiss dating goodbye. Which leads to the next point. ·

9. I lack dating practice. Sure you do. If you ask more than one woman out in a month they might say, "He's a player." Come on, ladies, give the men a break! The women's movement has done enough to emasculate men as it is; let's not discourage the guys from asking someone out and calling it a date. If they ask you for coffee, you probably don't have to take your small group with you. And if you have a second cup of coffee, don't start looking at the engagement ring catalogues. And if there is no third cup of coffee, get over it. And whatever you do, don't become one of the Silver Bullet Gang—the group of women who subscribe to the theory that he gets one silver bullet, and if he uses it on someone in our herd, he better not come hunting again for at least another year. Do you know what they call members of the Silver Bullet Gang? Single! When someone asks you out for coffee, the usual response should be a nice smile and the magical word, "Yes!" If he proposes at the bottom of the second latte, the answer should probably be "No! But thanks for asking."

10. All men/women are untrustworthy. This is a smoke screen to mask fear if ever I saw one. I have heard a few young men who have the presumption that lurking below that nice exterior is a nagging,

money-spending, gossiping, unfaithful, fickle vixen who, once the wedding ring slips on her finger, will turn into a blimp who sits in front of the TV and watches soap operas all day. Men, you don't have to marry your mother! Get over the issues you may have had with other women in your past and stop projecting them onto the fine, godly women you think you know. Women, likewise, project the notion that men carry size 15 Bibles to hide their axes and whips which will be used to bring unsuspecting women into subjection while these men ride in trucks to buy beers to drink in front of 97 inch TVs, while she, all the while barefoot, has to keep child number five from putting sticky fingers on daddy's wife-beater tee shirt. Wake up, men and women! Face your fear and deal with it, but not by pinning your long list of what could go wrong on the backs of unsuspecting men and women in your circle.

11. A spouse will limit my effectiveness for God. Genuinely pondering this question is a good thing to do...when you are 20. Yes, it is important that God comes first. It is critical that you seek first the kingdom of God. But you should be over this question by now. I won't delve into the many reasons to be married and the many ways in which single people can serve God. If this reason is an excuse for you, then you have probably overlooked the fact that a spouse is God's secret weapon # 1 to refine you into His image. He wants you married! Weapon # 2 in God's hands: children. There in your arms will be a helpless human being who is totally dependent on your becoming selfless, and you want to do it because you love them like you have never loved anything else before. When you become selfless, you become more effective for God. Make no mistake, having a baby does not make you a saint, but it can help in the process if we let it.

12. 1 Corinthians 7:7 – 'better to be single' i.e., 'I have the gift of celibacy.' Right! Thousands would believe you, but I have met relatively few, a very small fraction of a percent, to be specific, who actually have the gift of celibacy. If a pretty woman walks past you on the street and you are irritated because she is blocking the view

of a nice car, then maybe you have it. The fact of the matter is that, on occasion, people will box their fears, wounds, uncertainties and debts inside a box called Celibacy or Calling, hoping no one will take the lid off and look inside.

13. I'm not sure it's God's will for me. "In the beginning God said...it is not good for man to be alone." He hasn't changed his mind.

14. Old wounds, past hurts. Enough has been said on this topic to fill libraries, but it should nonetheless be mentioned because it is indeed one of the Top 15 Reasons why People Avoid Marriage. It may be lots of hurts, or just one hurt. It may have come from a father or a boyfriend or an ex. "God is the God of new beginnings." He can and does heal hurts.

15. There is a soul mate out there for me. In an article titled Great Expectations, freelance writer Polly Shulman says, "Now we want it all—a partner who reflects our taste and status, who sees us for who we are, who loves us for all the "right" reasons, who helps us become the person we want to be. We've done away with a rigid social order, adopting instead an even more onerous obligation: the mandate to find a perfect match. Anything short of this ideal prompts us to ask: Is this all there is? Am I as happy as I should be? Could there be somebody out there who's better for me? As often as not, we answer yes to that last question and fall victim to our own great expectations. That somebody is, of course, our soul mate, the man or woman who will counter our weaknesses, amplify our strengths and provide the unflagging support and respect that is the essence of a contemporary relationship." Polly goes on to quote Joshua Coleman, a San Francisco psychologist, "People are made to feel that remaining in a marriage that doesn't make you blissfully happy is an act of existential cowardice. It's a recent historical event that people expect to get so much from individual partners." It is not all about you.

# Calling an Obstacle to Marriage

Earlier I spoke about The 4-Cs: Calling, Career, Community and Creativity. They are meant to be integrated, not mutually exclusive. This sounds blindingly obvious, but I sometimes see young people ending a relationship with a potential spouse because "we don't have the same callings." One man had grown to love a woman who felt a call to China. He had no specific call of his own, but was not as enthusiastic about China as she was, so he ended it. Another man loves a woman but feels that his Calling may be more important than Community, i.e., he is putting off marriage because it may get in the way. There are a number of things that are wrong with this way of thinking:

» Very few people have their Calling completely settled before they get married. There are exceptions, but most often one's sense of a specific call evolves or becomes clearer over time.

» It is more the norm that a couple will discover Calling together. Each will shed light on the other's call, and because we are to lead lives of mutual submission, there is not doubt that your Calling will be altered in some part by who it is you choose to marry. So the reverse is true: you may not discover your true Calling until you get married!

» God, in his economy, keeps husband and wife interdependent. If one has their call all settled (at least in their minds) and the other has no clear calling, this can introduce an unfair imbalance into the relationship. Scripture attests that God is just, so my conclusion is that the one with the "crystal clear calling" needs to loosen up and be open to be moulded by a life partner.

» Some people make an idol of Calling. Yes, Calling is important, but when our rationale says, "God has made me so special, with such gifts and talents, that I have to forsake all else and maximize my gifts" we are in danger of placing Calling above Community. Remember, God is in the people business. He can find someone else smarter and more gifted than you if he likes. And he will if you glorify your gifts above the Biblical patterns of relationship and marriage. Remember the old saying, "God buries his prophets and finishes his work." You and your calling are not indispensable.

» Two can put ten thousand to flight. The multiplication factor that comes from finding a godly spouse is exponential. Marriage is not a divider of focus but a multiplier of effectiveness.

## Seasons of Relationship

The "four stages of relationships" have been used to describe male-female and many other forms of relationships:

| Forming | The honeymoon stage marked by flowers, candy, dates and humor. |
|---|---|
| Storming | Evidenced by idiosyncrasies, quirks, odd-isms and irritation. If doesn't happen well in advance of marriage, leads to buyer's remorse. |
| Norming | The settling in stage where the rose-colored spectacles are crushed in the pathway, and optimism is replaced with realism. |
| Performing | The era when the relationship is less inwardly focused and begins to produce results that benefit others. |

As helpful as these stages may be, they lack the essential pacing or regulation that a successful relationship needs. The development of an effective relationship is much like the drawing of a master painting. In our experience in counselling pre- and post-marriage couples, few have a good grasp of these concepts.

We once insisted that our daughter take a trip to South Africa with us to celebrate my mother's 70th birthday. With some reluctance she came. The way the flights worked, we had to return earlier and left Fay Maree with friends for an additional week. She called us from the Miami airport on the way home to California and excitedly told us that we had to talk when she returned. She had met a young man, and "It's a God thing." (As I mentioned earlier, God gets blamed for the most spurious of relational connections.) No big deal, except that Fay was all of 14 and the suitor a lofty 19, and I was the original founder of

FATBoys, Fathers Against Teenage Boys. Later Fay asked if the young man could come and spend a week with us. It was during that eventful week that Lyn and I sat them down and shared six important principles of relationship. The first one went something like this:

"Relationships are like painting a picture. You need three things, used in the correct sequence. First, there is the pencil of friendship," I said as I waved a pencil in front of them. "The broad outlines of the relationship are sketched out with a pencil. The boundaries are established, the price of making changes is low, and it involves some erasing and redoing."

"Second, is the black ink pen for adding detail and definiteness to the relationship. This is the season where you discover each others' spiritual gifts, and whether your giftings and passion for God are compatible."

Finally comes the color. "Color is added when the physical relationship begins. Generally, there is little chance of going back and picking up the pencil again, or adding black ink details once the physical gets fired up."

We shared how many of the kids in their circle of friends began with the color. Big blotches of color dropped indiscriminately on the canvas. Then later they try to add definition by adding pencil to a scene already out of control. Few have any concept of how to discover and develop spiritual compatibility.

We then discussed the price tag of each item. A dollar for a pencil, $2 or $3 for an ink pen, and $12.50 for the paintbrush (fortunately the price tag was still on it). The price of a relationship that gets off on the wrong footing can be enormous. Years down the road, the real price can be that neither husband nor wife ever experience all God had in mind for them. They picked the wrong partner or have a series of abstract paintings clouding the picture.

## Navigating Relational Waters

We discussed a number of other things with Fay and her friend that day. Since then we have dialogued many things with singles contemplating marriage.

» Different commitments are appropriate at different times. You should not expect to make the same commitments at 16 as you will when you are 26. Even if you are 26 or 36, make sure that the expressed commitment is appropriate to the level of knowledge about the person and the confidence you have that this is a good relationship.

» Regulate, regulate, regulate. A particular danger with e-mail relationships is that people are prone to say much more than they would in person. It is very hard to take your foot off the gas pedal without raising questions and destabilizing the relationship. So be careful not to go from 0 to 60 in four seconds.

» Live each day of the relationship without making life-long decisions together. Consider the short-term questions first:

  » Do I want to get to know him/her?

  » What are his/her personality traits?

  » What experiences in my life does he/she need (and not need) to know?

  » How much should he/she be a part of my planning?

» Learn to ask God questions first. Early in a relationship it is exciting and easy to talk. When problems arise we go to that person to get his/her counsel. But a time will come when God says, "When you have an issue, talk to me first." A big part of this is to ensure that we do not put our relationships with others ahead of him. Don't let the new relationship take you away from God, and if it does do so, then drop the relationship or do something radical to get God back at the center.

» Love God first and more. Matthew 6:33 says, "Seek first the Kingdom of God and his righteousness..." Then comes everything else. The world's way is to scheme to get your own way, then ask for God's seal of approval. If we go this route we harvest what we plant, and blessing is not a guaranteed result. God's way is that we get on with his business first.

» Get ready to be in a relationship: develop the personal life disciplines that will make you a "kingdom" husband or wife.

» Become super-real, and not super-spiritual. We know some wonderful people who would love to be married but they send out an "I am not available" message. Their faces do not mirror their hearts. They are so spiritual that no one without a gift of discernment would know they are interested in a relationship.

» Be friendly. This sounds simple, but for some reason, warm openness towards others is not readily practiced. I tell women that they have stenciled on their foreheads an Availability Index. Even the least intuitive man can read the Availability Index. If the needle is pointed into negative territory, there is little likelihood that the average man will even approach them. "But don't men like a challenge?" Yes, but with the ratio of Christian women to men being, in some cities, at 7:1, I would not risk it. On the other hand, if your Availability Index is all the way over to the "Too Available" side, then a man will stay away because he will think you are needy. Lyn believes most men lack confidence when it comes to dating (Okay, she actually says they are chicken) so they need women to "roll out the red carpet" for them. Give them some encouragement; drop a hint or two; telegraph your emotions somewhat while leaving the initiative for pursuit to them.

» Enlist yourself to pray against The Singleness Syndrome. This will prepare your heart, and the life of your future spouse. We know groups of men and women who meet to pray pro-actively that God will raise up future mates.

» If you have a list with great expectations, burn it. One evening we sat around the dining room table. A number of **rēp** people had popped in and we ended up talking about "the list" that some people have regarding the ideal husband or wife. We are not advocating that you settle for a slob, but something in the conversation led Lyn to suggest that the single people pray a prayer renouncing their lists. Do you have a list that needs rethinking... or burning?

» Discover his/her views on the big areas of life beyond the staring-me-in-the-face relational issues. What is their worldview?

## Uncovering Worldview

Recently I had a long conversation with a man who was some months into exploring a relationship with a woman whom he had decided was one of a kind. The only problem was that he was unsure whether they shared the same passion when it came to following God. It is not that easy to uncover worldview. Even though they had many discussions about work and family and faith, he was not sure that he was getting to the bottom of things. What if they got married and he discovered he had not covered all the bases? I encouraged him to have discussions with her along these lines: imagine that you are planning a town together that has all the elements of a healthy society. Your dreams, assumptions and priorities for each component might reveal quite a bit about worldview. For example:

| | | |
|---|---|---|
| » | overall layout of the town | your world view |
| » | the post office, internet cafe | how you communicate |
| » | the bank | what you feel about finances |
| » | the schoolhouse, university | your thoughts on education |
| » | the church | views on the church and philosophy of ministry |

| » | the hospital and elder care facilities | health care, aging, value of life |
|---|---|---|
| » | the park, green spaces | thoughts on recreation and the environment |
| » | the movie theatre | your ideas on entertainment |
| » | the police station | how you think about law and order; personal security versus other factors |
| » | the business center | your thoughts on career and making money |
| » | the town hall | your views on government, patriotism and nationality |
| » | the homes | the importance of family, having children, child rearing. |

You get the picture. Having these types of discussions can be useful as the relationship develops. When we frame a relationship with physical involvement and we are on a course of commitment without understanding these fundamental things, we radically impair the likelihood of success. And what is success in marriage? It is not enough to choose a spouse; we will one day have to re-choose them.

# (Re-) Choosing Your Spouse

"If I choose my wife correctly," asked the young intern, "can I avoid having to re-choose her later?" I laughed. "No way," I said. What do we mean by re-choosing your wife or husband?

Let me begin with our own story. Lyn and I had begun praying and ministering together before we started dating. While we had seen each other around the small valley of Llandudno since we were seven years old, we hardly knew each other, although once when I was young—I remember it clearly—I looked at her and wondered whether I would marry her one day.

Having said this, we hardly saw each other over the next twelve years. Occasionally we rode on a school bus together, once she wrote me a note and passed it on via a friend, and we attended a Scripture Union camp together one weekend when we were sixteen.

Around January of 1975 I had just completed my military service and attended a Youth for Christ youth group that Lyn and a friend had started in Hout Bay, a suburb of Cape Town. At the end of the evening, after having assessed the situation, I arrogantly said to Lyn, "What this youth group needs is some good leadership." Implied was, "And here I am." She thought she discerned some arrogance, but I was just functioning in my consulting gift, of course!

By the time I came to really know Jesus around the time of my 19th birthday, I was very involved in the group and Lyn's leadership team. Lyn and I began to spend time praying, leading and dialoguing together daily. We attended leadership training together, joined YFC's Associate Staff program, planned events, and drove places together (with the normal 20 to 30 teenagers with us). We wrote each other notes, shared things God was saying to us in our "quiet times" as they were called back then, and led meetings together.

I had my spiritual antennae up asking God whether this was someone with whom I should be having a more serious relationship. There was nothing that seemed to fall into the category of "guidance." I saw neither a red light nor a green light. I felt the freedom to build a friendship, but not to take the relationship any further.

The tricky part was that our relationship was growing. When you have so much time invested in each other, it would be odd for the emotional side not to develop.

I liked what I saw in Lyn. She was good with children, honored her parents, was a strong leader, and had a well-balanced sense of God's grace, especially in areas where I would have been more performance-oriented and legalistic. She was also interesting. While to some she may have appeared to be a compliant "religious teenager," she had a strong sense of who she was. Lyn followed God in ways that less secure teens were unable to do.

Things were happening at two levels in my life. One was the emotional growth of a healthy relationship. Since I was car-less and Lyn had use of her mother's car, she occasionally drove me to the University of Cape Town. We planned youth meetings, shared perspectives on life, and had the opportunity to understand each others' dreams and passions. Both of us loved people. We were, as I recall, mostly willing to put the needs of others ahead of our own, and together we learned to hear God's voice about the small things.

Lyn's feelings for me were becoming obvious. She wears her heart on her sleeve, which is one of her nice qualities. Meanwhile both of us had separately told God that we did not want to enter into another flirtatious relationship. No more castles to conquer, no more mind or heart games. The next person we dated, we had to be willing to marry. We were the ripe old age of 19. We spent time together over a nine-month period and I observed this quality person in numerous settings. I watched her teach kids in Sunday School, observed the way she related to her family, looked at the decisions she made about where to invest her time, noticed her kindness to older people, and saw her in good and bad situations. Subconsciously, I was weighing whether this was God's woman for me.

In early October of 1975 I was nearing the end of my first year at university and staying with a friend, Art Wouters, in his uncle's cottage. Art and his fiancé, Miranda, were having a few difficulties communicating. Being the third wheel in the party, I assumed the problem was me. I went outside to pray about it. As I was praying I thought, "Why am I worrying about this? This is God's problem, not mine." Just then God spoke to me saying that I was trying to manage my own relationships. I had been in control, and usually the results weren't good. So I repented and surrendered my relationships to God, one by one. At the end of the prayer, my relationship with Lynelle Möller came to mind, and I added, "...and also my relationship with Lyn." It wasn't uppermost in my mind. This was a life transaction with God, not a discussion about Lyn.

The next Sunday, October 5th 1975, Lynelle and I went for a stroll in Hout Bay. It turned out to be a historic walk for us both. Before a housing development ate away one of the last functioning dune systems in the Western Cape, we climbed the steepest dune that overlooked the lower Disa River and Hout Bay beach. Our conversation soon drifted to a series of letters we'd written each other in the preceding week or two. As we perched above Hout Bay that Sunday afternoon we began to unpack those letters. Somehow I managed to get Lyn to fully explain her letters to me and "fess-up" that she loved me before I told her that I loved her too. I know it's not very manly. It was pretty sneaky, but that's the way it happened.

That Sunday night she went off to church and I stayed home to study. I was over the moon. Much of my delight lay in the start of a new relationship in a new way. I was love-struck, and pleased that I had not followed the pattern of past relationships. I was also beginning to get a handle on the pattern in which God was speaking to me. As a new follower of Jesus, this was exciting. After years of knowing about the Almighty, Incredible God, about his Word, about his dealings in history, he was dealing with me, he was speaking to me, he was leading me along a path. After years of seeing through a fog, I was beginning to see more clearly. I was beginning to catch on. How incredibly exciting!

So from the early stages of our relationship we have done things together, and, hopefully, together with God. When we came to the United States we took a break from any formal role in ministry. The previous five years of pastoring while working at Price Waterhouse had left us in need of a rest. We decided on a one-year sabbatical. The one year became six, and the highway we traveled together in earlier years became two separate, parallel roads. During this season much happened in our lives separately: skills building, addition of gifts, some real desert experiences, internal integrity. Each of us was growing. We were not growing apart. But there was enough space for us to grow separately. This did not create a problem. The challenge was the re-integration of ourselves.

# Re-Choose or Crisis

For the many valid seasons of our life, the devil has a counterfeit. Nowhere is this more evident than in the so-called mid-life crisis. There are jokes about it, movies inspired by it, car advertisements suggesting its cure, and millions of men to attest that it happened to them. So we assume every man will have a mid-life crisis, and it's nothing that a sports car won't solve. But there is an alternative.

God's antidote to a mid-life crisis is Re-choosing your Spouse. In fact, Re-choosing is the real deal. The mid-life crisis is the counterfeit. You may be thinking, "That's fine for men, but women don't have a mid-life crisis." I beg to differ. The symptoms may be different, but the root is the same. This is how it goes. Around the ripe young age of 40 there is an attack on our identity which, if responded to correctly, can press us closer to God. We should graciously accept this rite of passage into a season that should find us basking in new abilities, maturity and limitations. It's all part of God's master plan of how we relate to him, others, and his world.[86]

Unfortunately we have bought the media-myth that we don't need to age. Worse, we have believed that it is wrong to age. Younger is better. Firm forever, flabby never. Now, I have no qualms with physical fitness. I am heart-broken, however, to see godly people fail to step through the door into the next season of their lives because they think they can be "forever young." We even have new language to explain away the inevitable. "The forties are the new twenties." It sounded good to me when I turned fifty, "Don't worry, Brett, the fifties are the new thirties!" What? Do I have to do all that again?

In the first letter of John, he writes to three groups of people: children, young men, fathers:

---

86    Os Guinness offers an alternate explanation for the mid-life crisis, contending that it is the result of making early career choices inconsistent with our Call. By the time we get to 40, the dichotomy has worn us out. Good point!

I write to you, dear children, because your sins have been forgiven on account of his name. I write to you, fathers, because you have known him who is from the beginning. I write to you, young men, because you have overcome the evil one. I write to you, dear children, because you have known the Father. I write to you, fathers, because you have known him who is from the beginning. I write to you, young men, because you are strong, and the word of God lives in you, and you have overcome the evil one.[87]

People desperately lack "fathers" because there are many who would rather cling to the mist of youth than own their age, maturing to a new season of effectiveness. A leader of a local church had a health scare that nearly killed him. I told him I sensed that God was taking him into the next season of his life; he was becoming an old man or father. I counseled him to find strategic things to do that leveraged his "father" status, and to shed some of his current responsibilities and give them to able "associate pastors." My observation is that he denied the life change, but I saw him from time-to-time and thought, "You are becoming an old man." Like it or not, there are passages and seasons. We too can deny the change that takes place in our lives, refuse to change how we live, fail to recognize that the focus of our authority has shifted, and fail to pass on new things to young men and children. Or we can embrace the life stage, and extract all of its lessons.

## Rediscovering Your Spouse

A key part of this season is re-discovering your spouse. It is fair to assume that you and your spouse have both grown as people since you were married. With this growth comes new gifts, a greater ability to hear God, a new understanding of Jesus. The God you were following 20 years ago is the same, but you know and experience him in a different way. So he gives you an opportunity—I think an imperative—

87      1 John 2:12-14

to rediscover and then re-choose your spouse. This is the true antidote for the mid-life crisis. Just as the insecurities about ourselves as teenagers are designed to press us into God where we discover our true identity, so our insecurities as 40-somethings are crafted to drive us closer, in Christ, to our mate.

Husband, are you a student of your wife? How well have you discerned her thought patterns lately? What gives her joy and excitement? When does she feel most alive? What wears her out? How is her self esteem? Do you know her love language? What gifts does she have? Where does she have wisdom and insight that complement your own? What are the best ways to engage her in the things of God with you?

## Salad Tongs

While attending a Business 2000 seminar at University of the Nations in Hawaii in 1995, Lyn and I received several clear messages of the need for us to re-integrate. As a team of people prayed for the delegates, someone had a mental image of us as silver salad tongs; not the separate fork and spoon joined at the centers by a rivet or screw, but a single piece of silver, separate yet connected, moving vast quantities of fresh green salad.

This was followed by someone different sharing a picture of a stallion (evidently me) and a rider (the Holy Spirit) and Lyn as the bit and bridle. They challenged me to not take "the bit between my teeth" but to listen to my wife, working in collaboration with her.

Finally as a friend drove us to the airport that evening, he shared his image of a road that had been together, separated for a season and run in parallel, then joined together again. And the overall word for us was "Integration."

That should have made it easy. We had a clear message to reintegrate, so we could just get on with it. Well, it has not been so simple. We have spent much time since then struggling through the implications of that three-pronged message to us. Why is it hard?

Men and women sometimes shy away from re-discovering each other for fear of getting smothered. He has been busy career-building; she has built a family, a career, a home... and all without much help, thank you very much. Now, suddenly, he needs her. He is aware of his vulnerabilities and feels a stirring to draw closer to his family. She runs the car pool, the social life, the checkbook and the household. Everything is ticking nicely, and she is not wild about his advances to "tong together" or "integrate." After so many years developing their own identities and functions, it is tough for a husband and wife to hear a call to subject themselves to each other.

From our own experience, we know that the Re-Choosing season is tough. Neither of us is high on the Meek/Submissive scale. We love each other, we communicate readily, and we interact well around projects and ideas. We are proud of each other's accomplishments and progress, and are each other's cheerleaders. But when it comes to the business of Convergence, which is so tightly linked to our identities, it does not work unless we discover a new combined identity with each party having the assurance that they will be represented.

## The Timing of this Season

I have been reflecting on the timing of this season in our lives not so much in relation to other seasons, but in relation to major life decisions that tied into our Calling. Looking back, Lyn and I began this deliberate season before we heard God say, "Start an institute." It came before Lyn said, "You should do this outside of your present employer." Re-choosing preceded the dormancy and rebirth of **rēp**. I do not think we would have had the foundation in place for the work we enjoy together today if we had not committed ourselves to the integration that is inherent in re-choosing.

I was recently at an all-male conference with notable speakers and seemingly successful men trying to figure out what God wants them to do with their lives. My hunch is that the vast majority were not factoring their wives into the equation from a "co-heir" perspective. If you are not sure about *your* calling, try discovering *our* calling—you and your spouse together. If you are waiting for your calling to arrive first, and then planning to invite your spouse to hop on with you, you may be waiting at the wrong bus stop for the wrong bus that isn't going to arrive. You may be like the proverbial blind man in the dark room looking for the black cat that isn't there. Can I be any clearer?

## A Caution to Women

Wives, you may be saying, "I just support Jimmy's ministry!"

Over the years, the Church's teaching on submission has resulted in passivity in some women when it comes to discovering their ministries, so it is hard for them to imagine having a ministry that is equal in stature and importance to that of a man, or that of their husband in particular. The idea of a combined ministry as co-heirs of God's grace with their husbands therefore doesn't register on their radar. Many couples are able to pray together, laugh together, love together, but Integration goes beyond these things. Supporting your husband is wonderful, but it won't protect you from the mid-life crisis. You need Integration.

## Myths and Truisms about Integration

As Lyn and I have worked through the dynamics of seeking a higher degree of integration in our lives personally and as we have spoken with couples wrestling with the same things I have noticed some truisms and myths concerning this integration. I define a truism as generally true, by the way, but not an absolute truth. [If you have the *Convergence Applied Learning* book, you may want to turn there and complete the related exercise before you read on.]

*Trust is important to Integration.*

This one is true—it is essential to have trust if we are to allow our identity to be closely intertwined with our spouse. If a woman believes her husband is just out to dominate and be "the head of the house" in a bossy way, she will smile, and stay independent. If a man thinks that a woman sees this as a way to cut down his golf time and tie him into her agenda, he will not pursue integration. Trust is essential.

*Personal wholeness is important to Integration.*

This is part truth, part myth. We come to greater wholeness as we re-choose our spouse because our identity is more settled in the process, and that which is broken is less of a threat. So it can be put on the table and dealt with in an environment of love. On the other hand, the more we have experienced healing in our lives, the easier it is for our spouse to relate to "the real us."

*I cannot be Integrated and codependent.*

This statement gets to the matter of integration being the healthy interdependence of a couple rather than a co-dependence which actually prevents the full growth of each person. So, in my book, this is "True."

*I must forego who I am to be Integrated.*

This is nonsense on the one hand, and true on the other. It all depends on how you define it. Jesus said that if we lose our lives we will find them. So serving our spouse while being willing to die to ourselves is good for everyone. But this does not mean that one is less of who one is: integration is not about making yourself nothing so that your spouse feels better about themselves. It is each of you bringing 100% to the partnership. As Nelson Mandela said, "There is no passion to be found playing small—in settling for a life that is less than the one you are capable of living."

*I cannot be Integrated if I do not believe I am equal.*

Strange as it may seem, I think this is true. Men and women need to understand that, despite the varying roles they may play, they are equal in God's sight. A wife or husband is a partner, a co-heir. The Malachi 2 passage is echoed in 1 Peter 3:7. God sees our wives as our partners. Do we?

*I cannot be Integrated and independent.*

This is a good point to debate because it brings up the question, "What do you mean by independent?" Integration recognizes inter-dependence as a healthy thing.

*I can achieve personal wholeness without Integration.*

I believe you can achieve a measure of personal wholeness if you are married and remain "un-integrated"—but only a measure. If you are single, you are fine. If you chose a spouse and yet you hold back from walking into the full potential of that relationship, you have, by definition, chosen to stunt your own growth. So this is a myth.

*I can achieve Integration without personal wholeness.*

We will die broken. This is not a doomsday prediction, but simply a matter of fact concerning the fallen nature of man. So if you think of wholeness as personal perfection you can have integration without personal wholeness. This is a truism. If you think of it more generally, however, then you could say this is a myth: it is clearly easier for more secure and whole people to integrate their lives.

*I have to have an equal career (to my spouse's) to achieve Integration.*

Nope. This is a myth.

*I must have financial flexibility in order to pursue Integration.*

Also a myth.

*My level of personal security affects my ability to Integrate.*

This is a truism. The more comfortable you feel about yourself the more ready you will be to blur the lines between your identity and the identity of your marriage.

*My level of personal security affects my desire to Integrate.*

I am not sure where I stand on this one. Somehow it seems that we have a built in longing for intimacy, regardless of our sense of worth or personal self-assurance. Chat about this with your spouse and friends.

*I need to be at peace with my past to achieve Integration.*

The essence of this statement is whether one can achieve integration with a spouse if there are hidden secrets in one's life. And does integration mean "I must disclose all"? My caution here would be that an absence of peace with my past might cause me to have lingering insecurities, and this may hinder my ability to integrate with my spouse as a co-heir of the grace of life. On the other hand, I see little sense in dredging up that which is forgiven and has been reconciled through the work of Christ on the cross.

*My spouse must be at peace with my past to achieve Integration.*

Go ahead and ask him or her. This statement gets to the matter or your spouse's wholeness. It is important to live in peace with each other if we are to achieve integration.

## Husbands Live Considerately With Your Wives...

"...so that your prayers will not be cut off or hindered."[88] Chauvinism is not a new disease. Christ came to challenge our presuppositions on many fronts. I know that until the day I die God will be tapping me on my shoulder and saying, "We need to chat about your thinking on _____." I can't name all the areas; indeed a detailed list would be a

88      1 Peter 3:7

little depressing. But we men need to be reminded, according to Peter, to live considerately with our wives.

Before you zone out with the, "This doesn't apply to me" trick, I am not implying that you are solely responsible for putting your wife in a cage. Society in many forms encourages wives to be little more than caged parakeets. Some of it is intentional; some of it is simply the result of sinful society going its own way, and perhaps some is of the woman's own making. Whether it was through the teaching of the church or the messages of the playground, there is no virtue in anyone, male or female, living a caged—i.e., less than full potential—existence. And this is precisely why Jesus came, "...to undo the works of the devil."

## For Husbands Only

» So how does your wife feel: "free as a bird" or "she's only a bird in a gilded cage"?

» Have your wife's wings been clipped in any way? If so, how?

» What does the scriptural challenge to "live considerately with your wife" have to do with your role in bringing her to new freedom?

## For Wives Only

» So how do you feel: "free as a bird" or "only a bird in a gilded cage"? And is your husband aware of your feelings?

» What is the thing you fear most about integration with your husband?

» What is the vision you have of an integrated function in society/ the body of Christ for you and your husband?

## A Note to the Singles

Before we move to our final season we must acknowledge that this season has a special face for those who, through no choice of their own, find themselves single for life, and for those who have chosen to be celibate. Others of you have been married and have lost a spouse before getting to the season of Re-Choosing. This is a season that you wish you could have experienced, but it never happened. If you look at the great army of people who have gone before you, there are countless many who have experienced this season in a different way. Some have, for very good reasons, decided not to choose a spouse. The obvious examples from New Testament characters are Jesus and Paul. In recent centuries, women have outnumbered men 2 to 1 on the mission field. Half of those women seem to have chosen singleness while doing God's work over staying home and hoping a husband will come along. Many still make the same choice today.

Singleness is not a disease or deficiency. If this season is not for you—this Choosing a Spouse—give yourself permission to move on with the great richness that life outside of marriage has to offer.

## Re-Choosing is a Choice

I will end this chapter with the simple reminder that re-choosing is a choice. This isn't a season about emotion or sentiment or whimsical moods. It is about choice. This season involves a deliberate, active exercising of one's will. "You obviously haven't met my husband... I can't re-choose him!" I admit that you may not be able to do it in your own strength, but that is why there is grace. When we say "Yes!" to re-choosing we are affirming, with Abraham, our belief in the God "who gives life to the dead, and calls things that are not as though they are." When you embrace the season of Re-choosing your Spouse you are saying, "This is not about me: this is about God showing his glory through our marriage in a way that surpasses our experience thus far." When you embrace this season and your spouse you are saying, "God, I hold my life open to you and to my spouse so that I will remain flexible, and my heart will not get encased by crusty old postures that inhibit the vibrant flow of your life in me."

"Choose this day whom you will serve."[89]

Choose this day with whom you will serve.

89     Joshua 24:5

## University Of The Desert

There is no avoiding the desert.

God has an infinite number of ways to shape us into people who come to a point of Convergence. The desert will therefore look a little different to each of us. The lessons of the desert have a common pattern, and a universal theme. In this chapter we will explore the landscape of the desert, examine the footprints of previous desert dwellers preserved in the historical writings, and read the certificates of U of D graduates. The desert is God's finishing school. It is the never-to-be-forgotten season. No matter what your recollection of other seasons may be, you will remember the desert, and many graduates remember it with fondness.

Are there those who oppose my views? Surely. A friend e-mailed to say that his time in the desert was not "alone with God" as I had predicted, but simply "alone." A waste of two years. Perhaps the Aarons, Jonahs and modern day melancholics would agree with him. Certainly a whole generation of Israelites who left Egypt and fell short of Canaan might see the desert as a waste. But the fruit of the desert was a nation of Promised Land-owners.

Many have navigated the desert gracefully. We have peeped at Abraham, Jacob, Joseph, Moses and David. Let's turn to some others and examine their story.

## Just Add Water

By all accounts he was a big cheese. He ruled nations, had a dynasty that stretched for thousands of miles, had coffers full of the finest, and people bowing and scraping left and right. Then he got cocky and made the mistake of thinking that somehow his own hand had achieved it all. A party, a prophet's appearance, and pretty soon Nebuchadnezzar is chewing grass like your garden-variety cow. For seven years. Compliments of University of the Desert.

Then there's the rising star. Fancy education in the best academic circles, on a career fast track, legendary among the elite. Then his horse sees its first traffic light, and he gets thrown. God gets hold of him. Now, had we written the script, he would have been giving his testimony at the Christian business breakfast the following week. Instead Saul gets the "Go straight to the Desert" card and there he stays; this brilliant mind seemingly drops off the radar for about 15 years.

He was a powerful prophet who challenged a strong woman, prayed for rain to be held back for years, challenged false prophets and called down fire from heaven. Then he holed up next to a stream called Cherith in, you guessed it, the desert.

Nehemiah's desert was palatial. But it was still a desert. Serving as an exile in the courts of a foreign king, sipping non-kosher wine to see if it was laced was not the career goal of a good Jewish boy from Jerusalem. But for years and years he did it. It was there he learned about empire building, nation building, authority, management and greatness. All this came in handy when, in the face of opposition he pulled off one of the first re-engineering projects in history.

Before you get to Convergence you will pass through a desert... maybe more than one desert. I have met people whose desert began when they lost money and made money. Some walked into a desert when they were fired, others when they were hired. Friends have lost a loved one, others have just had the gas run out of their spiritual tanks. Whatever it is that gets you into the desert, there is, as far as I can see, only one thing that gets you out of it. I will speak to this at the end of the chapter.

Let's dig a little deeper into the desert season. Consider your own life and mark the points of identification that you have with those listed below. The items that I will cover in this chapter are not academic. All of them come from my own desert season which was as glorious as it was painful. Many positive things happened in my parallel seasons of Skills Building and Internal Integrity. God's medicine often comes with a glass of fresh water. I am sure you will identify with these things "that are common to man"—just add your own water, and the story will be yours.

## Why Do We Need The Desert?

That's a fair question: Why do we need the desert? Surely when we became followers of Jesus, we became "a new creation; the old has gone, the new has come!"

Not so fast. A preacher once told his congregation that as long as he was their pastor, they would not get out of Romans chapter 7. Romans 8 is full of life-in-the-Spirit things; Romans 7 is quite clear about our sinful nature. "I know that nothing good lives in me, that is, in my sinful nature. For I have the desire to do what is good, but cannot carry it out."[88] I remember preaching on this verse once and an elderly, straightforward Dutch lady in the congregation raised her hand and asked, "Do you really believe dat in you is no good ting?" "Yes", I replied. "Then you are a bloody liar!" said she. Sometimes even others (except our mothers) find it hard to believe that in us "is no good thing." Why?

In the early days of our relationship with God it seems he does some interior decorating. New paint, tidied wardrobe, air freshener, no smoking signs, stripped wallpaper, cleaned up library, less TV, etc., etc. By the end of the first six months we think we have been through the ringer and, looking scrubbed up enough to be invited back to the average church, we secretly wonder, "Is there anything left to change?"

Then comes the structural work. Drainage, finding the source of subterranean rot, re-wiring, taking apart and healing the stimulus and response system, foundation repair, tackling the skewed walls of our personalities at their source: bad foundations. And while some of this work goes on, the house can be unlivable. When God jacks up your house to recast the foundations, it's hard to keep going with religion-as-usual. When he strips you down to the studs, don't try to wallpaper. When he takes off your roof to tackle the leakage, the rot and the heat loss, you're better off in the desert.

Why do we need the desert? Because we need to become more like Jesus. And the everyday clutter of life usually anesthetizes us to our need for fundamental fixing.

I have pondered whether to expand the rest of this chapter to give more of an explanation but have concluded that those who have lived

88    Romans 7:18

through the University of the Desert need some concise reminders, not a detailed topography, and those who have yet to get to the desert... why ruin the surprise? So what follows is an encouragement to sandy sojourners—you are not alone; there is life after the desert.

## What Are The Objectives of the Desert?

God seems to have a Help Desk of angelic travel agents with a core competence in planning desert seasons. The amazing thing is that they tailor the experience to suit the unique needs of each traveler. Despite this, there are some common objectives that are true for most desert dwellers.

> To make me more grounded in God
> and his grace
> so that in the future I may serve him
> more broadly,
> and more safely,
> and more deeply.

## Methods of the Desert

God has an infinite number of ways to accomplish his purposes in us. He is more interested in our deep-down growth toward his likeness than he is in securing our comfort. In the West we believe that life will be easy, and when something goes wrong, we do all we can to get back to a state of ease. Many of our prayers are slanted towards removing discomfort. In other parts of the world the premise is that life is tough, and believers pray for grace and courage to endure. The desert is tough. These are some of the things that seem common to the desert experience:

» Loneliness

» Being misunderstood

» Minimal use of talents and spiritual gifts

» The frustration of seeing what ought to be done, but having no influence or invitation to do it

» Start-and-stop friendships (as would-be friends pass you by for association with those who are "more successful")

» Financial stretching

» More time in the gospels than in the letters or Acts—more emphasis on being a follower than on doing great works or churchy accomplishments

» Uprooting

» Spiritual insignificance - this often follows uprooting: remember, no one knows who you are and what you have accomplished in the past

» Pruning, to the stump

» A dislocated hip

...and, failing all else, the old Foot-of-God-on-the-Neck trick.

## Characteristics of Desert University Students

It's easy to spot them on the campus of life. They often seem a bit drifty; when you talk to them you recognize that they are "convinced that God brought me here... but I don't know why." They seem to be coasting a bit, and the smart ones don't respond readily to appeals for action or subtle guilt trips. Frankly, they don't have the energy. Here are some of the symptoms of those with desert fever:

» Not enough spiritual energy to blow their nose

» Care free

- » Few great "words from the Lord" for others

- » Saying "No" more than "Yes"

- » Freedom from needing man's approval

- » More clues about five years from now than about tomorrow

- » Watching God make things grow without busily slapping up their own scaffolding

- » Significance derived from God in them, not God through them

- » Slowly unfolding vision

- » Reticence to touch what emerges from the dust

- » Walking with a stick.

## Challenges of the Desert

Given the choice, most of us would rather avoid the desert. We are afraid that it will last forever, and we have plenty of suggestions for God about better ways to achieve the same results. Once we have experienced the desert for a while, we may be so comfortable that we decide to stay there. So there are challenges at both the desert entrances and exits:

- » Resisting going in

- » Self-pity (for the melancholics)

- » Withdrawal from things you should be connected to

- » Attempting to stay connected to things from which you should be withdrawing

- » A short term focus (Neglecting to ask, "How long, O Lord" up front)

» Maintaining basic spiritual disciplines when there's no audience to keep you on your toes

» Bugs creeping out from under rocks you thought were safe

» Waking up from the big yawn

» Becoming a crusty old cynic

» Resisting coming out

Like much of life, God's sovereignty seems to be the determinant of when we go in and when we come out of the desert. Elijah is a classic example:

> Now Elijah the Tishbite, from Tishbe in Gilead, said to Ahab, "As the Lord, the God of Israel, lives, whom I serve, there will be neither dew nor rain in the next few years except at my word."[89]

> Then the word of the Lord came to Elijah: "Leave here, turn eastward and hide in the Kerith Ravine, east of the Jordan. You will drink from the brook, and I have ordered the ravens to feed you there." So he did what the Lord had told him. He went to the Kerith Ravine, east of the Jordan, and stayed there. The ravens brought him bread and meat in the morning and bread and meat in the evening, and he drank from the brook. Some time later the brook dried up because there had been no rain in the land. Then the word of the Lord came to him: "Go at once to Zarephath of Sidon and stay there."[90]

89    1 Kings 17:1-8

90    1 Kings 17

## Prizes of the Desert

Why submit to the desert? Perhaps the greatest reason is simply to be a Father pleaser. Obedience is the main reason; the prizes of the desert are secondary, but important. What are some of these prizes?

» Less concern about the little things that don't really add up to anything

» More God-centric and less spiritual-resume-centric (especially hard for clergy)

» More caution about who you entrust yourself to (especially those that don't have dust on their clothes)

» Deliverance from Charismatic-Answeritis, the affliction of having to have God's "word" on everything at all times

» Being more organic than institutional (being more focused on real life than structure, on substance rather than form)

» More eagerness to know Jesus than to have answers about him

» Simply, Jesus.

The writer of Hebrews says:

> No discipline seems pleasant at the time, but painful. Later on, however, it produces a harvest of righteousness and peace for those who have been trained by it.[91]

Enjoy the training. It is an essential piece of Convergence.

## Not Every Speed-Bump is a Desert Experience

It is important to recognize that not every automobile accident, not every consequence of our own stupidity or sin, and not every bout of

---

91    Hebrews 12:11

influenza is our desert experience. A friend told the story of a woman who arrived late for a Bible Study and proclaimed, "I ran out of eye liner; isn't that just the devil!" It takes more than missing face paint to constitute a desert. Some might need to be cautious to not develop a "woe is me" desert complex. How God deals with you is, after all, his business.

All of the above points are drawn from my season in the desert. Outwardly, things looked just fine. And inwardly I was at peace. But if I had tried to break out of the season before God was done with his pruning and shaping and re-rooting, I would have short-changed myself. While in my desert, occasionally people would come to me and say things like, "You could be contributing so much more. Your ministry is needed." It was not always easy, but I managed to "Just say No" to the expectations of others during this season. I could do it because I sensed the season. And looking back, I have been able to serve those same people in ways that were not possible before. Staying private (versus going public too soon) has been for my benefit as well as theirs.

Don't fight the desert. Let it complete its work in you. "Wait patiently for the Lord. Wait patiently for him to act." I suspect that if we insist on making appearances while we are supposed to be in the desert, God will let us come out early. But we should beware; we'll simply have to go back later. Having said that, my own experience was that God used me powerfully in the lives of others very sporadically while I was in my desert season, as if to encourage me by saying, "My gifts have not left you."

When you put your "pedal to the metal" in the desert, you simply spin your wheels. When you spin your wheels, you sink deeper into the desert sand. When you sink into the desert sand, instead of roaming its recesses peaceably, you become frustrated and crusty. You can try to take a dune buggy with you into the desert, but God has a slew of creative ways to exhaust your gas supply. The desert requires patience and grace. The desert is done on God's terms.

As we saw in Elijah's story, God provides in the desert. So enjoy your desert season and stay there "until the brook dries up."

## A Word to Those Who Have had Public Ministries Prior to the University of the Desert

Some of your biggest critics will be those for whom you previously filled some pastoral or spiritual leadership role. When our season of obvious public ministry was over for a while, even those who had encouraged us to take a sabbatical looked down their noses at our apparent "lack of ministering." There was more than one friendly interrogation session: "But what are you doing now? Do you think that God is still using you? Don't you miss the ministry? You are so busy with other things! When are you going to get back on track?"

Someone once told me that people with needs have no mercy on those who can meet their needs. Most likely, many of the people who asked these questions were more interested in what I could do for them (and now wasn't doing) than in me as a friend. The true friends who simply love us for who we are see the same set of circumstances quite differently. They say, "It is wonderful that you have the time to spend with pre-believers. You are being such a positive influence among us."

Why these seemingly opposing views over the same set of circumstances? A review of scripture (and the life experiences of many I know) indicates that the desert season is often a bridge that transitions us from one sphere of ministry to another. To be personal, my spiritual authority had come from my role as the pastor of a local church. Yet I have known since the mid-1980's that my Call lies beyond the boundaries of a particular local church. This was not necessarily apparent to others until much later.

Now, in Convergence, my influence draws on my experience as a pastor, but it is not the primary root of my influence. It also draws on my experience in business, but this is also not the source of my identity. I draw some on my experience as a leader of a not-for-profit organization; this, too, is not the well from which my identity springs. I now live in a wonderful place of non-dichotomized work that integrates career, call, creativity and community. One would almost have to invent a word for it: vocupation (vocation and occupation), bissions (business and missions)...the list could go on. None do it justice, so we speak of integration and of convergence. The point here is simple: you cannot easily flip-flop from one sphere of influence to another without some down time, re-tooling and good old-fashioned rest. When we feel we 'just have to be ministering' it is a warning sign that the work of the desert has yet to run its course.

The fact that words like "clergy" and "laity" get thrown from pulpits like verbal hand grenades complicates this whole scenario. "First class, second class." Preachers beware. When we have inadvertently preached the Christian class structure, we understand our own season in the desert that much less. When a pastor asked me how I felt when I "left the ministry" to just do business. I replied, "I didn't leave the ministry."

The desert is the awkward in-between. And the best thing to do is to smile at your critics, and shut up and enjoy the desert. Pretty soon you'll be busier than you wanted to be and you will yearn for those long, warm evenings in the desert with Jesus.

## Most Frequently Asked Question

"How do I get out of the desert?"

The faces of many good friends who are or were in the desert pass through my mind as I recall them asking this question. When you are in a desert colored by loss, infertility, delayed promises, broken dreams, financial hardship—whatever the palette of your desert—you have a few things on your mind. Will I get out? When will I get out? How will I get out? When will my dead tree bud again? Will my dry creek run with cheerful water again? Is there life after the desert?

I want to encourage you that there is life—abundant life—after the desert. I must also stress that there is no formula for how God gets you out of your desert. The most common way he does it is this: he speaks. He speaks a *rhema* word—one that jumps up and down in your soul—and somehow it produces faith, and things spring to life. Simply put, we exit the desert when God speaks a word that draws us out of that season.

How does he speak that word to us? Having been privileged to be the tour guide standing at the **EXIT** sign of more than one person's desert season, my limited observations are that others may play a supporting role, but the initiative comes from God. He may send someone to validate our journey. Jessica had felt called to minister in the marketplace. When she shared this with spiritual leaders they told her emphatically, "You have your ladder up the wrong wall." Five years later she heard a talk that validated her call, infused hope, and prepared her to be escorted out of the desert by a past desert dweller.

One way God nudges us out of the desert is by taking away our present provision. This sounds counter-intuitive, but Elijah had his water supply dry up. It looked like a bad thing, but it moved him out of his desert confines. A second method is when Jesus answers a deep cry of our hearts. Sometimes it is interim provision; sometimes the big dream. Mary's Aunt Elizabeth is a good example. "It wasn't long before his wife, Elizabeth, conceived. She went off by herself for five months, relishing her pregnancy. 'So, this is how God acts to remedy my unfortunate condition!' she said."[92]

A third method is when God provides a community of like-minded people, a safe band of friends that emboldens you for the cross-border venture. You will no longer feel, "I am the only one thinking these thoughts, feeling this way." He may just whisper in your soul, "It's time to get back in the saddle, time to get back on the road. It is time for this season to end." Those who escort people across the U.S.-Mexican border are called coyotes. God has used me as a coyote-catalyst for one or two desert folks.

My friend, Brenda, had been through years of desert experience. After about five years of selfless obedience during which she gave away her business, moved to a new city, and poured herself out with little reward, she began to sense that the season was drawing to a close. One day we were talking and a strange picture came to my mind. It was a pizza with multiple layers. I sensed that God had completed his work on the base layer; the dough was spread out, the lumps were gone, and it covered the whole surface. Suspended above the base were other layers—the tomato paste came next. It too was spreading. Yet another layer had the toppings. The word I sensed God saying to Brenda was that the base was complete. In future seasons there would be no revisiting of the base, no going back to the desert. This particular season was over.

This word picture probably means little to you, for such is the nature of the personal way in which God speaks to us. The power of the word spoken is life-transforming to the person who hears it. My prayer for you is that when God finally does speak to you, you will be listening, you will receive his word with faith, and you will move out of the desert.

13

## Hindrances To Convergence

Our rights. One of Lyn's grandmothers often used to say, "Stick up for your rights, Lynnie." And in the normal course of things, it seems reasonable advice. But Jesus came along and upset the normal course of things. As the One who made it all—who dreamed it up, who brought it all into being, who had a rightful place of preeminence—he took on the nature of a servant. He gave up his rights. Convergence has nothing to do with getting your just desserts. It has more to do with obedience and grace and rest.

Song of Songs 2:15 is an interesting verse on relationships:

> Catch for us the foxes, the little foxes
> that ruin the vineyards, our vineyards that are in bloom.

Any venture has the potential of being thwarted in its initial stages. "Little foxes" rub against the blossoming vines and bump off the flowers so that the potential for a full harvest is frustrated. The same is true for the journey towards Convergence:

| The little foxes | The potential implications |
|---|---|
| Wrong concepts of God | For whatever reason, we think of God as less than he is, lack his loving authority, feel insecure, and push back with rebellion or rejection. We need to be convinced that God likes us, he is crazy about us, he is overflowing in grace and goodwill towards us. He is all for us. |
| Rights to your own Career | Looking good, but not feeling fulfilled, we make a string of job choices that never lead to Convergence. |
| Finding your identity in the wrong places | Pursuing work, relationships, money, fame and other substitutes for meaning instead of pursuing obedience. |
| Being hung up on significance | Getting caught in the cult of the individual. |
| Wrong definition of success | Defining self-worth as net-worth, we shoot at the wrong target, and end up ensnared in money. |
| Refusing to make graceful transitions | Getting what you longed for, hanging on to it too tightly, then watching it wither on the vine because you refused to move "with the cloud." |
| Lacking the faith to move into a position where God can bless you | Having a predictable income stream, a predictable upstream float, and being bored with it all. |
| Avoiding key seasons | Never being ready for Convergence. |
| Not seeing eternity | We live as if life on earth is what it is all about, failing to see the fact that this is just the pre-game warm-up for our real work in heaven. People who discover Convergence live attuned to eternity. |

# The Line in the Sand

We don't mean to, but we do it. On one side stands the Almighty God, a few feet away we stand and face him. And between us we have drawn a line in the sand. "I was willing to give up smoking, I was willing to stop this, I was willing to start that, but please don't ask me to ____."

I was proud of myself. I was nearly 19-years-old. Finally, I had come to a real relationship with Jesus, and I was doing well. Up at around 5:30 each morning, William Barclay commentaries, extensive note-taking. I remember thinking to myself, "I don't think I am holding out on God in any area. I am pretty much squeaky clean." Except for one thing: I loved to dodge the traffic lights when driving down Loop Street (prophetically named) in downtown Cape Town. If you timed it just right, you could hit all of the lights from one end to the other as they changed from red to green. I was on my way to a Youth for Christ camp. It was my birthday, and I was pushing my sister's 6-Volt VW Beetle "Sammy" down Loop Street about as swiftly as I could. I glanced over my shoulder to change lanes, and when I looked back in front of me the pale blue Ford Escort was stopped dead in its tracks. Wham! Happy Birthday! I had run into my line in the sand, the one thing I thought I wasn't ready to give to God.

The process of sanctification takes time. My arrogance made me feel I was near the end of the journey when I was crashing the vehicle on my first go round the track. Many other wrecks followed. Now I assume that there is still stuff embedded in me—lots of stuff—that needs rooting out.

In some respects this "getting rid of sin" part of sanctification is easy. The Holy Spirit reveals it, I pray I don't delay too long before owning and confessing it, and we move forward together. But we can easily draw a subconscious line in the sand when the issue is no longer bad behavior, but "Who's running the show?" Does God have a right to tell you where to live, what car to drive, what to name your child, where to work, whether or not to travel?

I have met many people who unwittingly have drawn a line in the sand, right in front of God's nose. Most often, nowadays, I see it around the challenge to be mobilized into God's army. Jesus said, "Go" and we said:

> "I am a neighborhood person...my neighbor is my mission field."
> "My kids are too young."
> "I don't have a husband."
> "My wife doesn't want to go."
> "I just got married."
> "I just started a new job."
> "I just started a new line of business."
> "I just bought a holiday home."

None of these are new to God. These excuses are right up there with "The dog ate my homework." In a weekly devotional titled *Who said "Go"?* I made these observations:

> Jesus resolutely set out for Jerusalem... (Luke 9:51)
> But the man replied, "First let me bury my father."
> "I will follow you, Lord, but first let me go and say goodbye to my family."
> "I have just bought a field and must go see it."
> "I have just bought five yoke of oxen"
> "I just got married, so I can't..."    (Luke 9:57-62, and 14:15-20)

What would you do if Jesus walked up to you, in the flesh, and said, "Follow me"? If you and I were like the general religious population in Israel at the time of Christ, we might have followed, or we might have been tempted to use these familiar excuses. Jesus still calls us to follow him. While we have these excuses, and a few more, we must get back to the question, "Who told us to go?" Let's unpack these statements, starting with one I have not listed here, but which I have noticed creeping around recently.

1. Not enough money

I have recently seen people use finances as a fleece to determine whether to go on a mission venture. I am wracking my brain to find a time in Scripture when Jesus, or Paul or God said, "Go, if the money comes through." What I see instead is Scripture saying, in effect, "Obey, and trust me for the provision." In Luke 22:53 we read, "Then Jesus asked them, 'When I sent you without purse, bag or sandals, did you lack anything?' 'Nothing,' they answered."

Gideon's fleece approach is a pre-Holy Spirit, "did God really say" approach that should not, in my view, be used as a litmus test for whether God is calling us to go on a faith venture. If God tells us to go, then we have to stand in faith, trust and obedience, and ask him to provide what is needed for the journey. We have to model the miraculous if we are to impart it.

2. Burying the dead

Staying for a family (make that your father's) funeral sounds like a plausible excuse. But Jesus told the man, "Let the dead bury their own dead, but you go and proclaim the kingdom of God." The man had a genuine case, a family responsibility that was the accepted thing to do, but Jesus had a higher claim: the Father's business. Recently one of our team faced pressure from her family to stay and bury her dead. Her father died two days before she was due to fly to Cape Town. God had clearly said, "Go!" Her family said, "Stay!" What would you do?

3. Delay of game

"No one who puts his hand to the plow and looks back is fit for service in the kingdom of God." We aren't doing God any favors when we sign up to do his will. He has the right to call us, and to sift us. Those who are willing to delay obedience might well be pulled off course, and never obey again. So Jesus cautions him to not "look back" even for a short while. I remember when I had the opportunity for a second **rēp** trip to the Ukraine back in 1993, but I was in the midst of a job change, so did not go. The opportunity has not returned. Perhaps **rēp** would have been a lot further along if I had not delayed the game. Are you delaying going to that which God has called you?

4.  Business opportunities

    The caution here is to not let a business opportunity get in the way of following Jesus. I know the command to "do business until I come." But this was a new business venture, an add-on to income producing capacity, a choice to get deeper into the business rather than follow Jesus. The man in Luke 14 just had to give that five-pack ox yoke a spin. "Jesus, I can't follow you because I just got a new toy!" "Jesus, I can't follow you because I have just got a new tractor, a new factory, a new product, a new whatever." Some man gave up the unique opportunity to walk with the Creator of the universe on a journey that would change him forever, so that he could tromp around in the dust behind ten smelly oxen that would make some short term money but potentially cost him his eternal purpose. The man made a margin choice: he gained financial margin, perhaps, but lost the time to follow Jesus. Sad.

5.  I just got married

    You may add, "And didn't God ordain marriage, say it was not good to be alone, and write in his book that a man shouldn't leave his wife to go to war in the first year?" Yes he did, and the book also says, "Let the bridegroom leave his room and the bride her chamber."[93] Joel says we should interrupt the honeymoon if God says, "Now is the time." He gets to decide.

So the big question is, "Did God really say..." or, "Who said 'Go'?" If it was just your idea to follow Jesus into some faith venture, then sort that out. But if he told you to go and you have leaned into any of these

93      Joel 2:16

212

five excuses, then beware, because you don't know when the window of opportunity will open again. We know God is gracious, but we must recognize that for some of these people, Jesus never passed by physically again, and they never heard him say again in person, "Follow me." How much better to have it written of us, "We have left everything to follow you!"

Take a close look at your index finger. See any dust there? Any dirt under the fingernail? Ask the Holy Spirit to let you know where you have drawn any lines in the sand. Not if, but where.

## Laziness

A major obstacle to Convergence is laziness, particularly in a world where we confuse activity and work.

"One who is slack in his work is brother to one who destroys."[94]

Meetings, cell-phones, crazy schedules all lull us into laziness in the midst of busyness. Convergence demands the focus to clear the decks of the divergent. Failure to muster the energy to unravel and make sense of the threads of life is a hindrance to Convergence. In addition, the absence of language, frameworks, markers and milestones will obstruct Convergence.

## Holes in Our Worldview

Our street, our Suburban, our school, our social network. Wherever you are, you are local, and life has to be lived out at the local level. But our particular locality must be a springboard to a broader worldview. We must understand not just the people beyond our Community, but the patterns, the trends and the meaning of the times at the national and international levels. This creates a grid against which we can examine our call, our career and our creativity. Even Community, for

94    Proverbs 18:9

an increasing number of people, extends well beyond their immediate locale.

And worldview is not just about geography and location. I think that when Jesus returned from the trips with his disciples and stopped in for tea at Martha's Vineyard, they probably chatted about what God was up to in the world and how they were a part of it. What on earth is God up to nowadays, and how can you get into his game? Good questions for those who want to get on the road to Convergence. Many people make the transition from "me in my world" to "God invited into my world." Few make the journey to "me in God's world." Decide what you want: a little God-sauce on your life...maybe on the side. Or do you really want to be subsumed in God's great plan for eternity? Recognize reality and you will see that the latter is true, whether you believe it or not. God has a master plan and he will accomplish it. The fact is that we can live pretending it is not there, or we can ask that he reveal what he is doing and how we can see things his way.

## Failure to Work a Long-Range Plan

In the early 1990s I brainstormed with friends about developing plans to transition from 60-hour weeks to something that would free up time for more direct Kingdom purposes. We drew diagrams of stepping down one's occupation to picking up one's vocation. I once received an e-mail from Doug, one of these friends, it read:

Brett,

While unpacking here in Kent, Ohio, I came across an old PFC [Professionals for Christ] newsletter. I read my first fund raising letter from '94 which said that I was starting a small consulting business that will eventually support me full time in ministry. I did not realize at the time how much God would use Add On Consulting. I merged my client base with another company this past year and I get a percentage of gross consulting hours paid monthly (which goes farther in Ohio $). This has truly freed me up to do this Vineyard Church plant. The process has taken just about five years as you said it would. I have learned a lot as an entrepreneur that is transferable to pastoring. I know I have said thanks before, but I just wanted to say so again: Thank you for helping me the way you have.

Doug had a long-term plan. He took risks to achieve it, leaving a secure job as an in-house Information Technology professional to start his own business. At the outset we worked together on **rēp**. Within a year his startup had grown to the point where it could support him fully, and he moved on. But he never let go of his dream of fulfilling his call to pastor. His e-mail tells the story of how he did what many just dream about. Dreams are great, but they need legs to get you places. Doug is a man with dreams that grew legs. How are your dreams? And do they have legs yet?

## Unwillingness to Act

Sometimes you must be willing to do it before you can see it. Sure we'll meet some folks who knew exactly what to do but they balked at God's possibilities. They are like a batter at the plate and God is throwing them lots of strikes. They stand over the plate twitching occasionally but unwilling to take a swing. None of the balls have yet looked just perfect. They are like cricketers at the crease who watch the fast balls whiz by but are afraid to play any strokes.

For many others the Call is not obvious because they are subconsciously unwilling to face the consequences of the Call. Their lives are filled with questions about Call: "Could God be saying this? What if it is God? What if it isn't?" They have collected many ideas. If they appear to be really talented, others have come to them with ideas. "What if you did this? If I gave you this money and that opportunity, you could..."

Changing the analogy, they are like a potential homeowner standing over a table covered in architect blueprints. Each one seems to be a wonderful plan. The longer they stand looking at the fine ideas, the more others try to help. Friends throw in plans, wives and husbands draw up plans, employers create plans, venture capitalists ask for plans, ministry leaders say, "God loves you and I have a plan for your life." Some of the plans come with strings attached. Others are plain good opportunities.

Over the years these people appear to grow more confused than ever, less sure of themselves, less confidant that they can build what's been presented to them. They say they don't know, but slowly a weight of evidence has been amassing. And God begins to craft situations to ready them for building and for going with the plan that is his.

Maybe it's a career diversion that is really a season of Skill Building. Back to the table. Still they make no choice. Then comes an Internal Integrity test, and she returns to the table a little more willing to do it God's way. Then there is a trip down a promising career track that, instead of success, delivers misunderstanding, being overlooked and even scorned. She comes back to the table more leery of man's plans and a tad more willing to ignore the glitzy game plan and go for the substantive steps of obedience.

God is quite patient. We can diddle and dawdle and claim we hear no call when the answer lies in plain view behind our fear. We have to ask ourselves, "What do I fear?"

» I won't be able to pull it off

» The Call will not look good enough to my friends

» I will have to give up a title

» My income may go down

» I will have to relocate

» It might not be the best thing for me or my family

» I don't know if I am worthy of such a call (Get over it. You're not.)

If we are still haunted by these types of questions, beware the University of the Desert. That desert has a way of weeding these things out of us.

On the other hand, you might genuinely want God's call, and you have experienced the Seven Seasons, yet you are still drowning in the cacophony of options. "Be still..." Consider what you have learned about who you are. Reflect on what you really value—what are your non-negotiables? Affirm again the few gifts that are you. (Separate these from the many things you could do if you had to.) "...and know that I am God." Remember what you have learned about God and his character. Brush the world's dust off the plate. Tune out the blare of the advertising on the stadium walls and the bright lights of seductive success or glamorous significance. Make a list of what you know about God and his dealings with you. Then take a swing at what comes your way.

If the sporting analogy leaves you frozen at the plate, go back to the drawing table. Reconsider the many plans you may have made. Reject those that simply make you look good; embrace those that resonate with a "deep calls to deep" quality. Assess where the weight of evidence is stacked. Your call may be more obvious than you think.

If God is good, his call is good. No fear!

## Who Am I?

For some portion of the population there is the tough obstacle of not knowing who they are. Obstacle might be too definite a word, because you can easily see an obstacle, and not knowing who I am is a tough one for me to see. In my discussions with people over time, my ears have become attuned to the statements "I have always wanted to..." "I have always believed..." and "I have always known..." This is no scientific fact, but I have discovered it usually means, "I have recently discovered about myself..." or more pointedly, "I don't really know myself, but if I drive a few stakes in the ground in the form of absolute statements

I will feel better about what I don't know." What has all this to do with Call and Convergence? If you don't know yourself, it is hard to know your Call. And if you don't know your God, it is hard to know yourself. (If this sounds a bit like you, and you glossed over the first season—Faith and Knowing God—you might want to re-visit the essence of who God is. A distorted view of God leads to a distorted view of ourselves.)

If I don't know myself, then I place an unrealistic burden on others to (a) know me, and (b) clarify my call on my behalf. This book can help clarify what one does and does not know about Career, Call, Creativity and Community, but it may not do the job if you haven't done the hard work of facing up to who you are and are not.

## The Time has Not Yet Come

The path to Convergence is usually clearer in retrospect. The same is true in the area of Call. Like Abraham, we may know where we've been called from before we know where we have been called to. More important, we may know who has called us better than why he called us. The area of Call is a mixture of mystery and certainty. Nonetheless our thinking can be aided if we are clear on what we know and honest about what we don't yet know. This is especially true when we are more than likely some years away from Convergence. Not all factors hindering Convergence in our lives are controllable. Our job is to obey, resting in the fact that "my times are in His hands."

## What's In It For Me?

Jeremiah was a famous prophet who lived in a time when Jerusalem was besieged. He had a sidekick, Baruch, who was his scribe. Baruch did a pretty good job going back and forth between Jeremiah and the king, delivering bad news. He was, however, faced with some of the same maladies that assail us. After lots of comings and goings and being shunted from Israel to Egypt and beyond, Baruch had had enough.

He had served Jeremiah well, delivering messages to unfriendly kings, writing and rewriting what God had revealed... and now he wanted to know, "What's in it for me?" Have you ever thought, "I have served God faithfully, I have done what I am supposed to do, and things are still not going well? I deserve more"? Have you ever complained about the trouble and pain and weariness of following God?

Baruch then gets a whole chapter in the Bible, Jeremiah 45, dedicated to setting him straight:

> The prophet Jeremiah gave a message to Baruch son of Neriah in the fourth year of the reign of Jehoiakim son of Josiah, after Baruch had written down everything Jeremiah had dictated to him. He said, "This is what the LORD, the God of Israel, says to you, Baruch: You have said, 'I am overwhelmed with trouble! Haven't I had enough pain already? And now the LORD has added more! I am weary of my own sighing and can find no rest.' Baruch, this is what the LORD says: 'I will destroy this nation that I built. I will uproot what I planted. Are you seeking great things for yourself? Don't do it! But don't be discouraged. I will bring great disaster upon all these people, but I will protect you wherever you go. I, the LORD, have spoken!'"[95]

That's it—that's the whole chapter. The punch line seems to be verse 5: "Are you seeking great things for yourself? Don't do it! But don't be discouraged." Following God is generally not a walk in the park. Spare yourself from the extremes of seeking your own glory and drowning in discouragement. The two go together: if you are on this journey for your own glory, you will get discouraged. There will seldom be the accolades to keep you going. You will also face discouragement because you have an enemy. You will have difficulties because you need to grow in strength. I particularly encourage those who have made a commitment to get mobilized and equipped for God's service to be

95    Jeremiah 45:1-4

encouraged, and to remember that it is for the completion of his plans, not the growth of your spiritual resume. Servants, make that bond slaves, don't generally ask, "What's in it for me?"

We only find contentment when we live inside the greater agenda of our Sovereign who says, "I will...I will...I will...I will...I, the Lord, have spoken!"[96]

## External Hindrances

Look back over this chapter. Most of the Hindrances to Convergence have been internal factors that lie within your control or decision making. Without giving too much credence to the difficulties we face, I do want to point out some external sources or types of opposition that will get in the way of Convergence.

### Vision Trimmers

There are always those who feel that it is their duty to cut your vision down to size. This normally means that they want to take something that is nicely impossible without God and make it pragmatic, doable. These well-meaning Christian humanists will right-size your vision and guarantee you a place in mediocrity.

### Values Vampires

Then there are those who look smooth and sound supportive, but they infiltrate your life and begin to erode the very values you hold to be important. They place doubts in people's minds, put sand in the gears of relationships, and eventually undermine your moral authority if you let them stay around long enough. You are hoping, "They will change... I should love them..." but when they have done enough damage or you have had enough so that you confront them, they leave.

### Spiritual Opposition

---

96      This first appeared as a Devotional on the rēp website in July 2006.

There is no question that we will encounter spiritual opposition. We are part of a conflict between good and evil, so we should expect it. The issue is how we are going to let if affect us. Jeremiah was a young man when God called him and he was immediately challenged with these words:

> Get yourself ready! Stand up and say to them whatever I command you. Do not be terrified by them, or I will terrify you before them.

The Message says it a little differently:

> But you—up on your feet and get dressed for work! Stand up and say your piece. Say exactly what I tell you to say. Don't pull your punches or I'll pull you out of the lineup.

Convergence is not some self-help routine that enables you to recite 4-Cs and name Seven Seasons and, hey presto, you are done! It is about putting some markers on a life path so that we undertake our spiritual journey with sound understanding and in God's strength and by his grace.

Many well known leaders faced early opposition from people close to them. There is often a one-two combination of ridicule and discouragement that is designed to take us out of the game. Winston Churchill was sent to a military academy. He thought it was because his father viewed him as a future military strategist; he later found out that his father thought he did not have the intelligence to pass the Bar. William Carey's wife would follow him around the indigo factory that he managed accusing him out loud of infidelity. Martin Luther King faced repeated beatings from his father. David's wife, Michal, ridiculed him when he danced before the Lord. Nehemiah's opponents made fun of his building efforts: "If a fox jumped on the wall it would fall down." Billy Graham was told by his seminary professor in no uncertain terms that he would fail.

I remember the weekend that we started **rēp**—we were heading to the Northern California coast to pray with good friends and "birth" the organization. We had emailed our friends back in South Africa asking them to pray for us and share any insights. Just before we left for Mendocino I received a fax stating that what we were doing was wrong, it was a "Polly Anna" effort, and it would not amount to anything. Looking back, the words were almost comical in their insult. It was signed by some of our closest friends, many of whom were people we had nurtured, leaders we had raised up. Opposition will come. What will you do with it?

# Convergence And Young People

I t's fair to ask about the relevance of Convergence to children. On the one hand, kids have a long way to go before their direct influence over Convergence becomes apparent. On the other hand, many people don't achieve Convergence simply because they fail to develop right patterns of decision-making when they are young. For a host of reasons, I believe it is important for teenagers or young adults to at least understand the questions they should ask as they squeeze through their rites of passage within four or five flicks of the annual calendar.

The goal is not to turn twenty one year olds into adults who have "arrived." This chapter tries to provide some glimpses into the possibilities and the hurdles that young adults will encounter on the road to Convergence. In exploring this we need to better understand the changes going on in the definition of "Who is a young adult?"

Since the First Edition of *Convergence*, articles have appeared about the challenges to growing up. New words have been invented to describe people who are neither teenagers, nor adults—"tweeners," "kidults," "twixters," "youthhood," and "adultolescents." Terri Apter, a psychologist at the University of Cambridge in England and the author of *The Myth of Maturity*, calls them "thresholders." She says, "Legally, they're adults, but they're on the threshold, the doorway to adulthood, and they're not going through it." *TIME* magazine, in its January 25th, 2005 Edition, had a cover story by Lev Grossman titled *They Just won't Grow Up* with the subtitle, *Meet the twixters. They're not kids anymore, but they're not adults either: why a new breed of young people won't—or can't—settle down.*

> Social scientists are starting to realize that a permanent shift has taken place in the way we live our lives. In the past, people moved from childhood to adolescence and from adolescence to adulthood, but today there is a new, intermediate phase along the way. The years from 18 until 25 and even beyond have become a distinct and separate life stage, a strange, transitional never-never land between adolescence and adulthood in which people stall for a few extra years, putting off the iron cage of adult responsibility that constantly threatens to crash down on them. They're betwixt and between. You could call them twixters.[95]

Others have also written on this theme. A *San Francisco Chronicle* article read:

95    Lev Grossman, *Grow Up? Not so Fast*, Time Inc., January 16, 2005

Who are these puzzling, twenty-ish tweeners who don't want to leave home? They're not really adults, at least by traditional standards, and they certainly aren't kids any more. Mocked by movies like "Failure to Launch," where two Baby Boomer parents finally hire a facilitator to blast their thirty-ish son out of the house, these reluctant adults are labeled "The Boomerang Generation," or "Peter Pans"—kids who don't want to grow up. Critics see them as pampered, aging slackers, who would benefit from a swift kick out of the nest. But the "kidults" have heard the knocks, and remain serene and unconcerned.[96]

A reader responding to this article commented:

I think one reason why we're not so inclined to move on and leave the nest is because the generation gap with our boomer parents is much less than any other generation in the past. So we don't mind being under their roof, especially when we're given free or nominally cheap food, lodging, utilities, etc. And parents don't want to let go either...even though we're technically full-fledged adults, they really don't want to let us get out of their sight. Student loan debt and low starting salaries may have something to do with it, but there are plenty of 25-year-olds out there who have upper middle class backgrounds and $50,000/year jobs but are still living with mom and dad.

Make sure you don't view this phenomenon as negative. "In my day we were married by 23, had a house and a dog..." The point is, if you are 50 years old, this chapter isn't about your day.

Why is it that young people need the thinking tools of Convergence?

» It is becoming easier to be "sophisticated" but harder to mature. Walk through a shopping mall and it is harder to distinguish a 14-year-old from a 19-year-old. Kids are informed, have spending power, and have adult-looking behaviors. While they may be demanding more freedom and money, and while double-jobbing, guilt ridden parents may acquiesce, this early enjoyment of life's pleasures delays rather than speeds true maturity.

» Information is available everywhere, but life-skills are hard to come by. It is a fallacy to think that more information results in better cognitive abilities. Common sense doesn't come with higher Internet bandwidth. Life skills are learned shoulder to shoulder from people who have them, and this takes time.

» Worldviews are in flux. The good news is that young people are more attuned to the issues in the world than were prior generations. This can cause them to tune out because they are overwhelmed by the mind boggling statistics of world troubles, or they can become world citizens. This will depend on how they are guided and how they are inclined.

» Career choices are hard to untangle. No longer do you choose something that takes you onward and upward; it is not unusual to find an entry point and move sideways through a variety of jobs while you get a feel for what you really want to do.

» College debt is crippling. The better your degree, the more the debt, the longer the delays in feeling adulthood is upon you. This is partly because being an adult, in some people's view, means having your own home and being married. The Center for Economic and Policy Research says that student debt is 85% higher than a decade ago.

» Young adults don't expect to live the lives of preceding generations. They don't want some of the negative things that went before them, and they realize that they cannot have some of the affluence that their parent's generation had. As one blogger describes it, "The carrot is becoming smaller and the stick becoming longer." So the incentives to get on with life are few.

» Today's children face different and more direct social challenges than previous generations. Keeping track of how many millions are impacted by HIV/AIDS, human trafficking, modern day slavery and which countries are at war this week, not to mention famines, floods, tsunamis and earthquakes. Then there are the more internal challenges of Internet scams, being exposed to undesirable or "overly desirable" people on MySpace and other forums, and advertising bombardments. It is possible to be directly connected to hundreds, if not thousands, of people via the Internet, but still say, "I have no friends."

» Young people need to be anchored in order to weather the serious changes the Church is undergoing today. This is a comment I made in the First Edition of this book, and since then we have seen what is called "The Emerging Church" and articles with titles like "Christians outside the church." Some are predicting the demise of "church" as we know it. Others are optimistic that local churches will transform. Either way, when a young person considers what a local church is they do not see something that is without change. The point is not whether this is good or bad, but just that young people will continue to look for an expression of kingdom living that is real, anchored, current and timeless. To do so effectively, they must have a well rooted worldview where the kingdom of God is bigger than the local church.

The foundation for Convergence begins early in life and uneven growth in The 10-F's is much harder to counter in later years. We have seen the fruit of this in men who grew up without fathers and now lack basic life skills. I meet too many thirty-something year-olds who struggle to make decisions because they don't know who they are because there was no father at home to "call them out." I see parents who want teenagers to leave home too soon and teenagers happy to oblige. There are young adults returning to live with their parents at age 40, and some people simply never growing up. For many, the definition of growing up has changed permanently. Add to this the eternal youth syndrome and the increased incidence of millionaires under 30, and we have the recipe for undirected or passionless living.

## A Framework for Thinking About Life

In the late 1980s I began to create a model of personal planning that addressed the major components of my life. I soon became convinced that routine planning using this model was one of the most spiritual exercises I conducted. So as not to create the impression that I'm one given to rigor and personal discipline, I'll confess the planning was more grace than grit. I did not convert each goal into an activity on my calendar. But somehow just having thought-through, documented goals provided a Magnetic North to my daily life. The original model had five major areas:

I spent a few minutes most weeks setting goals in each area. Food-on-the-table covered my work goals, Fresh Thinking was intended to keep me growing beyond my current mental models. The social side of life was covered by Friendship/Fellowship, and Family and Faith seemed to pick up the rest. It wasn't perfect, but it provided a framework.

Then in 1995, Lyn and I began to teach on the concept of Margin. The underlying reason was simple: if we didn't make space for God to do the uncommon in our lives, it might never happen. The alternative to this truism seems to be that God has to use a catastrophe, and we hoped to avoid that scenario. The series of presentations we developed for various **rēp** meetings expanded to include The 10-F Model® and The 10-F Gap Map.

In 1997, The Institute began working with Prison Fellowship Ministries to develop a program that would minister to children of prisoners on a year round basis. Dubbed "The Angel Tree Network" because it built on the successful Angel Tree program, the model needed a way to understand the needs of a child. So we adapted The 10-F Model and tested its application to children.

The 10-F Model recognizes that a variety of organizations are engaged in bringing things into the life of a person: TV, movies, school, sports figures, doctors... There are numerous contributors at each point of influence, namely, for each of the 10-F's. The subconscious role of the parents is that of network manager. Mothers seem best equipped for this task with an innate ability to juggle multiple balls, manage conflicts, and create the right alchemy of ingredients to benefit and nurture a child.

## It Takes a Network

The number and frequency of inputs into the lives of our children is exploding and becoming difficult to control. Billboards, newscasts, magazines, e-mails, pagers with secret codes, telephones, cell phones, wrist-watch beepers, chat rooms, teen-targeted web sites, push-advertising on the generic web browsers, smart pets, video games, internet gaming...and lest we forget, the old nemesis, TV. Yikes! Add to this the tendency of teenagers to go overboard on something until they are sick of it, then drop it, and we have an input management crisis. How can we counter-balance the onslaught of this megaphony of other inputs? In our experience, it takes a network to impact a child.

The Institute has developed the concept of an Impact Network. In its work with both non-profit and business organizations, we help design and develop a network (or collection of people and organizations) unique to each organization that will help it achieve some desired future Impact. By combining the network concept and The 10-F Model, we created the framework for placing children on a path to Convergence from an early age. This is the framework we used for Prison Fellowship.

The model was designed to help caregivers identify needs for input into the lives of children and adults, and then tap into good sources of such nurture and growth. It aims to move the business of raising responsible people from an unconscious to a conscious competency.

## In the Beginning... Was a Network

The network is not a new concept. It can easily be argued that the concept of both The 10-Fs and the network is inherent in the Triune God. God communicates, relates and functions cooperatively. Further, he places us in communities because that is where we get to know him best. The early Hebrews practiced community in many ways: family rituals, life at the synagogue, special celebrations, formalized instruction, personal relationships. All were part and parcel of their being. In very natural ways, the whole community contributed to the raising of the children. And at the center of much Jewish activity was the mother. In many respects she was the 'network manager' in that she oversaw the influences that shaped the identity of her most precious possessions, her children.

## Re-Shaping The Network

The rate of change in society is phenomenal. Due to the reach of the Internet and other media, especially mobile media, the increased flow of information and ideas is incredible. With this comes the entrance of new, daily influences on our 10-Fs. On top of this, we are growing and changing. The net result is that we have to rearrange the ingredients in our network frequently, but particularly as we transition from children to teenagers to young adults to adults. Consider the example of Who is managing the Network, and Who are players in the Network in the table below; note how some of the normal "defaults" appear to change as the child gets older:

| 10-F Area | 1-6 years of age | 7-12 years | 13 - 18 years |
|---|---|---|---|
| Friendships | Mother-managed network | Strong parental influence; limited child choices | Self-managed network with parental 'exception management' |
| Fun | Parent-managed | Higher child input | Child drives, parents react |
| Family | Family-centered activities | Child-event centered (sports, school, church) | Peer-centered |
| Faith | Home Sunday School | Sunday School | Youth group, Young Life, Christian School |

The traditional role of the family in the child's network has been challenged for some time. There are countries that believe that the state should have control over how children develop. There are school districts and systems that see themselves at the center. Quite often this "wanting to be at the center" springs from a worldview that says, in effect, "The Church no longer sets the agenda for the culture, so we want our domain to be the ones who do it." Everyone wants to play God:

> The future battle over our minds is a battle for the individual soul, the individual personality as perceived by itself, "What am I like? Who am I?" Where [the family] used to reign supreme, today it faces competition; in the future, this competition will be even stiffer. A 1997 survey asked American MBA students what things they considered most important in life. Heading the list was building a career (75 percent), but the family ran a very close second (71 percent). Responses from these young Americans reveal the increased competition; if they stick to the

ideals of their youth, these students will be facing a lifelong, daily challenge: job or family.[97]

In June of 1999 the National Marriage Project at Rutgers University released The State of our Unions—The Social Health of Marriage in America.[98] The statistics may not surprise us:

» Since 1970 there has been a decline of one-third on the annual number of marriages per 1,000 women.

» The percentage of "very happy" marriages has decreased; after 10 years only 25 percent of first marriages are successful (i.e., intact and reportedly happy).

» The percentage of children in single-parent homes has risen from nine percent in 1960 to 28 percent in 1998. Thirty-five percent of children now live apart from their biological fathers.

What is surprising, perhaps, is that against this backdrop of terrible statistics, the teenagers are hoping, or perhaps clutching, for something better. Of the teenage girls polled, 83.1 percent say that having a good marriage and family life is "extremely important" (up from 80.2 percent in 1980). The report goes on to say:

Nonetheless, there are some reasons for hope. For example, given the increased importance of marriage to teenagers, it is possible that this generation will work hard at staying happily married. The decline in the unwed birth rate is also a good sign. And there are stirrings of a larger grass-roots marriage movement. Churches in more than a hundred communities have joined together to establish a common set of premarital counseling standards and practices for engaged couples.

97    Rolf Jensen, *The Dream Society* (1999) McGraw-Hill

98    David Popenoe and Barbara Dafoe Whitehead, *The State of Our Unions: The Social Health of Marriage in America* - http://marriage.rutgers.edu

This hopefulness suggests a window of opportunity for adults to play a role in shaping the values and strengthening the dreams of teenagers. It also underscores the importance of deliberately building the right network to support today's children.

## There's Many a Slip

"It's a holding ministry."

About 500 children passed through our hands over the ten years that we led the youth group in Hout Bay, South Africa. After we had driven the last of the children home after youth group on a Saturday night, we often said to each other, "It's a holding ministry." Many late nights, many years of planning, praying and counseling; not always much to show for it. The risky areas seemed to be the passages from pre-teen to teen when they had outgrown Sunday School but not yet connected with a youth program. Likewise the transition from teenager to adulthood was risky as they went to the army, university or their first job, and lost touch with their previous support network. There's many a slip in the passages of life.

What's worse, today the passages are becoming less predictable, and more slippery. Columnist Dave Barry's statement may be more than humorous: "What I look forward to is continued immaturity followed by death." Pre-adolescents are maturing at odd ages. Teenagers are assaulted with adult stuff. Young Adults think they're still teenagers. The baton gets dropped at the hand-offs precisely because we don't see the hand-offs coming. Age-appropriate, regulated, transitioned growth is rare.

All of these changes are leading some to predict that the standard age categories are going to be redefined. "Teenagers" are a creation of the second half of the twentieth-century; they may disappear as a market or societal segment as teenagers become part of a new group called... "screenagers." These are the emerging products of the Internet era who are defining their life-maps using a set of inputs that none of their preceding generations had.

The 10-F Model® (with a long-term eye on Convergence) can help to secure the hand-offs by providing an understandable framework for all ages, and providing parents with a level of compassion about the difficulty in making life transitions:

> Most of the problems that twixters face are hard to see, and that makes it harder to help them. Twixters may look as if they have been overindulged, but they could use some judicious support. Apter's research at Cambridge suggests that the more parents sympathize with their twixter children, the more parents take time to discuss their twixters' life goals, the more aid and shelter they offer them, the easier the transition becomes. "Young people know that their material life will not be better than their parents." Apter says. "They don't expect a safer life than their parents had. They don't expect more secure employment or finances. They have to put in a lot of work just to remain O.K." Tough love may look like the answer, but it's not what twixters need.[99]

## Increasing the Density of Responsible Adults

When we came to the United States I realized how much we missed the support structure we'd enjoyed in South Africa. We'd been busy there: a full-time job at Price Waterhouse and a full-time job leading a local church. There were elders' meetings several times a week, sermons to prepare, clients to audit and consult, people to counsel, administration to perform, worship to lead, friends to reach out to. But there was also an organic network of support: people to cook meals, watch our children, trim trees, fix cars, plan vacations, guide our children, pray for us, counsel us in many areas, support our (very young) leadership.

99   Lev Grossman, *Grow Up? Not so Fast*, Time Inc., January 16, 2005

Without that network in the U.S., as a father I had to dedicate much more time to the day-to-day routine of my family.

Over the years we have made a conscious effort to expose our children to the company, thinking, prayer and worldview of godly people. When our friends have come to stay with us they ask our kids questions, spot things we do not see, and take the time to pray for, and sometimes with, our children. We have tried and still do try to give them time so that they can talk about stuff that is not easy to broach with Mom and Dad. They laugh with each other, get mad at each other, cry with each other, and love each other. We also send our children away to stay with others when this makes sense. They relate differently to each other when we are not around to hog the conversation. We spend money on going places, and having others come to us. We nurture the network. Our kids have not always seen the method in the madness; they have seen it as another occasion when they have a house full of visitors from another city or continent. But our hope is that they will look back and see a rich heritage of relationships with quality people that have influenced their lives for the better.

John Dilulio and other researchers claim that disadvantaged children are most helped by "increasing the density of responsible adults" in their lives. The same holds true for "regular kids." As they go through their teenage years, other adults will be key to your children finding themselves. Don't let the network happen by accident; actively build your child's Impact Network.

## Life Management Skills

I spoke on Convergence in Dallas at two conferences organized by different groups. One was Campus Crusade and the other was Cisco, the networking company. The first exposed people to the concepts of integrating Career, Calling, Creativity and Community. The second exposed people to the inevitable convergence of voice, data and video on the same networks. Our kids intuitively understand the convergence of camera, mobile phone, web browser and calendar on one device. Will they understand the integration of the major facets of life? What will the next century feel like for our children? What are the one or two big decisions they will have to face in regard to their Call, Community, Creativity and Career? And who is equipping your children to make the big decisions that come along?

They will live in a world where there is a confluence of previously separate streams. It is not just limited to mobile devices. Here are some other examples:

» Nations and economies: there is a shift from nationalistic borders to economic borders. Ethnicity is a factor, but commerce is an increasing factor. The old David Livingstone motto may ring true for them: "Christianity, Commerce, and Civilization."

» Language barriers: the common language for business and the Internet is English, in various forms. In India they call it Hindlish. The fact is that your children will see a blurring of language as a barrier.

» Time boundaries: no longer do they just relate to people in their own time zone. They live in world of 24x7 chat rooms and connectivity.

» Barriers between people and technology: miniaturization and ubiquitous technologies are making technology more transparent.

» Cultural barriers: America's #1 export is culture and the MTV generation looks and sounds quite similar around the world.

» Convergence: communications, content and computing are all melding.

But will our children find Convergence in the area that matters the most? Will we overcome the fragmentation, and model a new way of living out our faith? Or will the flaws of our own faulty foundations leave gaps in the walls of their lives?

# What Can be Done to Prepare Them for the Future?

In the old days, kids knew what their parents did for a living. Butcher, baker, candlestick maker. Farmer, doctor, engineer, teacher. They could see what mom and dad actually did. Today we are lucky if our children know the name of our company, let alone the industry we are in. If they don't know what we do, it is no surprise that they have few clues as to what they want to do when they grow up.

So how do we balance these seeming conflicts when:

» we recognize that our children are growing up earlier than we did?

» we understand that they have few clues about the uncertain future?

» the statistics say that children are getting older but not maturing?

» technology-skills are developing at a pace that can outstrip character development?

First, parents need to become their children's network managers and take steps to understand what that network should look like.

Second, we have to teach them the nitty-gritty process of figuring out what God wants on a daily basis. Our experience thus far is this: involve them in decisions, seek their counsel, expect them to hear God on behalf of the family. Our children, by way of example, have been the instigators in a few big property decisions. Fay started chatting to an elderly man outside his house one day; she was six-years-old. He complained about taxes, government and living in California. He said he wanted to live in Oregon. We bought his house without it even going on the market.

Eight years later we needed to rent a larger house. We checked the rental listings and discovered four houses in a forty-mile stretch that met our criteria. We prayed and Lyn felt our children would lead us to the next house. A few days later they came home and said some kids were leaving town and their rental would be available. It didn't go on the market either and within a short period we moved in. We have come to expect that sometimes the only guidance we will get is going to be from our children.

Third, try to model integrated living for them. Sure, they may still want to break out of the mold and do their own thing. They may want to live a fragmented life for a while. But they will have been ruined for the ordinary if they have seen you model the components of life in an integrated whole.

Fourth, teach them to ask the right questions. In the planning supplement to this book there are some tools that help in asking the right questions. Consider how these may apply to your children.

Fifth, take deliberate steps to instill your values in your children. In the normal course of events, they will take on your values just through being with you. But don't rest on your laurels. Deliberately ask questions and make observations about their values.

Finally, seriously evaluate whether the mad dash to college is right for your child. Our observations over 25-plus years is that many teenagers need a break after high school before they dive headlong into college. We are not talking about a party break, but a bookmark in the routine of study. I recommend that this be considered for a series of reasons:

» High school does not always do a great job of preparing students for college. Junior colleges have become finishing colleges, completing the work that high schools would have done in the not-too-distant past. According to the US Department of Education, one-third of undergraduates must take remedial coursework because they did not graduate from high school with the skills to perform well at the college level.

» Parents are not finished preparing their children for their role in the world. While in high school, the bearers of the Holy Grail are twenty-something-year-old teachers. Your children are turning to them for answers sometimes in a way that closes them to hearing from you. So many kids leave high school without having basic life skills. Yet these same children start at age 14 talking about how they can't wait to get their own apartment and do their own thing. Their fixation with leaving (and the American parents' desire to get them out of the nest quickly) can easily have the opposite of the desired effect. The goal is for them to grow up; the result is that the last season in the cocoon which is designed to bring them strength, is short-circuited. Instead of growing them up, they are ill-prepared for adult responsibilities.

» Many children are growing up too quickly physically and socially, without the character, emotional and spiritual development to complement this early development. The training we provide to warn them of various ills means we have to expose our children to things earlier than we would like. There is some premature loss of innocence. But some things cannot be rushed, and often we are too quick to push our children into the world half-armed to fight the battles they will face.

» Many children are shielded from service opportunities. Society places great virtue in establishing a regimen of school, sports, arts, dance, karate, music and more. We are dizzied by our children's activities. And all of this can leave little time for them to learn how to serve others. Even in church, they have programs tailored to them and youth ministers hired to serve them, and they are not asked to consistently serve others.

You might have guessed that some of this comes out of our own experience. In the churches we attended as youth, we began teaching three and four-year-olds as soon as we became teenagers. We were conscripted and trained to be part of the staff—unpaid, of course. At age 16, Lyn started a youth group in her home. For years, many of the young people who attended were older than she was. Service was expected.

When we graduated from high school, boys in South Africa—we were allowed to call them boys then—generally spent a year or two in compulsory military training before going to college. Compulsory military training draws on a cross-section of society. We were forced to bungalow with people we didn't even know existed. We were taken outside of our cultural comfort zone, physically, socially and mentally. I noticed a huge difference between the level of maturity of those who went to college directly from school, and those who did their military stint first. Some people wasted that time and did unsavory things. Most boys just grew up. Was the army good for everyone? No. Could everyone "be all that they could be?" Not at all. But the notion of serving people you didn't want to serve and doing things you didn't want to do, all for three bucks a day, had some merit.

I am not advocating that we send our kids off to the military. Given the choice, I would have avoided it. I am suggesting that they volunteer a year of their time between high school and college and enter a formal program where they can be discipled, equipped and taken into service opportunities, preferably in other nations.

This won't guarantee Convergence at a later stage, but it will help stretch their worldview beyond the narrow confines of their high school or college campus. It will fire their imagination for what God is doing in the world. It will provide a channel for their gifts to the needy. It will heighten awareness of their own privileged position on this planet. It will underscore the reason for later academic training. These things may help them lessen the struggle with Convergence when they are older.

## Contend for Your Children

We recognize that when we marry there is this new entity, our marriage, and we have to contend for its survival. But how many of us contend for our relationship with our kids? There is a vast difference between contending with your child and contending in the spirit, making a stand in prayer and intercession for your relationship with your son or daughter. Your relationship with your children has an enemy. Teenagers are not the enemy. Their friends are not the enemy. Satan, however, comes to "steal, kill and destroy." Fight for your relationship with your children. Ask intercessors to join you; call on family and friends; stand against the work of the real enemy; and stand for your relationship with each child. It is too easy to get hurt, to hurt; it is a commonplace to cower at the pain, to inflict pain. As your children become adults, it is the path of least resistance to give up, instead of standing up. It is easier sometimes to give in rather than make a stand. Contend. Contend not just for your children, but contend for this special thing, this relationship with each child. And, while you are at it, pray that they too will experience Convergence some day.

## Convergence and Clergy

Shouldn't the most fulfilled people be those who have dedicated their lives to serving God? Then why is it that the turnover rate of pastors is so high? The average tenure of a senior pastor is five years. A Barna survey goes on to say, "Our work has found that the typical pastor has his or her greatest ministry impact at a church in years five through 14 of their pastorate." Most pastors don't stay long enough to have a fruitful ministry. This may strike you as a shocking statistic, but there are many reasons why this is the case. Over the past 25 years I have counseled many church leaders and found that their Career issues are no less complex than those who minister in the marketplace. Clergy have no guarantee of Convergence.

Before I get too far into this chapter I have to add a disclaimer: the title of the chapter was a trick to lure the "professional ministers," those who have a seminary background or who have followed a path to pulpit ministry. I do not believe that there should be a distinction between "clergy" and "laity." I don't believe that people who get paid by churches are necessarily any more in ministry than those who get paid by a business, or don't get paid at all. I think that the language used in many churches is unhelpful, particularly when we talk about "full-time service" and "pastor" and "minister" and "priest" and so on. I had to get your attention, however, so the title of this chapter is *Convergence and Clergy*. Besides, preachers like their alliteration.

At the same time I want to say that I am for you. Yours is a wonderful, but sometimes tough and thankless job. The needs of people never end, and the demands on your life can be overwhelming. (I do not believe they need to be, but an uneducated church can wrongly assume that you are there to meet their needs rather than equip them for a life in the army.)

Many who read this will not be from "majority nations"—or whatever the politically correct term for first world nations might be—and probably hold down multiple jobs, one in "the church" and one in "the world." When I was in the Ukraine I asked the head of a major denomination, "What percentage of your pastors have other jobs?" His reply surprised me: "99.9%". There are also increasing numbers of people pursuing "missional" work, and some of these are clergy or missions leaders. The desire for work being worship runs deeper. Hopefully this chapter will help the many pulpiteers who are striving to speak a positive message about work, vocation, and ministry *through* business. It will also validate those who are generating income from "secondary sources" in order to free them up to do what God has called them to do for the Church, but which they cannot do from within the wineskin of a local church. Also, many churches are recognizing the growing ranks of businesspeople who want to minister where they are with the gifts that they have. Let's delve into this by starting with the easily identifiable Pastor's Pitfalls to Convergence first.

# The Dragon of Dichotomy

The Dragon of Dichotomy gets his best meals in church. The secular-sacred dichotomy is a severe form of segregation that has had devastating consequences for centuries. One of the outcomes of this bankrupt way of thinking is that resources that God intended to fully deploy in building the kingdom of God are either sidelined totally, or under-deployed in people that serve the programs of local churches, but do not fully utilize the gifts of pew people. Within the church, the best jobs are kept for those who are "on full-time staff." If you are a church leader, I can almost hear you saying, "I am OK; in my church we tell everyone that they are ministers. We even have a sign at the exit of our parking lot that reads 'You are now entering the mission field!'" I have seen those signs, and I have heard you say the words. But I have also read your business cards that say "Pastor" and seen your preaching schedule that has you doing most of the preaching, and I have seen the decision-making processes that give more weight to those on the church payroll than others. I have heard you talk about Marketplace Ministry, but most of what you said revolved around witnessing and giving, the two starting points least likely to succeed.

Wake up, Church! The rest of the world is becoming increasingly integrated about spirituality and life in general. The institution that should preach, with and without words, integrated living—that all things are God's—should also make it a reality within its own body. As Church leaders we need to examine our own theology, language and practices to root out dichotomized thinking and practice. Let me tell you a story to illustrate my point.

This week I sat with a young professional woman whom I will call Ann. She is intelligent, works for one of the top companies in the world, and is a talented worship leader in her local church. Ann has an accountability partner, Zenda (also not her real name). Ann and Zenda met with their pastor recently to report back on their mission trips. Ann had gone to Africa to teach business leaders that their work is their ministry, business is a calling, and that they are ministers in the

245

marketplace. She helped a young business leader go through a total change of thinking about how his business can be used to advance the kingdom of God by serving governments throughout Africa. Zenda went with a group to China to teach English as a Second Language (ESL) in the hopes of reflecting Christ's love to the pre-believer students. After Ann and Zenda had each reported back excitedly on their missionary adventures, their pastor asked Zenda to share her ESL experiences with the businesspeople and older people (i.e. 40 +) in the church, and he asked Ann to stay away from them. Why? Among other things, he wants to lead a missions trip to China next summer teaching English as a Second Language. So what message was sent to Ann? He would prefer to have Vice Presidents of technology companies, working professionals, and business owners who are not teachers by trade attempt to teach English to people who cannot understand them, rather than figure out how to live out Biblical principles in their own work, and then disciple others in what they have learned and practiced. This is a ludicrous waste of resources.

What messages are you sending to the people in your congregation? Examine your announcements, the language in your sermons, church bulletins, and your conversations: are you baking bread for The Dragon? What percentage of the sermons preached from your pulpit are preached by members of the congregation who are not on staff? How much time do you spend at the workplace of your congregants helping them live the life of a disciple where they work?

## Bogus Career Plans

In speaking with Ann she concluded that the young businesspeople in her local church who are the most keen about church are the most dichotomized in their thinking. A major reason for this is that the church has laid out a career path that says, "If you are really spiritual you will quit your job and come and be the worship director, or administrative pastor/whatever. Then you will really be in ministry." So the aspiration of people who love God and want to serve him becomes

246

a choice between joining the staff of the local church or becoming a missionary, in the traditional sense. Anything else is second class ministry. You know as well as I do that this so-called spiritual career plan is bogus. If anything in your thinking or language implies or endorses this, then you have yet to slay the dragon of dichotomy.

Now let's move beyond your people to your own journey towards Convergence.

## Work and Ministry

One of the first factors is that clergy are stuck in a Career just like anyone in business, health care, government or teaching. While they call it "ministry" they view what they do as a job. They have job expectations, roles and responsibilities, measures they have to meet, and things they have to produce. On the one hand this is good. On the other hand, they can do all this while it drifts into simply being a job that pays the bills. When a wife explains where her husband is and she says, "Joe is at work" then you have some indication he is in this church business as a job. Being a pastor is just a job to some people. It is no longer their calling. This is dichotomized thinking and living.

The Hebrew word *avodah* makes no distinction between work and ministry. We have popularized the notion that some people have a ministry and some people don't. You may say, "But I teach people that they are ministers...we are all ministers. And I tell them my job is to equip them to do the work of the ministry." In most churches I have visited, even when these words are spoken, this is rhetoric and not reality. The reality is that the good jobs in the church are kept for the full-time staff people, often bearing the title of "pastor." Seldom do "lay people" from within the congregation preach. They get to do the more menial tasks, the second class jobs, but not the public ministry.

Our language perpetuates the two-tier system. "You are all ministers, but I am the pastor." Then we wonder why people do not believe that they are indeed ministers, and why they are not really equipped. Sitting in a pew and watching preachers do their thing does not prepare people for ministry. Equipping has a demand-pull component. In church-speak this means that you create a demand for people to grow when you give them really tough work to do that demands that they grow.

A friend told me of the reaction he had when he saw the CEO of a major oil company walking down the aisle of his church, passing the collection plate. His first thought was, "Wow! This man is humble." His second thought was, "We are wasting this man's talents." What jobs are you giving your businesspeople? Do you even have a good grasp of how God has gifted them, how he has invested in them? I do not need to look on your bookshelves to know whether your thinking and practice is bifurcated; all I need to do is observe your people. Are they practicing ministers inside and outside your church walls?

I met Jessica Pillay in Johannesburg on September 17, 2005 when she was at the tail end of four years in the desert. She had approached her church leaders some years before and they had demonstrated a clear lack of understanding of work-faith integration. She relayed her story to me:

> After about five years of working in the corporate world, for one of the largest mining companies in the world, it began to slowly dawn on me that my career could be a vehicle that God could use to impact the company and display His glory. My influence in the company had grown. I was moving quickly through the ranks and positioned to have direct influence with the Board of Directors. At the same time, I began to feel uneasy because I knew that I was learning corporate "worldly methods of interaction" with people to survive. The higher I went up the corporate ladder, the rougher it became. However, my love for God caused me to believe that there must be a God-centered way to do my job. I decided that if I had support and training from my church, I would be prepared to behave like a "Joseph" or "Daniel" and begin to have Godly influence in the company.

I approached my church elders with this request. They made it clear from our interactions that I seemed to be a bit wayward. Women didn't take on such roles except where there were "Jezebelic tendencies" at play. "The world system is corrupt," said the church elder. "Forget about thinking that you are going to try to change it. The only thing you can do to have real impact is to leave the world and join the ministry. You have your ladder up the wrong wall." I was devastated. Feeling rejected by the place from which I expected to receive acceptance and solace resulted in deep-rooted confusion. I wondered why God had given me these gifts if they were of no value to Him. As a result I began to believe that I had no value in His Kingdom. The next four years were lonely spiritually and I felt lost. However, God was faithful and he eventually connected me to like-minded people who believed that business belonged to God. They were able to provide me with the necessary support and guidance to use my gifts to help build His Kingdom.

Church leaders, be careful that you do not call "unclean" what God has called clean. Work is good. God worked before the Fall, Adam and Eve managed God's creation, God still works today, and we will all work in heaven. The fact that an organization other than a church pays for that work does not decrease the value of the work, nor the person doing it.

## Unrealistic Expectations

Whether they view their work as a calling or as a job, pastors have unrealistic performance expectations that are set by hiring committees. I have seen Senior Pastor job descriptions that would make Jesus nervous to apply for the position. I believe in accountability and order. It is important to have a clear sense of Who is doing What. But it is neither fair nor right to give church leaders unfillable orders.

One of the ways to counter this is to see the work spread across a team of people. I believe that the "best practice" in Scripture is to have a lead pastor/minister, or whatever your tradition calls him or her, who is a "leader among equals" and is embedded in a leadership team that is multi-faceted. They should not be a law unto themselves. I do not believe, however, that they should be neutered and left with a low probability of actually walking out their calling. Onerous job expectations can kill the dream. Have high expectations for the team, and reasonable expectations for individuals.

## Clergy Bypass

One of the downsides of having a clear sense of calling is that it can tempt one to skip the other seasons, such as Skills Building. There are situations where one has to pioneer and start from scratch. You may have to exhibit extraordinary capabilities at an early age. It may seem like you skipped a few seasons and went straight to the Finish Line. I have met relatively few people on the pastoral staff who say, "I always want to be the # 2 person." Most carry dreams of leading their own church one day, and the sooner they get there the better! One day I sat with two talented young men who carried the title of Associate Pastor. They both had great hearts and significant abilities. The problem was that their church was out looking for a senior pastor and their denomination did not allow promotion from within the ranks. So neither of them were candidates. I looked at them and told them pointedly, "When you are ready to lead this church, God will give it to you." Months later I received a general letter from the chairman of the church board saying that they had decided unanimously, and counter to normal policy, to call one of the young men as the senior pastor. The other young man remains as his lieutenant. It doesn't always work out this way. Many pastors-in-waiting get hurt when they are overlooked for promotion. They get frustrated and move on. Yet often this delay is not man's doing, but God's. "Promotion comes from the Lord." So there is a dual test in this phrase: first, that you try to bypass seasons, and second, that "the powers that be" try to bypass you. Guard your heart.

## Idealism

Idealism does not guarantee Convergence, of course, and those who go the church route are often more idealistic than those who pursue other professions. The realities of the job and the expectations placed on one by the institutional church can dull this passion. This can lead to "hope deferred" and then to burnout. If you are depending on your whole career to happen in one church setting you may be placing more weight on the church than it can bear. Similarly, if you place too much pressure on yourself to get it all done at once, you may likewise be disappointed.

## Internal Isolation

I have already expressed the belief that church leaders should function as a plurality of leaders. In everyday terms this means that there are no One Man Bands in the New Testament Church. None. Protestants sometimes criticize Catholics for having a hierarchical church structure, yet their own structures are generally just as hierarchical. Instead of Pope we call them Superintendent, Moderator, Bishop, Apostle, Bishop-of-Bishops...you name it. What is intended to provide guidance and accountability can create a false sense of context that results in pastors not relating closely enough to those in their more immediate circle.

We find Convergence in the context of Community.

## External Isolation

The previous paragraph talked about personal isolation. In this paragraph I am cautioning you about the danger of viewing the job or function of a pastor without regard to other ministries. The written Word of God contains this statement in Ephesians chapter 4 about the components of a healthy church:

> It was he who gave some to be apostles, some to be prophets, some to be evangelists, and some to be pastors and teachers,

to prepare God's people for works of service, so that the body of Christ may be built up until we all reach unity in the faith and in the knowledge of the Son of God and become mature, attaining to the whole measure of the fullness of Christ.[100]

For a variety of reasons relatively few local church leaders have a functional relationship with those who fit into the category of "apostles" and "prophets." Every now and then an "evangelist" may be invited to speak at the local church, but he or she is then doing very little to consistently equip the local believers to do the work of evangelism. The guest speaker is simply doing the job that the local believers should be doing. If you are a local church leader, whatever your title, you need to be in a relationship with what some call "trans local ministers" in a way that is more than some abstract reporting relationship. "I have a dotted line to the Moderator" will not cut it. You may not have addressed the issue even if you have a peer group or accountability group who has known you since seminary. Do you recognize these gifts to the Church given by Christ to complement your own ministry? You should take special note of them because your pastoral gift isn't even on the 1 Corinthians list!:

> Now you are the body of Christ, and each one of you is a part of it. And in the church God has appointed first of all apostles, second prophets, third teachers, then workers of miracles, also those having gifts of healing, those able to help others, those with gifts of administration, and those speaking in different kinds of tongues.[101]

Pastoring people is a tough and often thankless job. You will do well to be cheered, guided, prodded and coaxed by those who have a broader scope than you as a local church leader. Can you name an apostle, prophet, evangelist, and trans local teacher to whom you relate? If not, you are most likely experiencing external isolation.

---

100    Ephesians 4:11-13

101    1 Corinthians 12:27-28

## Following Jesus

I have led a church and I have led a business. It takes as much faith, if not more, to run a business. The economic model for a traditional church is simple. If you keep the pews full you can predict your revenue. If you manage expenses according to a budget, you should end the year in the black. Sure, you are dependent on the generosity of people, but if you total the income of all attendees and multiply by two percent you should be able to guesstimate your top line. This sounds pretty crude, and it is.

If, on the other hand, you are committed to following the prototype that Jesus modeled for us, then you are in trouble. You are walking away from the predictable model towards the life of faith. What I described above takes management, a few program tweaks, and an occasional big name speaker. If you go with John 5:19, however, you are in a different walk. Jesus said, and I think it was an example for you and me:

> I tell you the truth, the Son can do nothing by himself; he can do only what he sees his Father doing, because whatever the Father does the Son also does.

When you make a commitment to only do what you see the Father doing, you are following Jesus. This is an opportunity, but it may lead you to some lateral or downwardly mobile career moves. Following Jesus is a dangerous business.

## With or Without You

I end this chapter with a plea and a warning. The plea is that you, as someone who has a career in the church, fully pursue integration at every level of your thinking and life. This means that you will truly have to become an equipper and promoter and releaser of others. My warning is that, if you do not do this, you will wake up one day and find that the Church will not be where and when you thought it was. You may have center stage on Sunday mornings, but the real action will be in the AND places: *and* Judea, *and* Samaria, *and* the ends of the earth. It will be in the houses down the road *and* in the businesses on Main Street. The future is already now. God will do it with or without you.

Take some advice from Martin Luther King, Jr. who had this to say in a 1963 speech:

> We must face the fact that in America, the church is still the most segregated major institution in America. At 11:00 on Sunday morning when we stand and sing and Christ has no east or west, we stand at the most segregated hour in this nation. This is tragic. Nobody of honesty can overlook this.[102]

Why do I place this comment about legalized apartheid in America in the same chapter as The Dragon of Dichotomy? In both instances the Church has a real responsibility for addressing the root and fruit of these parallel plagues. We can learn from Dr. King's remedy in addressing the man-made segregation between "sacred and secular" and "work and ministry." Dr. King went on to say:

> Now, I'm sure that if the church had taken a stronger stand all along, we wouldn't have many of the problems that we have. The first way that the church can repent, the first way that it can move out into the arena of social reform is to remove the yoke of segregation from its own body. Now, I'm not saying that society must sit down and wait on a spiritual and moribund church as we've so often seen. I think it should have started in the church, but since it didn't start in the church, our society needed to move on. The church, itself, will stand under the judgement of God. Now that the mistake of the past has been made, I think that the opportunity of the future is to really go out and to transform American society, and where else is there a better place than in the institution that should serve as the

---

102    http://www.wmich.edu/library/archives/mlk/q-a.html

moral guardian of the community. The institution that should preach brotherhood and make it a reality within its own body.

I have heard some businesspeople say that they are forging ahead whether their pastors get on board or not. They echo Dr. King's statement, "I think it should have started in the church, but since it didn't start in the church, our society needed to move on." I, however, am not too worried about whether the institutional church will go away. First of all, large organizations routinely reinvent themselves. The church has done the same over the centuries. Second, Jesus said he will build his Church. I am concerned, however, that people should discover and walk out their callings. If they do not believe that they are ministers, as the Bible says they are, then their path to Convergence is fraught with difficulty. Your life as a church leader will be an obstacle or an encouragement to them. It all depends whether you are dichotomy-free.

I am also concerned that those who call themselves clergy or full-time ministers or pastors get so caught up in their ministry careers that they miss the mystery. Convergence is a state of rest. If Satan cannot derail you, he will bog you down with busyness. If you are laboring under the pressure to prove yourself, shred your resume, burn your job description, and hear your heavenly Father say, "Well done." Surrender your career, make sure your real community is not separated from your real work, and block off time to co-create with the God who called you. I am sure you do not want to be among the 80-90% of church leaders who intend to spend a lifetime at their work, but drop out within 10 years. Some say they die of over-commitment; I say that this is a symptom of fragmented thinking.

# A Huge Opportunity

A good friend who pastors a church in Texas told me that in recent years he has noticed a new phenomenon: businesspeople are coming to Christ and going to the nations (but not as traditional missionaries) within a year. There is no program, no great plan, and no real training. They are simply connecting the dots between who God says they are (ministers) and what they do in everyday work. If you are a pastor, go with them. Don't take them to do a Biblical tour of the Promised Land; have them take you to minister to their suppliers, customers and the rest of their household in whatever nations they do business.

If businesspeople in the faith community to which you give leadership are not going internationally, go to their places of work locally. Another pastor I know takes one full day every six weeks to go and "hang out" with businesspeople in San Francisco at their places of work. This is probably 30 miles from the church campus, so it requires some effort. When he gets to see their work first hand he is less inclined to draw them into his work (on the church campus) and more motivated to equip them to be "about the Father's business" right in their place of business.

The opportunity to team with business, government, education, healthcare and other leaders from your local church is huge. Jesus called Peter after he got in his boat, performed a miracle, blessed Peter's business, and used it as a floating pulpit. Team up with a marketplace minister; it just might be the starting point for changing your world.

## Telling your Story

People remember stories. They forget whole speeches, but remember the stories. They forget facts and figures, but can recall minute details of tales told. From children to juveniles in prison to old people, we like hearing stories. When we hear a good story, we inevitably find something that resonates with our own lives, for each of us has a story.

Not all of us understand the importance of telling it. Yet if we can tell of our past we can tackle our future. Often when I meet someone I ask, "Tell me your story." This simple phrase opens up a slew of history. The telling of one's story builds a bridge.

When getting to know someone I want to fill in the missing pieces of the jigsaw puzzle. Where did they live, what school did they go to, what were the formative experiences in their lives? Four of us sat around a table having dinner. I had met the other three people for the first time that day. We were discussing the purpose of their business and I then asked them about their own personal purpose. They were not so sure, but it soon became clear how important the sacrifices of grandparents and parents were to one of the women. She was the third generation of Irish immigrants who had sacrificed to raise the platform higher for their children. She herself had persevered to not drop the baton when she found herself a single mom with two young tikes dependent on her being there for them. "Stewarding an inter-generational family trust." She found her purpose in her multi-generational story.

We are living in an era where those in affluent countries are increasingly purchasing with their hearts. We are no longer buying just goods and services, but we are purchasing a piece of the story that is embedded in the products. You aren't just buying the watch, you are becoming the aviator or the polar explorer.

## Story-Telling Tools

I sat down for dinner with my cousin and some friends in Atlanta. After we had been together for an hour or so I turned to my cousin and asked her, "So how are you doing?" "What do you want to know?" she retorted. She looked like she was ready for a good conversation so I said, "I want to ask you about 10 areas." Without naming The 10-F Model I simply asked her one question in each category. Beginning with her Faith, we walked through all of The 10-Fs. Within about 20 minutes I had a good idea of how she was in all the important areas of her life. So I asked a waiter for a pen and a clean napkin and mapped out a radar or spider chart of her feelings about where she was in life. Next I suggested that she compare herself to her husband so she talked about their similarities and differences. I then mapped his coordinates on the same napkin, overlaying his chart on hers. By the end of the evening we had created their 10-F Gap Map. There were five or six couples at the table that night and when they saw what was going on, they were drawn into the exercise. The 10-F map can be a starting point for your story. On occasion I will redraw my own map just to get a handle on how I am feeling.

"Tell me your story." Another way that I phrase the question is to ask people about the journey they have taken through the seasons of life. I then introduce them to The Seven Seasons, not to share the model, but to get a quicker understanding of their pilgrimage. I recently had lunch with a brilliant woman from Iran. I wanted to know her story. We spoke about how she, like me, longs for the integrated life. I then took side plates and a few other items on the table and visually demonstrated the concept of increasing the overlaps between The 4-C's. This led to a discussion about The Seven Seasons. She, like many others I meet who are in their forties, had experienced most of them. What is particularly interesting to me is listening to people's perceptions of their present season, and the season they believe they are heading into next.

Take a while to consider which seasons you have experienced. What indicated the start and end of a season? Seasons often overlap: How have your seasons overlapped? When have you avoided seasons? Why did you avoid them? What is the story line that runs through your seasons?

## Dangers of Telling Your Story

I have lived in the U.S. for over twenty years, but in the last five years I have come to spend more time with my brother Doug, who still lives in South Africa. When we first began talking about things that happened in our childhood it seemed he remembered very little. (This could have been very useful if I had wanted to rewrite any of the past.) A few months ago we sat chatting again and he shared stories about his own encounter with God and I heard about things I had long forgotten. Now I was the one with historical amnesia. Observing my own children and their friends growing up and reflecting on their years thus far, I am convinced that most of us develop a sort of "life was tough" story. "I walked barefoot to school every day. It was twenty degrees below, and uphill in both directions." My kids actually confuse my story, which did include some bare feet by choice, with a man I knew who would walk barefoot to school and stop to stand in fresh cow paddies to warm his feet.

Telling one's story is very important, but it does come with some dangers:

**Revisionism:** Re-writing the past to make it sound better than it was. "This is a true story; only the facts have been changed to protect the guilty." After World War II Stalin had his favorite film producer make a movie about the war. Stalin was the hero, of course. During the pre-screening of the movie the producer sat with his heart in his hand, nervous about Stalin's reaction—this could be a career limiting film. Stalin's eyes were glued to the screen; his eyes were glued to Stalin. The climax of the movie came when Stalin flew to Berlin, and he triumphantly addressed the adoring crowd. Those present relaxed when they saw Stalin wipe away a tear from his eye. Patting the movie producer on the shoulder as he left the screening room Stalin was heard muttering, "If only I had gone to Berlin... if it had happened." In the movie Stalin had a triumphal entry; in real life he never made the flight to Berlin. Beware of revisionism.

**The blame game:** "My mother made me do it." While there may be truth to some of this, the purpose of telling your story is to understand how God has led you, what seasons you have been through, not to apportion blame for what you didn't do. As the saying goes, "Build a bridge and get over it!" Many great people had not-so-perfect parents. Churchill was sent to boarding school at seven and his parents did not respond to his pleas for them to visit him, even when they were visiting close by. He thought his father encouraged him to pursue politics so that they could work together; in reality, the father thought him too stupid to study law. Bill Clinton's father died when he was young and his mother then married an abusive alcoholic. As a youngster Clinton had to testify against the new father in court. Martin Luther King's father beat him as a child. Difficulty can be a bridge.

**Covering the trail:** Not every story is logical or pretty. In fact, many people fail to reach Convergence because they lacked the tools to make decisions that would lead them in the right direction. If your life is a trail of not-too-brilliant choices, own it. You don't make better decisions tomorrow by passing off yesterday's bad decisions as divine guidance.

**An end in itself:** On the one hand your story is important. On the other hand, God's story is the real story. We are mortal, he alone is immortal. We are finite, he is infinite. His story is before all stories. Our story begins and ends within his story. Because our story is a sub-set of his story, we are significant. Our story for its own sake is not that huge, but our significance lies in being part of his drama.

## Just Give Me the Facts

If you are a business person you must recognize that you face schizophrenia in story telling. In his book titled *The Leader's Guide to Storytelling: Mastering the Art and Discipline of Business Narrative*, Stephen Denning says, "analysis is what drives business thinking. It cuts through the fog of myth, gossip and speculation to get to the hard facts. It purports to go wherever the observations and premises and conclusions take it, undistorted by the hopes and fears of the analyst." He goes on to point out that "this strength is also a weakness... leadership involves inspiring people to act in unfamiliar and often unwelcome ways. Mind numbing cascades of numbers or daze-inducing PowerPoint slides will not achieve this goal...But effective storytelling often does."[102] So the first part of the story-teller-dichotomy is that corporations will tell you, "Just give me the facts." The second part of the equation is that we are rapidly moving towards a world of stories.

---

102    Stephen Denning, *The Leader's Guide to Storytelling: Mastering the Art and Discipline of Business Narrative*, Jossey-Bass, 2005

With hundreds of millions of home made movies flooding the Internet, any teenager with a movie camera can become a producer. People are becoming expectant of stories. Getting in touch with our own story and being willing to share it authentically is a key component of our life's journey. While there are dangers of storytelling, the bigger danger is that we don't tell our story.

# Developing Your Tapestry

I don't think I have the patience to create a tapestry—choosing just the right background color and fabric that will last for decades if not centuries; painstakingly creating an image for this blank piece of material; selecting the threads; deciding what to do first, what to do later; deliberating the richness of the image versus the time and skill it takes to weave the additional features; deciding on the fineness of the needlework; then hours of painstaking sewing, snipping, pushing and pulling.

Today we use computers to generate and transmit images, but the essence of creating the image is the same. We use phrases like "granularity of the pixels" or the "dots per inch" (dpi) that parallel the world of tapestry and cross-stitch... and painting by numbers. In a tapestry there are essentially three layers. There is a piece of fabric that is the base plane for the final product. Printed on this is an image that is much like a blue print. Then there is the actual stitching that is woven onto the fabric consistent with the pattern or blueprint.

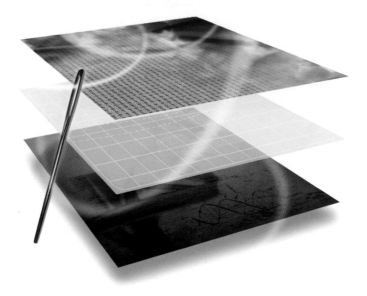

What we have explored in this book can be related to your development of a life-tapestry in at least three ways:

Each person is unique, created with the potential to bear God's image. Each life is the material that forms the background for the special tapestry God wants to weave. It may not be perfect, but it is enough for God.

God has a blueprint for our lives. When viewed in general terms it may not seem that helpful, but it is this: "To be conformed to the image of his own dear Son." God makes it come alive when, hovering above the fabric of our lives, this general vision for who we can be by God's grace starts to take form. It is a dream, a picture, a hope that will transform us. The sooner and the more completely we wrap our hearts and minds around the lines of God's blueprint, the better.

3.  Woven on top of the background of man's potential and the seemingly faint layer of God's plans "to give us a future and a hope" comes each person's tapestry, the real stuff of life. We see our life choices laid plain in the thoughtfulness and thoroughness and thickness of the threads. In one beautiful detail of our tapestry we see our obedience in following the Plan. In a corner a rusty needle dangles haplessly at the end of the dusty thread of neglect, brokenness or pain. In other spots we have woven "outside the lines" and it may look artistic, but it somehow doesn't flow with the rest of the picture. Some of our tapestries are rich with the blend of the Seven Seasons of life. Others are more color-scarce. Many of us have spent years creating tapestries that compartmentalize the major spheres of our lives. We walk through small gates between Career, Community, Call and Creativity, keeping them ever separate. Yet we admire those boundaryless tapestries where the everyday and the eternal flow easily together... where the majestic touches the mundane and transforms it.

## Why Create a Tapestry?

You and I each have a unique tapestry. Understanding our past can help us to more fully experience the future. As we move to greater understanding of our own journey towards Convergence, there are two equal and opposite errors:

»  taking such pride in our past that it blinds us to a different future

»  having such a poor understanding of our past that we waste decades re-inventing ourselves only to find that we have "created" a new us that looks like many of our ancestors.

God is indeed the God of new beginnings. Many of us are grateful for the fresh start and are happy to forget a few chapters from our past. Clinging relentlessly to family ties and history can actually impede personal growth. Yet our family history does impact us, and having some understanding of our roots can sometimes help us fashion a future that is deliberately different from—or that draws purposefully on—that past.

I have tried to convey the importance of understanding the story of my own tapestry. It can be an anchor that keeps us from being swept into despair, losing perspective, repeating poor family patterns and worse.

## In the Genes

One Friday evening I read my grandfather's unpublished memoirs. Joseph Lewis Green[103] had trained for ministry in the Baptist tradition. He had a start in the London business world as a teenager where he worked at the leading edge of the communications industry. (He sold Waterman fountain pens over the counter.) Some years later he was the Minister of a church in the East End of London:

> The activities of the various organizations were seriously restricted by the limited accommodation. We resolved to build a two storey institute at a cost of four thousand pounds which was a considerable sum for those days and a heroic venture for a working class congregation, most of whom were artisans, factory workers and clerks.

Later he went on to write:

> The stone laying ceremony of the Institute was performed by Sir Frank Dyson, Astronomer Royal, who was the son of a Baptist Minister. In spite of his eminence, Sir Frank was the

---

103    My grandfather later changed the spelling of his name to Joseph Louis Green, perhaps fancying his French heritage. His grandfather, Le Fort, had been a general in Napoleon's army. JL Green later moved to South Africa, and spent twenty years leading Rosebank Union Church. He was the head of the Baptist Union in South Africa for some time.

soul of modesty...Sir George Hume, the Member of Parliament for Greenwich, also participated in the service...In three and a half years nearly the whole deficit was liquidated.

Around 60 years later I found myself in a very different business community, Silicon Valley. When I sensed God was leading me to start The Institute, little did I know that J.L. Green had faced the same challenge; had I read his story a few years earlier, I would have been less surprised when I sensed God say, "Are you willing to start an institute?"

A friend, David Boyd, has a clear illustration of this in his own story. In his own words:

> Consideration of being Chancellor of a university never appeared on the screen of my consciousness for the first forty-four years of my life. Then an opportunity came to serve through this role in 1992 with the University of the Nations, Kona. A few years later I discovered something while reviewing the history of our family name and lineage in Scotland. A number of the forebearers of the Boyd name were found in similar roles in fields of education, missions and government. They even included one Robert Boyd (1578 - 1627) who held the Chancellor role in Glasgow University in 1615 and at the University of Edinburgh in 1622.

What is there in your own story that suggests what God may or may not have for you?

## The Core of Our Identity

I kneeled in front of a wheel from a Model-T Ford that was propped against a wall in an antique store. It had an old rubber tire, 12 sturdy wooden spokes, and a metal hub. I said to Lyn, "If it had ten spokes I would buy it." In an earlier chapter we introduced you to The 10-F Model. Think of each F as a spoke in a wheel. Each is needed for our completeness. At any point in time it seems as though repair or restoration is taking place on different spokes.

The hub is another key piece that keeps the wheel functioning. It represents our identity. We cannot easily come to Convergence without settling core identity issues. A good friend, Dr. Art Wouters, has written a paper in which he describes the seven things that lie at the center of our being.[104] Think of his "seven hidden P's" as seven ball bearings that are hidden, but enable the wheel to turn smoothly.

» **Presence:** "The first is the longing for the presence and availability of at least one other person who will always be there for us and who will desire a relationship with us no matter what happens or whatever we do."

» **Provision:** "The second is the longing for provision. My relational nature makes me dependent on others to provide for me, and others need me to help provide for them."

» **Protection:** "The third longing is to be adequately protected and to be able to protect those who need it."

» **Permission:** "The fourth longing is to be allowed to be ourselves. This is the most vital of all permissions needed from others."

» **Purity:** "The fifth longing for relationship is one of a desire for purity. Ever since Adam and Eve sewed fig leaves to cover their nakedness, humans have needed to know how to deal with their moral guilt and shame."

» **Power:** "The sixth longing of relationships concerns the dimension of power and control. Each individual is born for a purpose and with the capacity to make an impact on his or her world. To us has been given the authority to make an impact and we are all gifted in various ways to engage in personally and corporately fulfilling activities. Everyone needs to discover their Call and serve others

104    Dr. Art Wouters, "The Hub," The Institute, 2000.

and society in a responsible way. We can control some things and must learn to live with things that are not under our control. Many individuals either underestimate or overestimate their own power as a result of early defining disappointments. Whether you expect too much or too little from yourself, both options lead to a person failing to fulfill his or her potential."

» Partnership: "The seventh longing of relationships is expressed in the desire for meaningful partnerships. We need others to partner with us in the completion of meaningful activities and we long for genuine partnership with others."

Settling central identity issues can be a major help towards Convergence.

I have to consider the tapestry of my life: where might it have been woven differently if I were at rest with the seven hub/identity areas? Where would I have lived more, compensated less, given more freely, and been hurt less often? Until we settle our identity in our Creator, until we pattern our tapestry after him, we will be so busy "making something of ourselves" that we will probably fail to even see his design. Until we know God as our provision, our protection, and our purity; until we rest in his presence, his power (made perfect in our weakness); until we know his "Yes," his permission; until we take his yoke, his partnership...until then, Convergence will be hard to come by. Why? Because when we "do our own thing" we sub-optimize. Because our tendency is towards disintegration, not integration. Because left to ourselves, we don't get it together. We need to ask the Holy Spirit to remove the grit from the ball bearings that grind daily at the center of our person.

## Considered Living

By all accounts we should be a generation that has the freedom to pursue our dreams. Dishwashers, microwave ovens, vacuum cleaners, refrigerators, cell phones, fax, e-mail, PDA's, pagers, etc. We have more "mother's little helpers" than any other generation. We should have more free time than we do. In 1890 people were asked to list the items they considered essential to everyday life. They listed 16 items. In 1995 the list had grown to 89 items. When we don't have a clear purpose, the clutter of modern life will flood into the void. One of the issues here is that these "assistants" fill up our hands and our heads, but do little for our hearts.

Oftentimes we seem to be caught in a cycle of mechanical responses to the unending stream of information that the machine of life spews at us. Waist-deep in information we plod pedestrianly around the corners of the information maze that leads who-knows-where. Patterned reactions to the routine transactions of daily life on planet earth; random decisions aimed to cope, or at best to add some variety to our lives...these symptoms seem to be life in its normative form. But this treadmill existence is not considered living.

The road to Convergence demands time to reflect. It requires pausing to consider the end, resting to make inner mid-course corrections, journaling to live twice, re-tracing ones steps. It means saying "No" to the conforming, selecting carefully from the basket of threads offered to us each day, picking out the permanent from the transient, the substantive from the superfluous, the precious from the precarious. Convergence means making the choices that favor the long-term dreams you whispered to your heart when out of the malaise. Convergence comes by making room for God, by having margin. This is closer to considered living.

Only God knows everything, and I suspect he resists man's attempts to create simple formulae for life. But this does not mean that we cannot seek to live deliberately. And if we want to live deliberately, it helps to be people of context. We find part of our context in what Scripture says about our identity in Christ. The foundation of our identity and security is the sure love of Jesus. We find another part of our identity in the tapestry he has woven around us.

# Unpacking the Raw Materials for Your Tapestry

## The fabric of your life

Certain things about you constitute the "fabric" of your life. Even before a design is sketched on that fabric, even before the first threads are woven, there is you. What are the things that make up your fabric? In earlier chapters we touched on how you are woven. Where are you different? What makes you unique? How do you carry in your fabric the weave of the family?

## The Seasons

Taking the tapestry image further, the threads in your life are the Seven Seasons. They are like seven different colors woven in and out, back and forth, making the image of your life.

Which of the Seasons have you been through? What Season are you in right now? Does any pattern form in your mind as you consider the coming and going of seasons?

In my own life, the preparation seemed to take forever. Not that I did not love and pour myself into what I was doing at the time. But when Lyn and I were leading a youth group or pastoring a church, it felt like preparation, not destiny. And when I studied for about five years, this too felt like something I had to do to get a ticket to the work life. Academia was not my destiny. And even though I worked in some companies for fourteen years and others for three, in all those years I felt like I was living in a tent. I felt a sense of caution about trying to make any of them my long-term home. They were Seasons of Skills Building, Internal Integrity Testing, Gift-Discovery and Development, Fearing and Hearing God, etc.

Too often I have seen people trying to build a permanent home where God would have them pitch a tent. I see people trying desperately to make a career in a particular company when all of the indications are that they should be moving on. We need to be better attuned to why we are where we are at any point in time.

The opposite error is the career-hopping scenario where we do not stay long enough in any one place for God to get his work done in us. We assume that difficulty means that there is something wrong with our employer. In today's world of "Internet Years" that are shorter than "dog years", how will we experience the character building that is an essential pre-requisite to Convergence?

## The Silver Threads

Woven through those seven different colors are the clear Sovereign touches on your tapestry. It is as if God himself has periodically taken a needle and woven a splash of silver, a touch of gold into your tapestry. These have become points of light that you look back to often. When you are losing perspective, you step back from the daily weave and remind yourself of these points of light.

For some the silver threads come as life experiences, for others they are the written Word. Or it might be a prayer someone prays for you or an insight a complete stranger has into your life. Sometimes it is the quiet whisper of assurance in the morning after worrying through the night. Your life has those threads. Step back and see the silver.

## Your Career, Creativity, Community

So you have the fabric of your life, and you have experienced many seasons. But how does it form an image? The answer is simple: one stitch at a time. Which raises the question, "How do I know that the stitches are all working together?" At the level of our humanness, we can have goals, objectives, life mission statements and more. Then hope for the best.

At another level, it is about obedience and who is going to be at the controls. It is that simple: will we trust God, or do we think we can do a better job? In the world of mobile philosophy, one bumper sticker proudly says, "God is my copilot." The retort is, "If God is your copilot, you are in the wrong seat." So, which seat are you in?

As you look back on the Career/Community choices you have made, which ones would you like to change? How about Career/Creativity: are there choices you have made that have sacrificed your creative side for the sake of "getting ahead" in your career?

And what about the good choices you have made? What can you learn from them that can help you in the future?

## Your Call

Call. Even the word sounds like an outside-in sort of thing; something that happens to us, something we have to wait for. And this is true. But it is also true that "deep calls to deep." The external call is to the internal "us" as human beings, not as automatons. The call we receive is consistent with our story, and more importantly, with the "image of God" that is imprinted on the fabric of our lives. It is colored by our seasons, and touched with the silver threads of God's sovereignty.

Because "Call" can be hard to define for some folk, I like to ask people about their interests and passions. Ask the question in as many ways as you can. "What rings your bell? What gets you up in the morning? What do you care deeply about? What lights your fuse? What gets your motor running? What gives you deep pleasure? When do you feel most at peace?" About what do you say, "I could do this for a long time"?

If our Call is not clear, it can sometimes be because we are not ready to hear it.

# State of Readiness

When we are willing to do God's will, we are ready to hear it. There is good reason why the sun rises and sets in a cycle, why we eat three or so meals a day and sleep each night. There is a renewing possibility in daily life. Each day brings opportunity, but also the temptation to take an easy way out. Forget all this weaving; pass the spray paint! Forget the deliberate discovery of our God and his ways, let me just scan an image from a famous media, business or sports personality so I can be like him or her...and if he or she wears a cross, so much the easier. But being molded in the image of someone else—even an unrealistic image we have of ourselves—is a dead-end street.

Our readiness to obey needs daily renewing. If we are to avoid becoming crusty cynics or heartless theoreticians, we need to constantly re-assess our own state of readiness. If we are to avoid the discontentment that comes from fashioning ourselves after the successful, we must obey God not so that we too can be successful, but so that we can walk out our Call. This requires a continual state of readiness:

» How ready are we to choose the seasons?

» Are we willing to forego the shortcuts?

» Do we have a desire to have our minds renewed? Are we open to imagining our identity and our actions being in alignment with God?

» Are we ready to daily commit to integration?

## One Size

There is no "one size fits all" prescription to the journey towards Convergence. In fact, there is no prescription at all. There are principles that when wisely applied can make you better equipped to sift through the confusing options that you encounter. I have attempted to provide meaningful handles for life through the concepts of finding the overlaps between the Four C's of Career, Creativity, Community and Call and the embracing of the *kairos* seasons of life.

# The Ultimate Aligning Principle

There are many sections of our tapestry that will not make sense at the time. Each of us will die with questions we would still like to ask God. It is therefore fair to ask whether there is some simple principle this side of eternity that will keep the threads of our life from being wasted. Life is not about Do's and Don'ts. This is especially true of the Convergence journey. In another context, the Apostle Paul gives some advice to his readers:

> We want to live well, but our foremost efforts should be to help others live well. With that as a base to work from, common sense can take you the rest of the way. I'm not going to walk around on eggshells worrying about what small-minded people might say; I'm going to stride free and easy, knowing what our large-minded Master has already said. If I eat what is served to me, grateful to God for what is on the table, how can I worry about what someone will say? I thanked God for it and he blessed it! So eat your meals heartily, not worrying about what others say about you—you're eating to God's glory, after all, not to please them. As a matter of fact, do everything that way, heartily and freely to God's glory. At the same time, don't be callous in your exercise of freedom, thoughtlessly stepping on the toes of those who aren't as free as you are. I try my best to be considerate of everyone's feelings in all these matters; I hope you will be, too.[105]

The principle, attitude, or motivation that will keep the threads of our life intact is "to God's glory." When we are not sure what to do we can ask, "What will honor God the most?" When we have to make a tough choice we can inquire, "Father, what would give you the most joy?" When overwhelmed with choices we can get the highest common denominator by asking, "Jesus, what do you want me to do or be in this situation or season?"

---

105     1 Corinthians 10: 24-33 *The Message.*

# Where Do You Go From Here?

In an earlier chapter I described Convergence this way:

## The Process of Convergence:

The coming together of those threads woven into your life over the past 40-or-so years, resulting in the discovery and walking out of your life Call.

## The Activities of Convergence:

Your cooperation in understanding, preparing for, and walking into your Creator's life purposes for you. Your availability in God's hands as he pulls, knots, pushes and polishes the strands of your being.

## The End of Convergence:

The discovery of tapestry which, when turned over at a particular juncture in your life, causes you to say, "Yes! This is me, this is what my life is for."

Convergence is not necessarily about setting out to do great things. Convergence comes through setting one's face towards a walk of obedience that is carried to completion. My hope is that this book will help direct four separated areas of life towards a common center: Career, Community, Creativity, and Call.

The world around us is changing rapidly and radically. The only sure way to navigate the change we are encountering is rapid and radical obedience. People intuitively hunger for an integrated life. They hunger for a world where family does not have to be sacrificed on the altar of work, where creativity does not have to be neutered, where the deep call within finds expression without. And when they see it in you, they will believe it. My challenge to you is simple: take up the road towards Convergence. Abandon the shortcuts of orderliness and balance, and pursue obedience. Life is a life of faith: make sure your faith is in God. Deliberately move away from that which provides the escape of faith in a company, a church, a career-path, a stock market or your own smarts. They will not be enough. Submit yourself to the ways in which God disciplines you. Embrace the Seasons; grow in character. Make the small daily choices of obedience so that you learn the ways of God. Then when the big decisions come, you will be prepared for them.

God paid a high price for reconciliation. That reconciliation extends beyond our so-called spiritual lives. "For God was in Christ reconciling *all things/the world/kosmos* to himself..."[106] Our challenge to you: lay yourself on this template of truth so that all things in your life will indeed be reconciled, aligned, integrated with God, through his Son Jesus Christ.

Finally, Convergence is about resting, not arriving. When we know who we are, have marked our seasons with the ink of real life, and locked our pace with Jesus in pleasing the Father then we know what the writer of Hebrews meants when he/she said:

> There remains therefore a Sabbath rest for the people of God. For the one who has entered his rest has himself rested from his own works...let us therefore be diligent to enter that rest... [107]

---

106    2 Corinthians 5:19 (emphasis added)

107    Hebrews 4:9-11

# appendix

# 01

## Trends

The First Edition of *Convergence* contained a more detailed look at trends that impacted or were contained within The 4-Cs. Some readers enjoyed them, so I have included them in these Appendices for those who wish to dig into these topics in more detail. I have included comments on the status of these trends, where applicable. For example, I previously predicted that there would be a major shift in how Christ-followers defined and experienced Community. Since then, this has found expression in things with labels like "the emerging church" and "Christians outside the church." While these are not labels I endorse, they are evidence of a deeper trend that has come to fruition since the first writing.

# Career Trends

| Trend | Implication for Convergence |
|---|---|
| Globalization: People from around the world can compete for your job, and most of them will work for less money. | You have to continuously re-tool so that you maintain sought after skills. And there are new opportunities for the brave "across the ponds." Further, you will need to discover Convergence in a global context. |
| Family friendly policies: More and more organizations want to appear to be family friendly. Few employees feel the freedom to take advantage of these policies. | People recognize when there is a difference between stated policies and unspoken values. Don't believe everything in the policy manual. If you want integration between Career (work) and Community (including your family), get ready to make tough choices. They may be good choices, but they won't always be easy. |
| Work as Community: Some corporations are attempting to create a home-like atmosphere for work. Mrs. Grossman's Paper Company and AutoDesk allow dogs at work, some companies have on-site day care, workers decorate their factories any way they please. With job security no longer an option, smart employers are turning in other directions to make work seem more like a community. | The softening of the hard edges between home and work will allow the fortunate few to overcome the dichotomy between work and community. But ferns and fluffy pets won't be enough if the fundamental values of the organization are not aligned with the soft side of the company. |
| The shifting location of education: Education originally began in the home. Religious institutions then assumed the education role, with a later shift to public schools. | With the availability of home-accessible information via the Internet, corporations have taken on the role of educator. Will this fuel the shift of education back to the home? And with the growing information empowerment of The Millennial Generation (Y), will they self-manage more of their education? This emboldened self-management of education may be a pre-cursor to the self-management of Careers. |

| Trend | Implication for Convergence |
|---|---|
| Cashing out: Many have tasted success, not liked the aftertaste, and cashed in their stock options | People are starting to look for alternate careers earlier in life. The new millionaires are younger and less likely to know who they are. Career success can outstrip character development, leaving more questions than answers. |
| Cashing in: Those without the means to completely leave the workforce still have the wherewithal to cash in their stock options and pension plans and move to lower paying jobs. And many are doing just this. | Some people are content to take lesser paying positions that enable them to do meaningful work, often going to work for non-profits at a fraction of their former salaries. |
| Institutionalized philanthropy: corporations are integrating a philanthropic experience into the careers of people, allowing or requiring them to do some form of community service. | Employees have opportunities to experience a greater integration of Career and Call while maintaining their jobs.<br><br>The downside, in some countries pushing for "church-state separation" is that some employers will not allow stints at organizations that are "religious" in nature. |
| Home-based businesses: There has been a tremendous growth in home-based businesses in recent years. About 25,000 new businesses start in homes in the US each month; 80% of these are successful in the first two years (compared to the old statistic of 80% of new businesses failing in the first five years.) Of these new ventures, 60% are run by women. | Large corporations are no longer the only respectable career option. Gone are the tape-recorded background office noises, the muffler on the dog, and the long-winded explanations of why the client can't actually come to your office (a.k.a. Armando's Mailbox Service.) |
| Integration: "In the future, the distinction between work and spare time will wither away - because, increasingly, the demands we put on our leisure time will be the same ones we put on our work. We are approaching a fully integrated life." [1] | People will seek jobs with greater meaning and spend more time working at those jobs. But the distinctions between such work and play will blur. Working holidays will increase, people will find it harder to discern true priorities, and without a stable values base, people will be more sold-out than ever to their Career. |

1  Rolf Jensen, *The Dream Society,* McGraw-Hill, 1999.

| Trend | Implication for Convergence |
|---|---|
| Emerging college graduates in privileged countries are willing to work at less ambitious jobs and make lateral moves in order to find work that they really value. | On the one hand, this could be a good thing as fewer negative work patterns are put in place. |
| Push Pause: This is the flipside if Institutionalized Philanthropy where employees are taking the initiative and telling employers, "You cannot pay me enough to not have meaning in my work." They are either taking temporary breaks to do meaningful work among less fortunate people, or are placing careers on hold while they re-tool for the next phase of their career. | It is more acceptable to let an employer know that you are taking time off—even a year or two—to get a real world MBA in an environment that uses all of who you are, not just what the company expects. This bodes well for Convergence. |

| Trend | Implication for Convergence |
|---|---|
| Speed and superficiality replace longevity and depth: much of our world is becoming transient: our jobs, hometowns, technology, etc. This has a spillover effect on relationships. | We readily accept as normal the vacuous black hole that was once community. We have to rekindle hope in community because we find our Call in serving others, or in the context of community. |
| Roll-your-own community: We used to accept the menu of primary community-providing groups, such as a local church. More and more people are defining their own small groups and not paying much attention to the formal prescriptions of organizations. | Given that this trend is starting with teenagers, there could be an increased likelihood that we fail to grow up with a "balanced diet" of community. Whether it is big-picture oversight of a single point of community, or maybe just its pedestrian predictability, if this erodes we may be more susceptible to disintegration. Rampant personal consumerism could exact a high price. |
| Anonymous Community: This takes the Roll-your-own-community to the next level, where the community is online and often virtual. Think MySpace.com. | It is hard to tell what the outcome of this will be. On the plus side, people could develop the skills that make them meaningful collaborators in a productive sense. The downside may be no real community. |

| Trend | Implication for Convergence |
|---|---|
| Virtual Community at Work: Reporting to bosses you have never met, teaming with people you have never seen in the flesh. | Looking for other places to meet real people; increased spending on coffee at places with free WiFi. |
| Virtual Working Communities: The twist here is that companies are simulating future work scenarios before building out physical sites. Second Life is an example, where hotels or factories or offices are simulated online before money is spent on construction. | On the positive side, work can mimic real community.<br><br>On the negative side, you may have life as an avatar, but not as a real person. |
| Rediscovery of roots: Globalization makes us rootless... or does it make us hanker for our roots? With the lack of certainty on life's busy streets, many are retracing the path back home, not to live there, but certainly to know where there is. | Understanding your personal DNA can help you figure out your Call. This is good. On the other hand, a preoccupation with preserving the family heritage (especially if you think you come "from good stock" or if you were born with a healthy trust endowment) can lead to simply repeating negative family patterns instead of blazing new trails. Wisdom, please. |
| Resurgence of spirituality: The public admission of adherence to religion of all kinds is evident everywhere. There are books such as *A Spiritual Audit of Corporate America*, and *Spiritual Capital*... neither written from a Judeo-Christian faith-based perspective. | This popularization of spirituality can both open the path to Convergence and create the illusion of "any path will get you there." The theories of "the journey is the way" can sidetrack many from pressing in to find true Convergence. By the same token, the more public awareness of man's need for a spiritual foundation creates a forum for an inner dialogue about the "why's" and "wherefore's" of our lives. |
| Integration of family: There is a rising tide of "family first." I commonly meet with business people who are open about commitments to being home over the hour of doom - 5.30 to 6.30 p.m. - and reluctant to make appointments at times when they should be with their families. | We must overcome the destructive assumption that Call will take away from family. If we drag this deficiency from the world of Career to the other areas of life, we will be no less satisfied than we were before. The banner of "sacrificing for Jesus" is more likely wallpaper over our disintegrated thinking than God's call to isolated living.<br><br>On the positive side, people are jealous of precious time with their families. The deliberate integration of family into one's life paves the way to Convergence. |

# Creativity Trends

| Trend | Implication for Convergence |
|---|---|
| Innovation comes in small packages: One of the great strengths of the U.S. economy is its unstoppable innovation. Yet the bulk of innovation in the U.S. comes from companies with fewer than 19 employees. | We separately need creativity and innovation in our work and personal lives. While creativity might historically have been for recreation, now we need things that edify us incorporated into the fabric of our work lives. |
| What we might do tomorrow doesn't exist today: Many of the 21st Century jobs don't exist today. Rapid changes in technology will make obsolete many jobs we considered the "bedrock of society." | We need to pay closer attention to the creative side of our lives. Our ability to adapt, reinvent ourselves and nimbly follow God's initiative will be key to our success. |
| The quest for creativity in work and meaning in play. "In the Dream Society, free time will occasionally be difficult to distinguish from work and - above all - it will be imbued with emotional content..."[2] | On the down side, our children will see us as constantly working. ("That wasn't a vacation... you were working.")<br><br>On the plus side, there will be a vastly expanded number of opportunities to find or create jobs that embrace our creativity. |
| Purposeful Innovation: researchers have found zero correlation between spending on Research & Development and Innovation, but very high correlation between Purpose and Innovation. | This is an opportunity to introduce an eternal principle into organizations: you are more creative, more imaginative, more inventive when you are focused on serving those outside your organization. When business has a higher Purpose it gets better results. |

2  ibid

# Calling Trends

| Trend | Implication for Convergence |
|---|---|
| Working for a higher purpose: It's been said that if we can't enjoy our work, we should at least enjoy the reason for our working. But today people want both: they want meaningful, enjoyable work. | Employers are going to have to (a) create more enjoyable work environments and, more importantly, (b) craft a vision for their organizations that supersedes the processes and tasks of the organization. |
| A new understanding of occupation vs. vocation: "I fish therefore I am." "I work therefore I am." We've all seen the T-shirts. But the momentum nowadays is with the growing group who say "I am therefore I choose what I do." | Consider how much of what you do at work is consistent with how God wired you. One measure of this is your grace barometer: does your work build you up or let you down? How much call is there in your career? |
| Dissatisfaction with the temporary: Research shows that the satisfaction of a new purchase (such as a car) fades after just 21 days. We are increasingly dissatisfied with temporal things. | Watch out for the Convergence concealers. When the pursuit of things keeps as perpetually riding the 21-day curve, we will be less sensitive to the whisper that is Call. |
| Businesses with a Calling: This goes beyond *Business as a Calling* to companies discovering their real Purpose—their corporate call. This is a lot more than having a mission or vision statement. | This is the Call-Creativity interconnect. As businesses discover that they—a collection of individuals in organized form—can have a Calling, this opens up possibilities for stakeholders in the corporations to discover their own Calling. |

# appendix

# 02

## What happened to **equip**?

For thirty years God has had me live in the gap between local church, mission organizations and business, long before there was much of an intersection. In recent times the whole marketplace ministry or business-as-missions area has become almost popular. New organizations spring up routinely, and traditional mission organizations are donning a marketplace face. Some have a good grasp of business, some don't. Looking forward, I anticipate that this congregating in the marketplace will mobilize many businesspeople and other marketplace leaders, and I am thankful for this. I also believe that there is a distinct danger facing the marketplace movement.

The danger is that the movement will be neutered by well-intended participants who carry the DNA of old wineskins into this new era. Dennis Peacocke asserts that we may experience enough marketplace ministry to inoculate us, but not enough to transform us. When we began our journey of doing business plus church leadership plus missions work some decades ago, there were relatively few doing the same thing.

We were not entirely alone, of course, as God always has handfuls of people to whom he is saying the same thing, but in each one's native vernacular. In fact, while our focus is on recent decades, I believe that we don't know the whole picture when it comes to the silver thread that God has kept going through the centuries of those who integrated work and faith.

Let's explore this centuries-long thread further. We quickly talk about William Carey as the father of modern Protestant missions. My Indian friends will point out that he was preceded in India by Bartholomaeus Ziegenbalg, who started in India nearly 90 years before Carey. Sent by Danish King Frederick IV for evangelization in India, Ziegenbalg landed on July 9, 1706 at Tranquebar (known as Tarangambadi in Tamil). The area was a Danish colony at the time, located on India's eastern coast, 300 kilometers south of Chennai, or Madras as it was formerly known. Ziegenbalg aided Carey's work. The Moravians also began their missions thrust in the 1730's, about 60 years before Carey. For the first 100 years all of their missionaries were businesspeople. Who knows which business ministers preceded Carey, the Moravians and Ziegenbalg? I expect we will only know in eternity the people and groups who carried the baton of integration between work and faith beyond Paul and his New Testament friends to more recent centuries.

Back to our own story. We started our workplace missions organization in 1992 under the banner of "Professionals for Christ." People saw two aspects of the name that posed a problem: what is a professional, and isn't the name therefore restrictive, and, when you go to many nations, who is Christ? So we changed the name to **equip**.

In recent times the word "equip" has become so commonly used in the non-profit world that it is no longer distinctive. Many organizations seem to be equipping some group or another to change the world. In addition, there are one or two organizations claiming exclusive use of the name in the USA. Taking all of these factors together—the name issue, the muddying of marketplace ministry, and the generalization of the word equip—we have decided to do two things:

1. Move the work of Repurposing businesses and other key marketplace organizations into The Institute (www.inst.net).

2. Drop the **equip** name, even though it has been part of our story.

The new name of the line of business that repurposes companies based on Biblical principles is **rēp**, pronounced *reep*.


## The Institute

I remember meeting the Chief Financial Officer of a large U.S. non-profit organization. He asked me, "What are you?" I told him that The Institute has a threefold identity:

Head of a think tank,

Hands of a business,

Heart of philanthropy.®

His response was classic. "Well, I'll just think of you as a ministry then." He avoided having to integrate work and faith by classifying the product development we were doing as "ministry." It might have seemed easier to explain to the Board of Directors that the one million dollars they were spending was going "to a ministry." The reality is that we do not have the prerogative to separate work and ministry. God didn't, and we are not at liberty to do so either.

We are therefore integrating the work of **rēp** and The Institute, reinforcing that ministry and work are the same, and emphasizing the vastly more efficient operating model of a business—"the hands of a business"—to complete our mission. The work we have previously done as **rēp** is now being done through The Institute.

Our tag-line, which is a registered trademark of The Institute, aptly describes a core component of what we do:

## Repurposing Business—Transforming Society.®

The Institute has other divisions, such as Indaba Publishing, and over time the names of various products that we offer, including the Repurposing of businesses, will no doubt come and go.

We still have various non-profit entities around the world, and these will enable those who come alongside our family of volunteers to make tax deductible contributions to support them, where needed. Our preferred route, however, is that we practice what we preach, and fully blend work/ministry. (To reiterate, the Hebrew word, *avodah*, is the same word for work and ministry, and we see no difference between them.) We will charge different fees depending on what is fair in each marketplace, but the work is ministry, and ministry is our work.

Many years ago one of my colleagues asked me, "Are we a business or a ministry?" I replied, "Yes!" Thinking I did not quite understand him, he went on to add, "...because, if we are a business, we are governed by the laws of business, and if we are a ministry, then we are to live by the rules of ministry." The "laws" of all spheres of society are a subset of God's eternal principles which stem from Who he is. There is no bifurcation in our God, who is One. As mentioned earlier, one of the greatest giants we face in our work of Repurposing businesses is dichotomy. One manifestation of this is businesspeople, and others, who do not want to pay a fair fee for advice or services that are "spiritual." They reason that if it is "Christian" it should be free. I tell them, "Slay a giant—write a check." This is not a ploy for fund raising, but to further disciple them. It is incongruous that business owners will pay for legal fees or paper supplies, but when they get advice that will change the course of their business and impact their eternal destiny, they somehow think it should be at some spectacular discount. Somehow when one mentions the God who owns their business, or the Scriptures he gave to instruct them, the price must plummet. This is disingenuous, to say the least.

## The Right Wineskin

There are many other reasons why I believe that a business is the best wineskin for accomplishing the particular task we have been given. Businesses have open access anywhere in the world, provided that they offer a meaningful product or service. Businesses can generate capital of many sorts efficiently, with or without tax deductible donations. A business, properly purposed, can reach many people in authentic ways, if the business is intentional. For example, we have worked with two companies that each serve 40 million customers a year. Another business with just eight employees reaches 10,000 people—that is 10,000 new people every year!

Another reason why the nonprofit wineskin does not fit well is this: we must practice what we preach, modeling what we tell others to do. While the vast majority of our volunteers have regular jobs, we who serve in the core organization are not exempt from finding our own tents to make.

## Foundational Principles

I recognize that some will prefer to separate business and missions, and question how a business can have the heart of a mission. There is the danger that, when profits enter the equation, the motives of some become suspect. We have personally seen people get along just fine until there is money on the table. The answer, however, is not to avoid money but to purify our motives and deepen our understanding of both capital and working capital.

We attempt to mitigate greed and other hazards by being clear about our bedrock beliefs regarding business in general, and The Institute in particular. We call these beliefs our Foundational Principles, and these can be found in a booklet of that title on our website.

## Giving and Receiving

Jesus said, "It is better to give than receive." He did not add, "... except in a business." One of the hallmarks of kingdom people is that they are obedient givers. They have somehow cracked the code that says, "Things happen when people give." It should be no surprise that The Institute chooses to give time, resources and intellectual property to mobilize and equip businesspeople to be enlisted in God's great army of modern day business missionaries. The fact that The Institute is legally a "for profit" entity should not prevent other like-minded people from coming alongside the organization to co-labor in transforming business leaders, corporations, societies and nations. Provided that one has the guidelines for handling finances that are clearly understood by all, there should not be a barrier to people volunteering to serve, and being fully compensated for work done. Both are ministry; both are work.

For further information contact us at:

www.inst.net

or call us at 1-866-9INDABA

®Repurposing Business and **rēp** are registered trademarks of The Institute for Innovation, Integration & Impact, Inc.

# appendix

## 03

## More on Convergence

Over the past ten years we have offered readers the opportunity to dig deeper. This has generally taken place through public Forums, study groups, and Consultations in corporate settings. This appendix lays out some of the ways in which you can experience more of Convergence. The length of time and format varies depending on whether you are participating as an individual, or as part of a leadership team.

## Convergence Tools

1. **Convergence and Personal Planning:** This one day Forum focuses on the development of a personal plan against the backdrop of Convergence. We explore your assets and liabilities in light of yesterday and tomorrow, and help you

develop a personal plan using The 10-F Model and The 4-Cs. This offering is aimed at the working professional who is determining how to make a difference in a work life where you do not necessarily have influence over corporate direction. This will help set a personal trajectory for future Convergence. *Related Assessments*: 10-F Assessment from a personal perspective.

2. **Convergence and Couples:** Typically a weekend retreat, this Forum provides an Overview of Convergence, then digs into Choosing and Re-choosing your Spouse. Just to keep it interesting, we add a touch of LEMON Leadership so that each person can get a greater understanding of how they and their partner are wired.

3. **Corporate Convergence:** This is aimed at equipping leaders of organizations, be they businesses or other corporations, to discover a corporate calling. You will also find your voice as a leader and learn how to communicate the corporate Call. You will then learn how to build the organization into one where Calling, Career, Community and Creativity are integrated. During the Consultation you will analyze your current investments in these four areas, identify barriers to integrating Career and the other three areas, and tear down the walls that prevent the blending of these interdependent spheres. *Related Assessments*: Called Corporations Assessment.

4. **Convergence:** We offer a 10-part study which is a self-study series designed for group discussion by people who have read the book. You can order this study from the Products section of www.repurposing.biz and from www.convergencebook.com.

## Convergence Accredited Consultants

1. **Convergence Coaching:** The Institute Community includes those who are qualified to provide one-on-one coaching for leaders looking for someone to come alongside them in their

journey. This coaching is only offered once someone has participated in one of the Consultations or Forums.

2. **Business Coaching & Advisors:** We also have people who will come alongside corporate teams and guide them in implementing the truths of Convergence at the corporate level. This is a complement to the Corporate Convergence Consultation.

3. **Fresh Future™:** *Discovering fresh purpose for the season ahead.* Many people have significant transition points in their lives where there is a need to reassess who they are, and to determine what they do with the next season. *Fresh Future* is a unique combination of personal coaching calls, group meetings, projects and retreats for those wanting to move beyond the boundaries of past seasons. Convergence, together with wise counsel and other proven tools, is woven into the *Fresh Future* experience.

## Consultations & Forums

1. **Repurposing the Leader:** We learned long ago that as leaders we need to be repurposed if we are to lead effectively. This consultation emphasizes the discovery of one's life Calling. We help you develop a Personal Purpose statement, and then translate this into high level strategies to align all aspects of your life behind this purpose.

2. **Retooling the Leader:** Most leaders have a good blend of Competence and Character. The challenge, however, is that the yardstick for measuring these areas is taken from "best practices" that we find in the world's marketplace of ideas. Very few leaders have a solid grasp of what Scripture says about marketing, products or competitive positioning. In addition, the bankrupt philosophy of "balance" has given them just enough to know what to do, but not enough to empower them to actually do it. The 10-P Model and The 10-

F Model are looked at from the perspective of the individual, rather than the corporation as a whole. (The latter is done during the Repurposing your Business corporate consultation.) *Related Assessments*: 10-F and 10-P Assessment, from a corporate perspective.

3. **The Leader's Umbrella:** The work of a leader includes holding an umbrella over the organizations they lead. Traditional leadership materials do not address how the leader, as the head of a household, can hold an umbrella over the organization that protects it from harm and enables it to function optimally. You will leave knowing the 10 critical panels of The Leader's Umbrella and discover how to assess and remedy the holes in your umbrella. These ten areas correspond with the felt needs of people and the deep longings each of us has at our core, or hub.

## Study Programs

1. **MBA.M™:** Our Mentoring in Business as Missions program (MBA.M) is a longer term study where executives of a similar level walk through topics crucial to the integration of work and faith, with a particular emphasis on how this can take place in the context of the organizations they lead. This requires a group of six to ten peers working together over a longer period. The result is personal renewal and a retooling of the leader to function effectively as a Biblical businessperson.

For further information contact us at info@inst.net

www.inst.net

or call us at 1-866-9INDABA

# appendix

# 04

## The Author

**B**rett and Lyn Johnson founded The Institute for Innovation, Integration & Impact, Inc. in 1996. Brett's writings complement his work consulting business and social sector leaders on how to maximize Impact for today, and for eternity. He has over twenty-five years experience leading public accounting and management consulting firms, helping corporations from global multi-nationals to business start-ups and social sector organizations.

Brett was a Partner at KPMG Peat Marwick and at Computer Sciences Corporation. He spent fourteen years at Price Waterhouse working in the United States and South Africa. A sampling of Brett's clients include Apple Computer, Amgen, Cisco, Chicago Tribune, Cost Plus World Markets, Duty Free Shoppers, GATX Shipping, Incyte Genomics, Pacific Gas & Electric, Prison Fellowship Ministries, Safeway, Shell Oil, Sony PlayStation, Stanford University, University of the Nations, US Digital, Wells Fargo Bank, and Youth with a Mission.

He has worked extensively with executive teams helping them gain a greater Purpose, both personally, and for the corporation. Brett has helped them align their business with eternal principles, envision new futures, and ensure consistency between core operations and the new purpose. In addition, he has extensive experience in redesigning organizations and in coaching executive teams.

In recent years Brett and Lyn have worked with the team at **rēp** to train hundreds of businesspeople to use their business skills for a God's purposes. They have then traveled with these teams to nations around the world to help local business leaders repurpose their own businesses. The goal is that a critical mass of transformed businesses in each city will work towards the transformation of that society, hence the tag line, *Repurposing Business–Transforming Society*®

Throughout his career, Brett has used his business expertise to provide consulting services to charities and universities. He has worked with local NGOs through to international charities. At The Institute Brett has developed intellectual property and Web-based tools to rapidly analyze corporations and discover innovative ways in which to radically increase their impact.

*Convergence* was Brett's first book. He has also coauthored *I-Operations: the Impact of the Internet on Operating Models* with Gary Daichendt, the former EVP of Worldwide Operations at Cisco. The second edition of *I-Operations: How the Internet can transform your Operating Model* was released in February 2003. His third book is titled *LEMON Leadership*®. He has also authored numerous papers.

Brett is a Chartered Accountant and holds a Bachelor's degree in Commerce from the University of Cape Town.

Brett and Lyn have been married for nearly 30 years and have three children: Fay Maree, James Brett, and David Iain. Lyn has been in business for twenty years and leads a large team of businesswomen. Brett and Lyn travel, do business, minister and speak together around the world.